Security in the Gulf: Historical Legacies and Future Prospects

This book examines Gulf security in a holistic way seeing past the narrow military aspect and also trying to debunk the conventional narratives propagated by regional and external actors. In particular, the emphasis is on the historical legacy of Gulf security and the fundamental domestic and international vulnerabilities of the various states in the region. This approach proves important in light of the recent efforts by Gulf states to recast their position in the international arena trying to peddle an image of self-assertiveness and autonomy in the security sphere. These new diplomatic stances do not seem to be borne out by their current security policies that are marked by apparent continuity with past practices. In particular, the new Gulf-Asia nexus and the claims by Gulf monarchies that regional confidence building measures are appearing on the horizon are placed under critical scrutiny. This is done by a sobering examination of the balance of threat in the region, the historical amity/enmity patterns and the evolving American stance.

A shorter version of this book was previously published as a special issue of the *British Journal of Middle Eastern Studies*.

Matteo Legrenzi is Assistant Professor at the Graduate School of Public and International Affairs of the University of Ottawa. He has published articles on the GCC and on the international relations of the Gulf. He is co-editor of *Beyond Regionalism? Regional Cooperation, Regionalism and Regionalization in the Middle East* and the author of the forthcoming *The GCC and the International Relations of the Gulf: Diplomacy, Security and Economy Co-ordination in a Changing Middle East.*

This book has assembled many of the top analysts in Gulf security to address the complex and interdependent threats facing this volatile region. The analysis presented in these pages by these outstanding scholars should be required reading for academics, security policy professionals, and researchers, seeking to deconstruct the veils of complexity that complicate our attempts to understand this important region.
James A. Russell, Associate Professor, Naval Postgraduate School

A diverse and thoughtful collection of essays on the fundamentals of Gulf security. Separating myth from reality and challenging conventional stereotypes, this volume offers an informed and balanced analysis of the region's security architecture before and after 9/11.
Louise Fawcett, CUF University Lecturer in Politics, Oxford University

Security in the Gulf: Historical Legacies and Future Prospects

Edited by
Matteo Legrenzi

LONDON AND NEW YORK

First published 2011
by Routledge
2 Park Square, Milton Park, Abingdon, Oxon, OX14 4RN

Simultaneously published in the USA and Canada
by Routledge
711 Third Avenue, New York, NY 10017

Routledge is an imprint of the Taylor & Francis Group, an informa business

First issued in paperback 2013

© 2011 British Society for Middle East Studies

This book is a reproduction of the *British Journal of Middle Eastern Studies*, vol. 36, issue 3. The Publisher requests to those authors who may be citing this book to state, also, the bibliographical details of the special issue on which the book was based.

Typeset in Times New Roman by Taylor & Francis Books

All rights reserved. No part of this book may be reprinted or reproduced or utilised in any form or by any electronic, mechanical, or other means, now known or hereafter invented, including photocopying and recording, or in any information storage or retrieval system, without permission in writing from the publishers.

British Library Cataloguing in Publication Data
A catalogue record for this book is available from the British Library

ISBN13: 978-0-415-58776-1 (hbk)
ISBN13: 978-0-415-85052-0 (pbk)

Disclaimer
The publisher would like to make readers aware that the chapters in this book are referred to as articles as they had been in the special issue. The publisher accepts responsibility for any inconsistencies that may have arisen in the course of preparing this volume for print.

To Yossi: he genuinely bridged cultures

Contents

Introduction
Matteo Legrenzi   1

1. **From Here We Begin: A Survey of Scholarship on the International Relations of the Gulf**
   Fred H. Lawson   3

2. **The Power of Narrative: Saudi Arabia, the United States and the Search for Security**
   Patrick Conge and Gwenn Okruhlik   25

3. **La Longue Durée and Energy Security in the Gulf**
   Mary Ann Tétreault   41

4. **Jihad, Yes, But Not Revolution: Explaining the Extraversion of Islamist Violence in Saudi Arabia**
   Thomas Hegghammer   61

5. **Saudi Arabia and the Arab–Israeli Peace Process: The Fluctuation of Regional Coordination**
   Joseph Kostiner   83

6. **Dubai and the United Arab Emirates: Security Threats**
   Christopher M. Davidson   97

7. **Iraq's Gulf Policy and Regime Security from the Monarchy to the post-Ba'athist Era**
   Ibrahim Al-Marashi   115

8. **Islamic Utopian Romanticism and the Foreign Policy Culture of Iran**
   Arshin Adib-Moghaddam   129

Index   157

Introduction

MATTEO LEGRENZI

This book examines Gulf security in a holistic way, looking past the narrow military components and challenging the conventional narratives that have been propagated by regional and external actors. In particular, the emphasis is on the historical legacies of regional security and the fundamental domestic and international vulnerabilities of various states in the Gulf.

This exercise proves particularly important in light of recent efforts by some Gulf states to recast their position in the international arena by promoting an image of self-assertiveness and autonomy in the security sphere. These new postures do not seem to be borne out by crucial elements of their respective security policies, which are marked by significant continuities with past practices. In particular, the widely heralded Gulf–Asia security nexus and the prospect of confidence-building measures emanating from Gulf monarchies *vis-à-vis* Iran have yet to materialise. Proponents of a new security architecture in the Gulf will benefit by the sobering examinations of the balance of threats in the region, historical patterns of amity and enmity, and evolving American stance that are presented in this book.

Primary emphasis has been placed on the fundamentals of Gulf security and how these may or may not have changed in the aftermath of 11 September. Authors have been asked to assess whether these fundamentals were in any way altered by the momentous events of that day, and to reflect on the changed role of the United States in the region—its gradual shift from 'over the horizon' balancer to local player with an imposing physical presence. In contrast to what is often hoped for, or feared, on the two shores of the Gulf, the United States is becoming more deeply ensconced in the region. Decisions in Washington are increasingly taken in the name of force protection, which do not register on the political radar screen. By taking into consideration the historical legacies of Gulf security, contributors here have been able to escape the 'here and now' fallacies of much of the literature emanating from both regional and global think tanks.

Above all, the contributors to this collection have approached the subject of regional security from the point of view of their respective academic disciplines. Their essays offer insight into a subject that is all too often treated in impressionistic terms. Much can ultimately be gained by simply asking the same questions of the Gulf security complex that are routinely asked of other security complexes around the world, thereby eschewing the twin evils of sycophantic self-censorship and blanket vilification.

Acknowledgements

The editor gratefully acknowledges the support of the Centre for International Policy Studies at the University of Ottawa, the Centre for International Governance Innovation in Waterloo, Canada and the Security and Defence Forum of the Canadian Department of National Defence. Professor F. Gregory Gause III of the University of Vermont and Professor Bessma Momani of the University of Waterloo were exemplary discussants at our pre-publication workshop in Ottawa in December 2008. Professor Nicola Pratt of the University of Warwick made sure the project was completed in time. Finally, special thanks go to Lama Mourad, my formidable research assistant, as she embarks on what will certainly be a distinguished scholarly career: without her, this volume would never have seen the light of day.

From Here We Begin: A Survey of Scholarship on the International Relations of the Gulf

FRED H. LAWSON

ABSTRACT *Academic writing on the international relations of the Gulf has mushroomed over the last decade and a half, but for the most part the quality of work has not kept pace with the quantity. As a result, most literature on the topic adds little to our understanding of world politics, either in the region or in the world at large. This essay surveys the state of existing scholarship in three broad areas: foreign policy studies, security studies and the dynamics of interstate interaction. For the most part, it finds that works dealing with Gulf affairs are framed in terms of concepts and methodologies that lag far behind the times in each field, which makes it difficult if not impossible to integrate the region into larger theoretical debates. By indicating ways that literature on foreign policy, security and interstate interaction in the Gulf might close the gap with state-of-the-art scholarship, the paper hopes to encourage specialists in the region to pay greater attention to the kinds of arguments and research designs they employ, thereby raising the visibility and utility of their research beyond the narrow confines of Middle East studies.*

Introduction

There is now a massive body of literature on the international relations of the Gulf. Much of it takes the form of modern-day *nasihatnameler*, or 'advice to princes': explicit policy recommendations; critiques of past or current policies; and summaries of significant developments in regional affairs that are intended to inform or guide policy-making. A good deal of the rest concerns the great powers: surveys of broad trends in and specific aspects of United States, Russian, Chinese, European and Japanese involvement in the region; analyses of great power rivalry in and around the Gulf; and discussions of the efforts that have been undertaken by various external actors to construct some sort of security architecture in this persistently volatile part of the world.

Other writings deal with the international politics of hydrocarbons. Particular attention has been devoted to secular trends in the production and distribution of Gulf oil and gas, but relations between oil-producing countries and transnational petroleum companies have also received extensive treatment. More recent studies explore the ways in which revenues derived from the exploitation of regional hydrocarbon reserves have been transformed into substantial pools of investment capital, most notably the sovereign wealth funds that look poised to exert a major influence in global financial markets.

What remains after these three components of the English-language literature on the international relations of the Gulf have been filtered out is an extensive, but considerably more manageable, collection of studies that focus on the Gulf itself. Current scholarship on regional affairs can usefully be categorized in accordance with the three main sub-fields of academic work on world politics: foreign policy studies, security studies and international relations per se. This essay offers a critical overview of the existing literature in each of these sub-fields, along with some suggestions for future exploration that might help to integrate scholarship on the Gulf into ongoing conceptual debates and research programs in the larger discipline.

Foreign Policy Studies

Virtually all of the studies that analyze the foreign policies of the Gulf states remain idiographic in nature. This means, in the words of James Rosenau, that they 'tend to treat each international situation in which the society participates as unique and, consequently, to view its external behavior with respect to each situation as stemming from immediate and particular antecedents'.[1] Nevertheless, a pair of books represents a significant step forward in conceptual terms over the largely atheoretical narratives that commanded the field as late as the mid-1980s.[2]

Hassan al-Alkim's *The Foreign Policy of the United Arab Emirates* and John Calabrese's *Revolutionary Horizons: Regional Foreign Policy in Post-Khomeini Iran* share a pair of noteworthy features. First, they focus primarily on the policies that the state at hand has adopted toward its immediate neighbours, while devoting only subsidiary attention to relations with extra-regional great powers. Al-Alkim presents extensive discussions of the United Arab Emirates (UAE)'s dealings with Saudi Arabia, Iran and Palestine, which delineate successive stages in the federation's diplomacy with regard to each of these arenas; relations with the US and Soviet Union are relegated to a preliminary section devoted to the 'external milieu' within which the UAE operates.[3] Similarly, Calabrese concentrates on the Islamic Republic's posture toward the seven Gulf Co-operation Council (GCC) states, the post-Soviet republics of central Eurasia, Pakistan and Afghanistan; relations with the United States, Russia and Western Europe are mentioned only in passing.[4] By centering their analyses on each state's dealings with surrounding countries, the authors highlight the strategic problems that tend to be most salient

---

[1] James N. Rosenau, *The Scientific Study of Foreign Policy* (New York: Free Press, 1971), p. 103.

[2] Notable examples of such narrative studies include William Quandt, *Saudi Arabia in the 1980s* (Washington, DC: Brookings, 1981); Christine Moss Helms, *Iraq: Eastern Flank of the Arab World* (Washington, DC: Brookings, 1984); Nadav Safran, *Saudi Arabia: The Ceaseless Quest for Security* (Cambridge, MA: Harvard University Press, 1985); R.K. Ramazani, *Revolutionary Iran: Challenge and Response in the Middle East* (Baltimore, MD: Johns Hopkins University Press, 1986).

[3] Hassan Hamdan al-Alkim, *The Foreign Policy of the United Arab Emirates* (London: Saqi, 1989), pp. 67–89.

[4] John Calabrese, *Revolutionary Horizons: Regional Foreign Policy in Post-Khomeini Iran* (London: Macmillan, 1994).

for local leaders. Moreover, they emphasize matters that, to paraphrase Calabrese, capture the complexities and incongruities that characterize the regional policies of the UAE and Iran.[5]

Second, the two books grapple explicitly with concepts drawn from the broader field of international relations. Al-Alkim frames his analysis in terms of the extensive literature on foreign policy decision-making. Political institutions, societal interests and rivalries among the seven emirates that make up the federation are listed as analytically distinct features of the domestic milieu in which UAE foreign policy-making takes place.[6] Territorial disputes and historical links to Saudi Arabia, Iran, Iraq and Oman, along with 'superpower aims and objectives' in the Gulf, together make up the external milieu.[7] Furthermore, the bureaucratic machinery that produces foreign policy is broken down into its major components, and the relative influence that each agency exerts on policy outputs is stipulated.[8] Al-Alkim's book thus reflects current trends in the comparative study of foreign policy, which concentrate on the ways in which factors at various levels of analysis can be integrated into a coherent explanation for policy formation and implementation by large administrative organizations.[9]

Calabrese situates his study squarely in the context of scholarship that aims to reformulate the notion of 'national security', particularly as it pertains to the Third World.[10] He begins by outlining key aspects of Iranian security—or perhaps better, insecurity—during the 1980s and 1990s. These include deep-seated vulnerabilities arising from the absence of another superpower capable of offsetting the global predominance of the United States, the high level of excess capacity that characterizes the world oil industry, the spiralling arms race in the Middle East, the emergence of new, weak states along Iran's northern border and a number of other factors.[11] At the same time, the Islamic Republic's economy suffers the adverse effects of persistent 'distortions and imbalances', while its political system wrestles with increasing 'fragmentation and discontent'.[12] The conjunction of these external and internal difficulties creates severe 'cross-pressures' on policy-makers:

> The *impetus* for the Leadership Coalition to press ahead with economic reform and adopt a 'new' foreign policy has been supplied by the urgent need to act, given the dangerous convergence of the after-effects of a decade of upheaval and mounting adverse demographic trends. Yet, the *capacity* of the regime to drive policy has been constrained by the multiple political challenges and obstacles arrayed against it.[13]

---

[5] *Ibid.*, p. 2. In much the same way, Joseph Kechichian surveys not only Oman's relations with the states of the Arabian peninsula and northern Gulf, but also the sultanate's policies toward Russia, the former Soviet republics of central Eurasia, the People's Republic of China, Indonesia, Thailand, India, Pakistan, Japan and Somalia. See Joseph A. Kechichian, *Oman and the World* (Santa Monica, CA: RAND, 1995).

[6] al-Alkim, *Foreign Policy of the United Arab Emirates*, chaps. 2–3. See also Hassan Hamdan al-Alkim, *The GCC States in an Unstable World* (London: Saqi, 1994), pp. 20–21.

[7] al-Alkim, *Foreign Policy of the United Arab Emirates*, chap. 4; al-Alkim, *GCC States*, pp. 21–22.

[8] al-Alkim, *Foreign Policy of the United Arab Emirates*, chap. 5; al-Alkim, *GCC States*, pp. 23–25.

[9] See Valerie M. Hudson, 'Foreign Policy Analysis Yesterday, Today, and Tomorrow', *Mershon International Studies Review*, no. 39 (October 1995).

[10] This literature includes Edward E. Azar and Chung-In Moon (eds), *National Security in the Third World* (Aldershot: Elgar, 1988); Yezid Sayigh, *Confronting the 1990s: Security in the Developing Countries*, Adelphi Paper no. 251 (London: International Institute for Strategic Studies, 1990); Bahgat Korany, Paul Noble and Rex Brynen (eds), *The Many Faces of National Security in the Arab World* (London: Macmillan, 1993); Mohammed Ayoob, *The Third World Security Predicament* (Boulder, CO: Lynne Rienner, 1995).

[11] Calabrese, *Revolutionary Horizons*, pp. 6–18.

[12] *Ibid.*, pp. 18–22.

[13] *Ibid.*, p. 23.

Given these circumstances, Iranian foreign policy has tended to vacillate sharply, between pragmatic efforts to reduce the country's strategic vulnerability and heroic measures to advance the Islamic revolution.[14]

More conventional studies, by contrast, catalogue a wide range of factors that in one way or another shape the foreign policies of the Gulf states.[15] Among the most commonly adduced attributes are the hydrocarbon deposits that lie scattered throughout the region, and the revenues that state officials derive from exploiting these resources; the autocratic political systems that one finds around the Gulf littoral; the background, proclivities and perspicacity of individual rulers; the religious doctrines and principles that function as political ideology for a number of regimes in the area;[16] the size and composition of local military establishments; for the smaller states, a persistent fear of Iranian or Iraqi hegemony; and—more rarely—broad demographic shifts and connections among the region's disparate Shi'i communities.[17] Hassan Ali al-Ebraheem, Mary Ann Tétreault and John Peterson point out that Kuwait and Qatar are, after all, comparatively small states, which exhibit many of the predispositions and behaviours that one finds in such inherently vulnerable polities.[18] Marc O'Reilly adds that the economic liberalization programs currently underway in most of the Gulf states can be expected to have a profound impact on their respective foreign policies.[19]

Two recent books explicitly reject the positivist assumptions on which conventional scholarship rests, and propose instead a 'poststructuralist' perspective on foreign policy in the region. K.L. Afrasiabi argues that Iran's external relations after the 1978–1979 revolution can best be understood in terms of the innovative package of norms and institutions that the post-revolutionary regime put in place

---

[14] *Ibid.*, pp. 26–29.

[15] Notable examples include Abdul-Reda Assiri, *Kuwait's Foreign Policy* (Boulder, CO: Westview, 1990); Abdul-Reda Assiri, 'Kuwait's Dinar Diplomacy', *Journal of South Asian and Middle Eastern Studies*, 14 (Spring 1991); Bahgat Korany, 'Defending the Faith amid Change: The Foreign Policy of Saudi Arabia', in Bahgat Korany and Ali E. Hillal Dessouki (eds), *The Foreign Policies of Arab States* (Boulder, CO: Westview, 1991); Hooshang Amirahmadi, 'Iranian-Saudi Arabian Relations since the Revolution', in Hooshang Amirahmadi and Nader Entessar (eds), *Iran and the Arab World* (New York: St Martin's, 1993); William A. Rugh, 'The Foreign Policy of the United Arab Emirates', *Middle East Journal*, 50 (Winter 1996); Marc J. O'Reilly, 'Omanibalancing: Oman Confronts an Uncertain Future', *Middle East Journal*, 52 (Winter 1998); Joseph A. Kechichian, 'Trends in Saudi National Security', *Middle East Journal*, 53 (Spring 1999); Mehdi Mozaffari, 'Revolutionary, Thermidorian and Enigmatic Foreign Policy: President Khatami and the "Fear of the Wave"', *International Relations*, 14 (August 1999); F. Gregory Gause III, 'The Foreign Policy of Saudi Arabia', in Raymond Hinnebusch and Anoushiravan Ehteshami (eds), *The Foreign Policies of Middle East States* (Boulder, CO: Lynne Rienner, 2002); and Christin Marschall, *Iran's Persian Gulf Policy: From Khomeini to Khatami* (London: Routledge, 2003).

[16] James P. Piscatori, 'Islamic Values and National Interest: The Foreign Policy of Saudi Arabia', in A.I. Dawisha (ed.), *Islam in Foreign Policy* (Cambridge: Cambridge University Press, 1983); Roger Savory, '"The Added Touch": Ithna 'Ashari Shi'ism as a Factor in the Foreign Policy of Iran', *International Journal*, 41 (Spring 1986); and Cary Fraser, 'In Defense of Allah's Realm: Religion and Statecraft in Saudi Foreign Policy Strategy', in Susanne Hoeber Rudolph and James Piscatori (eds), *Transnational Religion and Fading States* (Boulder, CO: Westview, 1997).

[17] Joseph A. Kechichian, 'Unity on the Arabian Peninsula', in Joseph A. Kechichian (ed.), *Iran, Iraq and the Arab Gulf States* (New York: Palgrave, 2001); A.M. Haji-Yousefi, 'The Shia Factor in Iran-Iraq Relations and Its Regional Implications', *Iranian Journal of International Affairs*, 19 (Winter 2007).

[18] Hassan Ali al-Ebraheem, *Kuwait and the Gulf* (Washington, DC: Georgetown University Center for Contemporary Arab Studies, 1984); Mary Ann Tétreault, 'Autonomy, Necessity and the Small State: Ruling Kuwait in the Twentieth Century', *International Organization*, 45 (Autumn 1991); J.E. Peterson, 'Qatar and the World: Branding for a Micro-State', *Middle East Journal*, 60 (Autumn 2006).

[19] Marc J. O'Reilly, 'Oil Monarchies without Oil: Omani and Bahraini Security in a Post-Oil Era', *Middle East Policy*, 6 (February 1999).

to impose discipline on the highly mobilized citizenry.[20] This package included a heavy dose of religious doctrine and symbolism in the years immediately after the revolution, but shifted in a more pragmatic, routinized direction as the country's administrative structure gradually reconsolidated itself.[21] When economic problems mounted and popular discontent surged at the end of the 1980s, the post-Khomeini leadership undertook a fundamental reconfiguration of the institutional foundations of the Islamic Republic, pushed along by a major external threat—the 1990–1991 Gulf crisis—and an equally important external opportunity—the disintegration of the Soviet Union. Tehran's more accommodative posture toward Saudi Arabia and the other Gulf Co-operation Council states in the early 1990s thus reflected a dramatic new 'conception of Iranian power' in regional affairs, which accompanied the emergence of 'dual leadership' consisting of President Akbar Hashemi Rafsanjani and Supreme Leader 'Ali Khamenei'.[22]

Along parallel lines, Arshin Adib-Moghaddam argues that the diplomacy of the Islamic Republic has been driven by 'a "utopian-romantic" meta-narrative permeating the Iranian foreign policy culture'.[23] He defines the country's foreign policy culture as 'a structured system populated by intersubjective knowledge, e.g. ideologies, norms, identities, institutions, and other cultural artifacts' which, taken together, 'transcends the concrete minds of its agents.'[24] More specifically, he argues that the utopian ideas of Jalal Al-e Ahmad and 'Ali Shariati coalesced into 'a religiously framed, anti-imperialist discourse' that became the 'central ideological precepts of the [post-revolutionary] state'.[25] This discourse was buttressed by the institution of the Supreme Leader, creating a situation in which 'inevitably, the Islamic Republic felt destined to change what was perceived to be an overbearingly hierarchical world order'.[26] Occasional deviations from the confrontational policies championed by 'the followers of the Imam's line', such as the halting rapprochement with Saudi Arabia and steps toward 'détente with the European Union', reflect not a latent shift in meta-narrative but rather the impact of scattered opposing 'counter-cultures'.[27] Consequently, the overriding thrust of Iranian foreign policy continues to derive from 'certain grand strategic preferences that transcend the faultlines of day-to-day politics'.[28]

Where both newer work and standard studies usually fall short is in connecting causal factors to particular shifts or patterns in the foreign policy of the country concerned. In some cases, the discussion of causes remains at such a general level that it is impossible to explain the adoption of one policy as opposed to another. Calabrese, for instance, asserts that

> Iran's efforts to build closer links with the Arab states of the Gulf originate in its unsteady domestic political conditions, and constitute the external elements of a policy devised

---

[20] K.L. Afrasiabi, *After Khomeini: New Directions in Iran's Foreign Policy* (Boulder, CO: Westview, 1994), p. 14. See also Suzanne Maloney, 'Identity and Change in Iran's Foreign Policy', in Shibley Telhami and Michael Barnett (eds), *Identity and Foreign Policy in the Middle East* (Ithaca, NY: Cornell University Press, 2002).
[21] Afrasiabi, *After Khomeini*, pp. 26–31.
[22] *Ibid.*, pp. 108, 74–77.
[23] Arshin Adib-Moghaddam, *Iran in World Politics* (New York: Columbia University Press, 2008), p. 32. See also Arshin Adib-Moghaddam, 'Islamic Utopian Romanticism and the Foreign Policy Culture of Iran', *Critique*, 14 (Fall 2005).
[24] Adib-Moghaddam, *Iran in World Politics*, p. 33.
[25] *Ibid.*, p. 54.
[26] *Ibid.*, p. 57.
[27] *Ibid.*, p. 69.
[28] *Ibid.*

to alleviate them. More specifically, they proceed from Iran's urgent need to pursue economic reconstruction; consist of bilateral transactions as well as proposals for multilateral co-operation; and signify an acknowledgement of the indivisibility of security and development.[29]

Adeed Dawisha similarly remarks that 'security and stability ... are paramount in Saudi thinking and calculations' concerning foreign policy, and then goes on to say that the Kingdom's 'domestic and foreign policies have been influenced by an equally powerful force, rooted in the historical legacy and cultural traditions of Saudi society as a whole—the religious and moral values of Islam'.[30] Joseph Kechichian asserts that after '1990, Omani foreign policy has entered a new era that recognizes intrinsic interests, but aims to increase the standard of living of every Omani citizen. As such, it is adaptive, pragmatic, and motivated by long-term objectives'.[31] And Abdul-Reda Assiri observes that 'Kuwait's concern about its military capabilities, both quantitatively and qualitatively, became a focal point in the mid-1970s, as a result of Iraqi threats and as a part of total national development schemes'.[32]

Other studies fail to spell out the precise combination of causal factors that produces a particular outcome. In other words, they gloss over what Rosenau calls the 'relative potency' of conjoined independent variables.[33] Graham Fuller thus traces the Islamic Republic's diverse policies toward Iraq, the GCC states, Russia, Turkey and south Asia to an admixture of 'Iran's historical experience, the character of its creative culture, its tradition of statecraft, the nature of its social interactions, the role of the individual and the family under highly authoritarian rule, and the experience of Iran with the West'.[34] David Long writes that Riyadh's policy toward its smaller neighbours 'is based on a convergence of interests from a variety of sources and with a varying degree of priority which have caused the Saudis over the years, and especially the last few years, to focus on the Gulf'. He concludes that 'a combination of external and internal political, economic and military factors have [sic] led them toward more cooperation, culminating with the creation of the Gulf Cooperation Council'.[35] O'Reilly proposes to account for Oman's policy of simultaneously 'balancing internal and external threats' in terms of the sultanate's strategic location, the proclivities of its 'one-of-a-kind leader', domestic economic prospects, looming demographic crisis, growing scarcity of fresh water, pervasive administrative corruption and uncertainty over the ruler's succession.[36] Moreover, Adib-Moghaddam claims that 'pro-Palestinian sentiments, anti-Zionism and anti-imperialism, Islamic communitarianism, "third-worldism", and cultural and political independence [all] functioned as the ideational points of fixation [sic] reconstituting the Iranian self during the revolutionary process of the 1960s and 1970s, and are not easy to discard', even

---

[29] Calabrese, *Revolutionary Horizons*, p. 73.
[30] Adeed Dawisha, *Saudi Arabia's Search for Security*, Adelphi Paper no. 158 (London: International Institute for Strategic Studies, 1979), pp. 7–8.
[31] Kechichian, *Oman and the World*, p. 60.
[32] Assiri, *Kuwait's Foreign Policy*, p. 78.
[33] Rosenau, *Scientific Study of Foreign Policy*, p. 109.
[34] Graham E. Fuller, *The 'Center of the Universe': The Geopolitics of Iran* (Boulder, CO: Westview, 1991), p. 12.
[35] David E. Long, 'Saudi Arabia and its Neighbors: Preoccupied Paternalism', in H. Richard Sindelar III and J.E. Peterson (eds), *Crosscurrents in the Gulf* (London: Routledge, 1988), pp. 185, 195.
[36] O'Reilly, 'Oil Monarchies without Oil', passim.

in the early years of the twenty-first century.[37] In almost all cases, chapters or sections that set out to analyze concrete policy changes quickly lapse into straightforward narrative, rather than offering a coherent explanatory argument that accords specific weight to each causal factor.[38]

Debates generated by the literature on Gulf state foreign policy consequently gravitate toward practical rather than conceptual issues. Perhaps the most heated of these controversies concerns whether or not the Islamic Republic is predisposed toward expansionism. Those who argue that Tehran is bent on regional expansion claim that in the years since the 1978–1979 revolution, the regime has directed relations with surrounding states toward the overall objective of 'creat[ing] a political order in various countries in the area that either resembles the Islamic Republic of Iran, or, at least, is acceptable to the Khomeini regime'.[39] With respect to foreign affairs, such writers insist, the post-revolutionary leadership, 'while changing a great many things, did not in any way alter the long-held ambitions of Iran in the Gulf region'.[40] The Islamic Republic's aggressive tendencies are reinforced by its advantageous geographical position: Laura Guazzone observes that 'Iran does not need to invade Kuwait or Saudi Arabia to compel or deter militarily the GCC countries: all their strategic targets are within air reach of Iran, and Tehran could easily contend control of the Gulf waterways with the littoral states.'[41] Anthony Cordesman adds that Iran poses an even greater threat to surrounding states in the years following the death of Ayatollah Khomeini, due to the government's success in improving operational co-ordination between the Revolutionary Guards Corps and the regular armed forces, along with its ongoing efforts to build up the country's conventional arsenal and develop unconventional weaponry.[42] Consequently, 'a voluntary shift by [Iran's] leaders from their well-known mission-oriented regional

---

[37] Adib-Moghaddam, *Iran in World Politics*, p. 71.

[38] See, for example, Afrasiabi, *After Khomeini*, chap. 3; Marschall, *Iran's Persian Gulf Policy*, chap. 3; Hermann F. Eilts, 'Foreign Policy Perspectives of the Gulf States', in Sindelar and Peterson, *Crosscurrents in the Gulf*; Anoushiravan Ehteshami, Gerd Nonneman and Charles Tripp, *War and Peace in the Gulf* (Reading: Ithaca Press, 1991), chap. 3; Habib Ishow, 'Relations between Iraq and Kuwait', in Derek Hopwood, Habib Ishow and Thomas Koszinowski (eds), *Iraq: Power and Society* (Reading: Ithaca Press, 1993); Andreas Rieck, 'Iraq and Saudi Arabia: From Rivalry to Confrontation', in Hopwood, Ishow and Koszinowski, *Iraq*; Andrew T. Parasiliti, 'Iran and Iraq: Changing Relations and Future Prospects', in Amirahmadi and Entessar, *Iran and the Arab World*; Pirouz Mojtahed-Zadeh, 'A Geopolitical Triangle in the Persian Gulf: Actions and Reactions among Iran, Bahrain and Saudi Arabia', *Iranian Journal of International Affairs*, 6 (Spring-Summer 1994); Shahram Chubin and Charles Tripp, *Iran-Saudi Arabia Relations and Regional Order*, Adelphi Paper, 304 (London: International Institute for Strategic Studies, 1996); Mohammad el-Sayed Selim, 'Arab and Iranian Policies Towards Middle Easternism and Gulf Security', in Khair el-Din Haseeb (ed.), *Arab-Iranian Relations* (Beirut: Centre for Arab Unity Studies, 1998); Henner Fuertig. *Iran's Rivalry with Saudi Arabia between the Gulf Wars* (Reading: Ithaca Press, 2002); and Elham Manea, *Regional Politics in the Gulf: Saudi Arabia, Oman, Yemen* (London: Saqi, 2005).

[39] M.E. Ahrari, 'Khomeini's Iran and Threats to Gulf Security', in M.E. Ahrari (ed.), *The Gulf and International Security* (New York: St Martin's, 1989), p. 10.

[40] Mohammad al-Rumaihi, 'Arabian Gulf Security', *American-Arab Affairs*, no. 23 (Winter 1987–88), p. 50.

[41] Laura Guazzone, 'Gulf Co-operation Council: The Security Policies', *Survival*, 30 (March–April 1988), p. 139. See also Dan Caldwell, 'Flashpoints in the Gulf: Abu Musa and the Tunb Islands', *Middle East Policy*, 4 (March 1996).

[42] Anthony H. Cordesman, *Iran and Iraq: The Threat from the Northern Gulf* (Boulder, CO: Westview, 1994). See also Patrick Clawson, *Iran's Challenge to the West* (Washington, DC: Washington Institute for Near East Policy, 1993); Michael Eisenstadt, *Iranian Military Power: Capabilities and Intentions* (Washington, DC: Washington Institute for Near East Policy, 1996); David Menashri, *Revolution at a Crossroads: Iran's Domestic Politics and Regional Ambitions* (Washington, DC: Washington Institute for Near East Policy, 1996); and Jamal S. al-Suwaidi, 'Gulf Security and the Iranian Challenge', *Security Dialogue*, 27 (September 1996).

policies and discourse and from their domestic authoritarian practices is unlikely. The critical obstacle is the externally imposed inability to pursue these policies'.[43]

Others counter that Iranian aggressiveness has moderated significantly as the country's post-revolutionary regime settled into a more routinized system of governance.[44] It is true that after the 1980–1988 Iran-Iraq war, the Islamic Republic found itself in the throes of a severe domestic crisis. No leader has been able to fill Khomeini's shoes; economic reform has turned out to be both elusive and disruptive; 'there is growing instability in peripheral regions with large refugee populations, porous borders and unstable neighbors'; and the country faces the threat of an 'ethno-sectarian dispute between the Sunni populations and the Shi'i Iranian state'.[45] In addition, the foreign policy bureaucracy remains disjointed,[46] while Western governments have consistently turned their backs on Iranian diplomatic initiatives.[47] But these circumstances have led the leadership in Tehran to take fundamentally defensive steps to shore up its deteriorating strategic position by embarking upon a comprehensive rearmament program. In particular, state officials have earmarked scarce resources to rebuild and upgrade the air force and navy, both of which might help to dissuade outside powers from launching strikes against Iranian territory. Furthermore, 'Iran's experiences in the [1980–1988] Iran-Iraq War and the lessons of the [1990–1991] Gulf War have led it to attempt either to produce or acquire weapons of mass destruction to obtain a deterrent and retaliatory capability.'[48] Michel Nawfal summarizes the resulting situation:

> Iran finds itself now—even without being interested in the arms race—forced to rebuild and modernize its military forces, and develop its military industries. Iran cannot rely (as Kuwait and Saudi Arabia did) on protection from Western states in the event of a renewed Iraqi attack. Nevertheless, it is rather difficult for the Arab Gulf countries to view this Iranian armament with comfort, even if it is not necessarily directed against them.[49]

Policy-makers in Tehran recognize the underlying dilemma, and have made repeated overtures to surrounding governments in an attempt to reassure them that the Islamic Republic harbours no aggressive intentions.[50] Furthermore, Iran conspicuously refrained from taking advantage of the 1990–1991 war to

[43] Ghassan Salamé, 'Assessing Alternative Future Arrangements for Regional Security', in Geoffrey Kemp and Janice Gross Stein (eds), *Powder Keg in the Middle East* (Washington, DC: American Association for the Advancement of Science, 1995), pp. 70–71. See also Philip L. Ritcheson, 'Iranian Military Resurgence: Scope, Motivations and Implications for Regional Security', *Armed Forces and Society*, 21 (Summer 1995); Adib-Moghaddam, *Iran in World Politics*, pp. 69–71.

[44] Mohsen M. Milani, 'Iran's Gulf Policy: From Idealism and Confrontation to Pragmatism and Moderation', in Jamal al-Suwaidi (ed.), *Iran and the Gulf: A Search for Stability* (Abu Dhabi: Emirates Center for Strategic Studies and Research, 1996); Patrick J. Conge, *From Revolution to War* (Ann Arbor: University of Michigan Press, 1996), pp. 65–88; Stephen M. Walt, *Revolution and War* (Ithaca, NY: Cornell University Press, 1996), pp. 211–268; and Shireen Hunter, 'Iran's Pragmatic Regional Policy', *Journal of International Affairs*, 56 (Spring 2003).

[45] Ahmed Hashim, *The Crisis of the Iranian State*, Adelphi Paper no. 296 (London: International Institute for Strategic Studies, 1995), p. 5.

[46] *Ibid.*, pp. 30–32.

[47] *Ibid.*, pp. 34–35.

[48] *Ibid.*, p. 51. See also Shahram Chubin, *Iran's National Security Policy: Capabilities, Intentions and Impact* (Washington, DC: Carnegie Endowment for International Peace, 1994).

[49] Michel Nawfal, 'Arab-Iranian Relations in the Islamic World', in Haseeb, *Arab-Iranian Relations*, p. 552.

[50] Mohsen M. Milani, 'Iran's Post-Cold War Policy in the Persian Gulf', *International Journal*, 49 (Spring 1994), pp. 338–339.

improve its precarious strategic position,[51] and acted in an equally circumspect fashion in response to the US-led occupations of Afghanistan and Iraq 12 years later.[52]

Resolving debates about the true intentions and motivations of states in an anarchic arena is notoriously hard to accomplish. Even the most aggressive-looking external policies may well be undertaken due to defensive motivations.[53] Students of the international relations of the Gulf would therefore do well to devote more sustained attention and effort to the crucial task of disentangling the various factors and processes that determine foreign policy in this part of the world, and spend less time and energy arguing about what measures policy-makers should adopt in order to change the actions or attitudes of countries in the region.

Dimensions of Regional Security

Three intellectual currents have swept through the field of security studies over the last two decades.[54] First-wave studies postulate the existence of autonomous, competitive states whose overriding priority is to protect their strategic interests in the face of exogenous threats; the primary purpose of first-wave analyses is to explicate actual and potential security challenges, and indicate what measures states might implement in order to parry them. Second-wave studies broaden the twin notions of 'security' and 'threat' to incorporate a wide range of economic, societal, environmental, demographic and other challenges that play little or no part in first-wave accounts; second-wave studies also wrestle with the sticky question of whether security-producing programs tend be precipitated by threats to the interests of states or instead result from threats to the stability of regimes. Third-wave studies focus on the cognitive, discursive, organizational and socio-cultural processes whereby particular events or trends come to constitute security threats, that is, how and by whom threats get 'constructed'. Examples of each of these three intellectual currents can be found in the extensive literature on Gulf security, although the great majority of writings on the subject continues to fall somewhere between the first and second waves.[55]

First-wave studies are epitomized by Anthony Cordesman's comprehensive overview of *The Gulf and the Search for Strategic Stability*. The survey is premised on the claim that

> the smaller conservative Gulf states lack the territory and population to act alone [in regional security affairs]. Their geography makes them vulnerable to Iran, South Yemen,

---

[51] Mohsen M. Milani, 'Iran's Active Neutrality during the Kuwaiti Crisis: Reasons and Ramifications', *New Political Science*, 21–22 (Spring-Summer 1992); Hooshang Amirahmadi, 'Iran and the Persian Gulf Crisis', in Amirahmadi and Entessar, *Iran and the Arab World*; Afrasiabi, *After Khomeini*, chap. 2.

[52] Anoushiravan Ehteshami, 'Iran-Iraq Relations after Saddam', *Washington Quarterly*, 26 (Autumn 2003); Anoushiravan Ehteshami, 'Iran's International Posture after the Fall of Baghdad', *Middle East Journal*, 58 (Spring 2004); and Kamran Taremi, 'Iranian Foreign Policy towards Occupied Iraq, 2003-05', *Middle East Policy*, 12 (Winter 2005).

[53] Charles L. Glaser, 'Political Consequences of Military Strategy', *World Politics*, 44 (July 1992).

[54] A somewhat different view is presented in Keith Krause and Michael C. Williams, 'Broadening the Agenda of Security Studies: Politics and Methods', *Mershon International Studies Review*, 40 (October 1996).

[55] For an important catalogue of earlier work, see J.E. Peterson, 'Security in the Arabian Peninsula and Gulf States, 1973–1984', Occasional Paper no. 7 (Washington, DC: National Council on US-Arab Relations, 1985). See also J.E. Peterson, *Defense and Regional Security in the Arabian Peninsula and Gulf States, 1973-2004: An Annotated Bibliography* (Dubai: Gulf Research Center, 2006).

or Iraq. Their only hope of finding strength that approaches their wealth lies in collective action and in cooperation with Saudi Arabia.[56]

Whether or not security co-operation is likely to occur is held to be a function of the degree of interoperability of the armed forces of the smaller Gulf states, the amount of combat experience these forces manage to gain, the degree to which future equipment purchases create balance among various branches of their respective military establishments and the extent to which 'nepotism or "politicisation"' shapes the process whereby commanding officers are promoted, along with unspecified 'political' problems that have discouraged 'collective security efforts' in the past.[57] The formation of the Gulf Co-operation Council mitigated but did not resolve basic strategic incompatibilities among member-states.[58]

Equally first-wave in conception is Joseph Kostiner's analysis of the campaign to construct a collective defence arrangement in the aftermath of the 1990–1991 war. Kostiner demonstrates that persistent conflicts of interest among the Gulf states prevented them from coming up with a mutually acceptable security structure to replace the amorphous Damascus Declaration.[59] As a result, several of the smaller Arab Gulf states, most notably Kuwait and Bahrain, initiated bilateral defence agreements with the United States and Britain.[60] The new pacts heightened longstanding tensions over territorial boundaries, and at the same time encouraged the Islamic Republic to take steps to increase its influence in regional affairs.[61] Divergent responses by Arab governments to renewed Iranian assertiveness further undermined strategic co-operation among the GCC states.[62] Kostiner concludes that

> 1992 was marked by the escalation and subsequent diminution of conflicts in the Gulf region, developments that were exacerbated by the failure to achieve a comprehensive security arrangement and in turn impeded efforts toward reaching such an agreement. Strategies of defense cooperation which appeared as security options for the GCC states in early 1992 turned out [instead] to be major sources of security danger.[63]

---

[56] Anthony H. Cordesman, *The Gulf and the Search for Strategic Stability* (Boulder, CO: Westview, 1984), p. 41

[57] *Ibid.*, pp. 488–490. See also Mazher A. Hameed, *Arabia Imperilled* (Washington: Middle East Assessments Group, 1986); Andrew Rathmell, *The Changing Military Balance in the Gulf*, RUSI Whitehall Papers no. 38 (London: RUSI, 1996); Sean Foley, 'What Wealth Cannot Buy: UAE Security at the Turn of the Twenty-first Century', in Barry Rubin (ed.), *Crises in the Contemporary Persian Gulf* (London: Frank Cass, 2002); Saideh Lutfian, 'A Regional Security System in the Persian Gulf', in Lawrence G. Potter and Gary G. Sick (eds), *Security in the Persian Gulf* (New York: Palgrave, 2002).

[58] 'Abd al-Hadi Khalaf, 'The Elusive Quest for Gulf Security', *MERIP Middle East Report*, no. 148 (September-October 1987); Michael Sterner, 'The Gulf Cooperation Council and Persian Gulf Security', in Thomas Naff (ed.), *Gulf Security and the Iran-Iraq War* (Washington, DC: National Defense University Press, 1985); Turki al-Hamad, 'Imperfect Alliances: Will the Gulf Monarchies Work Together?' in Rubin (ed.), *Crises in the Contemporary Persian Gulf*. More optimistic accounts of the GCC's prospects include Joseph Wright Twinam, 'The Gulf Cooperation Council: The Smaller Gulf States and Interstate Relations', in Charles F. Doran and Stephen W. Buck (eds), *The Gulf, Energy and Global Security* (Boulder, CO: Lynne Rienner, 1990); John Duke Anthony, 'The Gulf Cooperation Council: A New Framework for Policy Coordination', in Sindelar and Peterson, *Crosscurrents in the Gulf*; Fred H. Lawson, *Dialectical Integration in the Gulf Co-operation Council* (Abu Dhabi: Emirates Center for Strategic Studies and Research, 1997); Matteo Legrenzi, 'Did the GCC Make a Difference?' in Cilja Harders and Matteo Legrenzi (eds), *Beyond Regionalism?* (Aldershot: Ashgate, 2008).

[59] Joseph Kostiner, 'The Search for Gulf Security: The Politics of Collective Defense', *Middle East Contemporary Survey*, 16 (1992), pp. 230–233.

[60] *Ibid.*, pp. 233–234.

[61] *Ibid.*, p. 236.

[62] *Ibid.*, p. 238.

[63] *Ibid.*, p. 241. A parallel analysis of other proposed Gulf security arrangements can be found in Anwar-ul-Haq Ahady, 'Security in the Persian Gulf after Desert Storm', *International Journal*, 49 (Spring 1994).

David Priess offers a less orthodox first-wave explanation for the formation of the Gulf Co-operation Council. Building on Stephen Walt's *The Origins of Alliances*, Priess argues that states adopt security-producing programs not so much in response to changes in the distribution of power as to increases in the level of threat that they face.[64] Threat levels are determined by four factors: 'aggregate power, geographical proximity, offensive power, and aggressive intentions'.[65] States can be expected to take steps to resist the initiatives of neighbours whose relative power is growing, who have the capacity to strike first and who evidence a willingness to resort to force. On the other hand, they are apt to collaborate with neighbours whose power is stagnant or decreasing, who cannot carry out a first strike and who demonstrate co-operative intent. In early 1981, the six smaller Arab Gulf states found themselves facing an overtly revisionist Iran which, although concentrating its armed forces on the war with Iraq, had begun to encourage or sponsor subversive movements throughout the region, and therefore posed a direct and proximate threat to their continued existence. They consequently put aside their rivalries with one another and set up the GCC. Priess concludes on the basis of this case that 'the role of perceptions of aggressive intentions, an integral yet perhaps still underemphasized aspect of balance-of-threat theory, should be given more attention' in the broader field of security studies.[66]

It is notable that in the wake of the 1990–1991 war, scholarship on the Gulf seldom treated United States military intervention as a threat to regional security. One of the very few scholars to broach the topic is Saleh A. al-Mani, who lists four ways in which the presence of the US armed forces effectively undermined the stability of the Arab Gulf states. First, the stationing of American troops in Bahrain 'fueled public resentment against a foreign army' on the islands.[67] Second, US policy tended 'to negate [. . .] calls for political openness and increased mass participation' in the GCC countries, and pushed them 'further along the military paradigm, and away from the mercantile interests of an essentially trade-oriented society'.[68] Third, US efforts to promote the sale of sophisticated weaponry to local governments drained resources that might otherwise have been used to encourage economic growth through the expansion of light manufacturing and trade.[69] Fourth, al-Mani observes that 'the declared US policy of [military] engagement and isolation of both Iran and Iraq (dual containment), may have succeeded in hurting these two countries. However, it also seems to have arrested attempts by GCC states to normalize relations with Iran'. So long as the GCC states and the Islamic Republic continue to gaze at one another 'through an American lens', al-Mani argues, the potential for conflict in the area remains considerably higher than it would otherwise be.[70]

---

[64] Stephen Walt, *The Origins of Alliances* (Ithaca, NY: Cornell University Press, 1987).
[65] David Priess, 'Balance-of-Threat Theory and the Genesis of the Gulf Cooperation Council', *Security Studies*, 5 (Summer 1996), p. 148.
[66] *Ibid.*, p. 171.
[67] Saleh A. al-Mani, 'Gulf Security and Relations with Our Neighbors', *Security Dialogue*, 27 (September 1996), p. 296. See also Hassan Hamdan Al-Alkim, 'The Arabian Gulf at the New Millennium: Security Challenges', in Kechichian, *Iran, Iraq and the Arab Gulf States*, pp. 418–420; Abdullah Alshayji, 'Gulf Views of US Policy in the Region', *Middle East Policy*, 5 (September 1997).
[68] al-Mani, 'Gulf Security', p. 297.
[69] *Ibid.*
[70] *Ibid.*, p. 298. See also Abdullah K. al-Shayeji, 'Stability in the [Persian] Gulf Region: Clash of Visions', *Iranian Journal of International Affairs*, 8 (Summer 1996). On the US policy of dual containment, see F. Gregory Gause III, 'The Illogic of Dual Containment', *Foreign Affairs*, 73 (March-April 1994) and Gary Sick, 'Rethinking Dual Containment', *Survival*, 40 (Spring 1998).

Second-wave studies introduce a wide variety of dynamics that could jeopardize the security of states and/or the stability of regimes in the Gulf. These include domestic political challenges, particularly the demands for greater popular participation in policy-making that were voiced in most of the Arab Gulf states following the 1990–1991 war;[71] the liberal use of coercion by state officials to suppress such challenges;[72] the economic difficulties that accompanied the postwar stagnation of world oil prices;[73] the sizable populations of expatriates that reside in the region;[74] the increasing number of young people and the growing shortage of fresh water throughout the region;[75] and the continued exclusion of qualified women from senior positions in government and business.[76] What remains unclear is precisely how these dynamics interact with the exogenous threats that are posited in first-wave writings: do factors such as rising domestic political challenges or escalating economic difficulties come into play only when the level of external threat is comparatively low? Or are there specific ways in which internal and external threats continuously interact with one another?

One essay that proposes a direct link between domestic and foreign security dynamics is Shahram Chubin and Charles Tripp's 'Domestic Politics and Territorial Disputes in the Persian Gulf and the Arabian Peninsula'. Chubin and Tripp note that the relationship between territory and patriotism remains 'problematic' in virtually all of the Gulf countries.[77] More precisely, the conjunction of the end of the Cold War and the consolidation of 'state-based nationalism' in the region is likely to have 'infuse[d] territorial issues with greater significance and, in the early phases of self-definition and self-identification, this may be particularly sensitive and volatile'.[78] At the same time, the spread

[71] Joseph A. Kechichian, *Political Dynamics and Security in the Arabian Peninsula through the 1990s* (Santa Monica, CA: RAND, 1993); F. Gregory Gause III, *Oil Monarchies: Domestic and Security Challenges in the Arab Gulf States* (New York: Council on Foreign Relations Press, 1994); Gawdat Bahgat, 'Military Security and Political Stability in the Gulf', *Arab Studies Quarterly*, 17 (Fall 1995); Clive Jones, 'Saudi Arabia after the Gulf War: The Internal-External Security Dilemma', *International Relations*, 12 (December 1995); Gerd Nonneman, 'Security and Inclusion: Regime Responses to Domestic Challenges in the Gulf', in Sean McKnight, Neil Partrick and Francis Toase (eds), *Gulf Security: Opportunities and Challenges for the New Generation*, RUSI Whitehall Papers no. 51 (London: RUSI, 2000); J.E. Peterson, *Saudi Arabia and the Illusion of Security*, Adelphi Paper no. 348 (London: International Institute for Strategic Studies, 2002). Internal threats from sectarian and ethnic minorities in the GCC states are detailed, and effectively dismissed, by J.E. Peterson, 'Security Concerns in the Arabian Peninsula', in Ahrari, *The Gulf and International Security*.

[72] Jill Crystal, 'Social Transformation, Changing Expectations and Gulf Security', in David E. Long and Christian Koch (eds), *Gulf Security in the Twenty-first Century* (Abu Dhabi: Emirates Center for Strategic Studies and Research, 1997).

[73] Gawdat Bahgat, 'Regional Peace and Stability in the Gulf', *Security Dialogue*, 26 (September 1995); F. Gregory Gause III, 'The Political Economy of National Security in the GCC States', in Gary G. Sick and Lawrence G. Potter (eds), *The Persian Gulf at the Millennium* (New York: St Martin's, 1997); Paul Stevens, 'Declining Oil Revenues in the GCC States: A Threat or an Opportunity?' in McKnight, Partrick and Toase, *Gulf Security*.

[74] Andreij Kapiszewski, *Nationals and Expatriates: Population and Labour Dilemmas of the Gulf Cooperation Council States* (Reading: Ithaca, 2001); Paul Dresch, 'Foreign Matter: The Place of Strangers in Gulf Society', in John W. Fox, Nada Mourtada-Sabbah and Mohammed al-Mutawa (eds), *Globalization and the Gulf* (London: Routledge, 2006).

[75] Geoffrey Kemp and Janice Gross Stein, 'Enduring Sources of Conflict in the Persian Gulf Region', in Kemp and Stein, *Powder Keg in the Middle East*; Michael E. Bonine, 'Population Growth, the Labor Market and Gulf Security', in Long and Koch, *Gulf Security in the Twenty-first Century*; Mai Yamani, 'The New Generation in Saudi Arabia', in Potter and Sick, *Security in the Persian Gulf*. See also Kamran Taremi, 'The Role of Water Exports in Iranian Foreign Policy toward the GCC', *Iranian Studies*, 38 (June 2005). For the case that water shortages provide important incentives for regional co-operation, see Asghar Ja'fari Valdani, 'Iran and the Persian Gulf Countries: Prospects for Cooperation', *Iranian Journal of International Affairs*, 8 (Fall 1996).

[76] Mai Yamani, 'Health, Education, Gender and the Security of the Gulf in the Twenty-first Century', in Long and Koch, *Gulf Security in the Twenty-first Century*.

[77] Shahram Chubin and Charles Tripp, 'Domestic Politics and Territorial Disputes in the Persian Gulf and the Arabian Peninsula', *Survival*, 35 (Winter 1993), p. 5.

[78] *Ibid.*, pp. 7–8.

of territorial nationalism removes the possibility of settling border disputes by means of what Chubin and Tripp call 'the rules of sheikhly exchange'.[79] Disagreements about borders become even more complicated 'when there is genuine popular participation in the political process. Under these conditions, territory and its associations assume a genuine power in politics and cannot simply be picked up, dropped or given away to suit the immediate priorities of the regime'.[80] Threats related to territory are therefore likely to become more salient in the near future, and will grow in importance to the extent that the citizens of the Gulf states gain 'an awareness of the *res publica*, the state as common property'.[81]

Another way to connect internal and external security dynamics makes use of the notion of 'two-level games'.[82] During the last quarter of 1980, Arab Gulf governments took seriously the possibility that Iraq's unexpected military thrust into southwestern Iran might reinvigorate radical movements throughout the region. At the same time, non-ruling family elites had an interest in defending the economic and political prerogatives they had been granted over the course of the preceding decade. Under these circumstances, the rulers of Saudi Arabia, Kuwait, Bahrain, Qatar, the United Arab Emirates, and Oman faced a choice between, on the one hand, augmenting the concessions that they had already made to local notables and, on the other, limiting, or even curtailing, these prerogatives. At the same time, non-ruling family elites confronted an equally difficult choice: whether to join the regime in suppressing radical activists or to express sympathy, and perhaps even support, for the radicals' demands. Given the two parties' shared interest in avoiding the emergence of a revolutionary situation, the interaction of rulers and elites was most likely to result in a perpetuation of the reforms that had been implemented in the late 1970s. But as in all such 'Chicken' games, mutual co-operation represented an inherently unstable outcome.[83] Non-ruling family elites continued to have an incentive to encourage radical challengers in a bid to seize the initiative in local politics, while rulers harboured an equally strong incentive to revoke earlier concessions as a means of perpetuating the existing social order. Were either of these two actors to defect by moving in the direction of its most preferred state of affairs, the other would have little alternative but to acquiesce in order to avoid the chaos that would almost certainly accompany mutual defection.

Meanwhile, on the international level, Saudi Arabia had two options regarding how to respond to the threat to Gulf stability posed by the Iraqi invasion of Iran. First, it might have insisted that whatever security arrangements were set up accord it a pre-eminent role in regional affairs; second, it could have advocated some form of truly multilateral institution, predicated on a more equal distribution of power among the prospective member-states. The Kingdom's potential partners, on the other hand, faced a choice between accepting and rejecting whatever security structure the Saudis might propose. Given Riyadh's expressed determination to play the leading role in Arab Gulf affairs, the most likely

---

[79] *Ibid.*, p. 21.
[80] *Ibid.*, p. 22.
[81] *Ibid.*, p. 26.
[82] This argument is developed in Fred H. Lawson, 'Theories of Integration in a New Context: The Gulf Cooperation Council', in Kenneth P. Thomas and Mary Ann Tétreault (eds), *Racing to Regionalize* (Boulder, CO: Lynne Rienner, 1999).
[83] See Glenn Snyder and Paul Diesing, *Conflict among Nations* (Princeton, NJ: Princeton University Press, 1977), pp. 118–119.

outcome was one in which the remaining emirates acquiesced in a Saudi-dominated regional security arrangement. Nevertheless, this outcome was no more stable than the one obtained in domestic affairs: Riyadh's strategic partners could be expected to take steps to distance themselves from a Saudi-dominated security structure just as soon as it became safe for them to do so.

In short, the winter of 1980–1981 saw Kuwait, Bahrain, Qatar, the United Arab Emirates and Oman confronting a major external threat, yet reluctant to acquiesce in the emergence of a Gulf security arrangement that institutionalized Saudi hegemony. At the same time, non-ruling family elites throughout the region stood to gain more from encouraging radical challengers than they did from rallying to the support of their respective regimes. As a way out of the internal and external impasses they faced, the six rulers devised an innovative set of integrative institutions that promised to satisfy the interests of local entrepreneurs and professionals. The multilateral components of the proposed Gulf Co-operation Council—most notably the abolition of restrictions on investment and employment across the borders of the member-states—gave local notables a strong incentive to refrain from supporting radical movements, even as they sweetened the pill of heightened activism on the part of local security services. It was thus the synergy generated by the conjunction of simultaneous internal and external challenges that sparked the unprecedented burst of Gulf regionalism that occurred in 1981–1982.

Rosemary Hollis offers a second-wave alternative to Kostiner's explanation for the failure to create effective collective security arrangements in the Gulf following the 1990–1991 war. Whereas Kostiner emphasizes fundamental conflicts of interest among the smaller Gulf states and the unintended consequences generated by the security policies that these states pursued in 1991–1992, Hollis argues that

> the GCC states also had economic reasons for wanting to backtrack on the expectations implicit in the original Damascus Declaration. They had war debts to settle, reconstruction costs to meet (especially in the case of Kuwait) and rearmament plans to implement. With these as their priorities and short-term cash-flow problems, they were not ready to lavish economic aid on Egypt and Syria in return for their continued provision of troops. In fact, the continuance of that military presence began to look like a liability.[84]

When the majority of contracts for postwar reconstruction projects ended up being awarded to US and British companies, Egypt became disenchanted with the idea of maintaining troops in the Gulf and announced that it intended to pull its forces out of the region.[85] Kuwait and Bahrain then negotiated bilateral basing and prepositioning agreements with the US and Britain to complement the reconstruction contracts.[86] Subsequent attempts by Egypt and Syria to revive the Damascus Declaration were politely but firmly rebuffed.[87]

Third-wave studies of Gulf security are just beginning to appear. One essay that makes use of concepts central to the third wave is Michael Barnett and Gregory Gause's account of the peculiar trajectory that one sees in the development of the Gulf Co-operation Council. Barnett and Gause argue that

---

[84] Rosemary Hollis, "'Whatever Happened to the Damascus Declaration?': Evolving Security Structures in the Gulf", in M. Jane Davis (ed.), *Politics and International Relations in the Middle East* (Aldershot: Elgar, 1995), p. 41.
[85] *Ibid.*, pp. 41–42.
[86] *Ibid.*, pp. 44–46.
[87] *Ibid.*, p. 48.

even though 'Gulf leaders constructed the GCC for statist purposes, its very existence has encouraged, however unintentionally, greater mutual identification at the societal level'.[88] This came about largely because even though 'the Gulf states did not emphasize publicly internal security issues when forming the organization, [...] one purpose of the GCC was to provide Gulf citizens with a rhetorical and an institutional alternative identity (beyond their state identities) that would compete with Iran's Islamic revolutionary and Iraq's secular Arab nationalist platforms'.[89] The innovative 'khaliji' identity has had a much greater impact on regional affairs than have the formal structures of the GCC itself: by the mid-1980s 'the GCC states began to use the institution to successfully handle border disputes and other areas of disagreement. And the populations of the GCC were beginning to interact and imagine themselves in new ways'.[90] Events associated with the 1990–1991 war 'provided a strong boost' for the new identity, which took on a more pronounced 'us vs. them' feeling in response to widespread Arab criticism of Western-led retaliation against Iraq.[91] More importantly, it is conceivable that local rulers will in the future redefine state interests so as to reflect the growing sense of regional identity,[92] thereby laying the foundation for a viable 'security community' in the Gulf.

Many of the themes that are advanced in third-wave security studies can be teased out of George Joffé's survey of divergent notions of sovereignty in the Gulf. Joffé traces the origins of current rivalries involving Iran, Iraq, Saudi Arabia and the smaller Arab emirates to differences in the meaning and practice of sovereignty in this part of the world. Whereas, in the case of Iran, sovereignty has long been intimately associated with control over a particular territory, along the southern Gulf littoral it inhered instead in the ability of rulers to maintain the loyalty of their political allies and collect taxes on commercial transactions. Furthermore, with the important exception of Saudi Arabia, the sovereignty of the Arab Gulf sheikhs 'did not involve any statement about the religious legitimation of the ruler's authority, merely an assertion of his power'.[93] Consequently, the emirs of the Trucial Coast found themselves constantly forced to parry efforts by Iran (and Ottoman Iraq) to extend a territory-based notion of sovereignty into adjacent areas. This challenge became especially intense in the islands of the Gulf, where the connection between rulership and a clearly delimited territory proved easier to transplant. Contests over the meaning and practice of sovereignty also precipitated recurrent conflict between Ottoman (and later British) Iraq and Kuwait.[94] British policy in the region confused the situation as much as it clarified things, particularly along the Trucial Coast.[95] Only with the arrival of foreign oil companies in the early twentieth century did a territorial conception

---

[88] Michael Barnett and F. Gregory Gause III, 'Caravans in Opposite Directions: Society, State and the Development of a Community in the Gulf Cooperation Council', in Emanuel Adler and Michael Barnett (eds), *Security Communities* (Cambridge: Cambridge University Press, 1998), p. 162.
[89] *Ibid.*, p. 170.
[90] *Ibid.*, p. 179.
[91] *Ibid.*, p. 186.
[92] *Ibid.*, p. 193.
[93] George Joffé, 'Concepts of Sovereignty in the Gulf Region', in Richard Schofield (ed.), *Territorial Foundations of the Gulf States* (London: UCL Press, 1994), p. 80 and p. 86. See also Mahmood Sariolghalam, 'Arab-Iranian Rapprochement: the Regional and International Impediments', in Haseeb, *Arab-Iranian Relations*.
[94] Joffé, 'Concepts of Sovereignty', pp. 86–87.
[95] *Ibid.*, pp. 87–89.

of sovereignty gain the upper hand.[96] Spelling out the specific ways, whether parallel to or divergent from the patterns adduced by Joffé, in which national interests and security threats have been constructed in the decades following Britain's withdrawal from the Gulf constitutes a pressing third-wave research project.

Explaining Inter-state Interaction

Systematic analysis of the dynamics that characterize interaction among the Gulf states remains in its infancy. Some of the earliest essays on the topic turn out to be more definitional than explanatory.[97] Others summarize the most important dynastic, territorial and ideological conflicts that shape international relations in the Gulf, but make no attempt to formulate theoretical propositions regarding the ways in which such conflicts shape regional affairs. John Duke Anthony, for instance, concludes one such summary by remarking that 'these forces—whether in the form of territorial rivalries between all of [the smaller Arab Gulf states], or of dynastic rivalries between the ruling families of the traditional regimes, underscore the complexity of this area in terms of regional and international politics and serve as a foundation conditioning how these states relate to one another politically'.[98] And to be sure that readers do not come away with the idea 'that a greater degree of cleavage than co-operation exists among the states concerned', Anthony goes on to list

> four categories of shared interests which transcend [these states'] rivalries and competition for influence in the area. Briefly, their interests are in: (1) the perpetuation of their respective conservative monarchical regimes; (2) the prevention of radical groups from gaining a foothold in the area; (3) the continuation of an uninterrupted flow of the Gulf's oil resources to markets outside the region; and (4) the procurement of the maximum revenue in exchange for their oil.[99]

Nevertheless, he claims that, in the end, 'individual states and groups of states have undermined efforts to achieve greater stability and co-operation, if not integration, among the states of the Arab side of the Gulf', and both the leaders and citizens of these countries have a tendency to blame Iran for this unhappy state of affairs.[100]

David Long offers a thumbnail sketch of relations among the Gulf states that represents a preliminary step toward explaining regional interaction. In the first place, the

> ideological and nationalistic confrontations in the gulf tend to balance each other in restraining any of the larger gulf powers from seeking to impose its will on the smaller states. For example, Iraqi aspirations in the gulf are checked by conservative Saudi Arabia and [Pahlavi] Iran, whereas Iranian national aspirations are restrained by Arab nationalist sentiments which are shared by the conservative Saudis and the radical Iraqis alike.

---

[96] *Ibid.*, pp. 90–91.
[97] William D. Anderson, 'The Persian Gulf as a Regional Subsystem', in Mohammed Mughisuddin (ed.), *Conflict and Cooperation in the Persian Gulf* (New York: Praeger, 1977).
[98] John Duke Anthony, 'The Persian Gulf in Regional and International Politics: The Arab Side of the Gulf', in Hossein Amirsadeghi (ed.), *The Security of the Persian Gulf* (London: Croom Helm, 1981), pp. 174–175.
[99] *Ibid.*, p. 179.
[100] *Ibid.*, p. 193. See also Abdullah K. Alshayji, 'Mutual Realities, Perceptions, and Impediments between the GCC States and Iran', in Potter and Sick, *Security in the Persian Gulf*.

The resulting equilibrium allows the smaller Gulf states some scope for independent political decision making, probably much more than they otherwise would have.[101]

Second, and 'at the risk of oversimplification, one might say there is a tendency for shaykhdoms to be at odds with their immediate neighbors and to have good relations with the next shaykhdom over'.[102] Rather than demonstrating how these twin dynamics determine the course of particular episodes of Gulf diplomacy, however, Long turns to an description of territorial disputes and radical movements across the region.

Shahram Chubin offers a perspective on regional affairs that is rooted in two cardinal assumptions: first, that the Gulf states have grown more and more interdependent, a trend that sets the stage for high levels of mutual 'entanglement and for shifting coalitions on different issue-areas and [therefore] breed[s] restraint' in their dealings with one another; and second, that 'international politics [in the Gulf] have taken on the aspect of a mixed-interest (or positive variable-sum) game rather than a (constant) zero-sum game'.[103] Unfortunately, he immediately stipulates that 'interdependencies mean vulnerability'.[104] Under these conditions, higher levels of interdependence become incompatible with positive-sum games: efforts by any one state to reduce its own vulnerability usually increase the vulnerability of others. This conclusion is apparent from Chubin's discussion of the problems that Gulf states have confronted when they have tried to set up a regional security pact. He points out, for instance, that 'from the point of view of the smaller powers, any regional grouping is bound to be dominated by the larger powers (Iran, Saudi Arabia and Iraq) perhaps at their expense (Kuwait's reaction to the Iran-Iraq rapprochement [of 1975] is indicative of this)'.[105] Still, Chubin makes the important observation that 'quite apart from motivation and capability, Iraq is constrained from intervention in the smaller states by the reaction of Saudi Arabia and Iran, Saudi Arabia by that of Iran and Iraq, and Iran by that of all the Arab states'.[106]

Gregory Gause pushes this line of argument a bit further. He observes that 'patterns of conflict and alignment' in the region exhibit a general tendency: 'Balancing behavior has predominated in the Gulf, but it has not been against military power per se. [...] Regimes have opposed and balanced against what they perceive to be the most serious threat to their domestic political stability, even if that meant aligning with another state whose military power could pose a future threat.'[107] Furthermore, 'domestic political challenges have been as important as those posed by disparities in military capabilities in driving regional international politics. Decisions on war and alliance made by the Gulf states can be understood only in light of both kinds of threats'.[108] Faced with a combination of serious external and internal threats at the end of the 1960s, for example, the new Baathist regime in Iraq attempted to mobilize neighbouring states into a collective security

---

[101] David E. Long, *The Persian Gulf* (Boulder, Colo.: Westview, 1976), p. 45.
[102] *Ibid.*, p. 46.
[103] Shahram Chubin, 'The International Politics of the Gulf', *British Journal of International Studies*, 2 (October 1976), p. 216.
[104] *Ibid.*, p. 218.
[105] *Ibid.*, p. 224.
[106] *Ibid.*, p. 226.
[107] F. Gregory Gause III, 'Gulf Regional Politics: Revolution, War and Rivalry', in W. Howard Wriggins (ed.), *Dynamics of Regional Politics* (New York: Columbia University Press, 1992), p. 26.
[108] *Ibid.*, p. 27.

arrangement directed against Iran; when the other Arab Gulf states failed 'to rally to Baghdad's call', Gause argues, Iraq initiated a campaign to overthrow their existing political systems and ordered its armed forces to advance into Kuwaiti territory. Saudi Arabia and Iran immediately came to Kuwait's defence, forcing Iraq to back down, 'although the border issue was not settled and Iraqi troops did not leave the area until July 1977'.[109] By the same token, after Iraq stopped supporting radical movements and the post-revolutionary regime in Iran started to encourage Shi'i activism throughout the region in 1979–1980, Saudi Arabia shifted sides and aligned itself with Iraq.[110]

Another insightful line of argument highlights the dynamics of strategic bargaining and deterrence among the key countries in the region. Bjørn Møller points out that Iraq, Iran and Saudi Arabia all augmented their armed forces during the 1980s, in both quantitative and qualitative terms.[111] By the mid-1990s, the Gulf approximated 'a situation of fragile balance, i.e. a situation where everybody (at least the three great powers) [found themselves] in a position to hurt everybody else (including the small powers), but where neither [sic] side is capable of defending itself against a determined surprise attack'. The resulting state of affairs, as Møller labels it, is 'a "mutual offensive superiority" stance', in which 'all three major states may be able to retaliate after any attack'.[112] The common inability to defend themselves against a first strike might well be expected to inject an element of stability into Iraq-Iranian-Saudi interaction, as predicted by mainstream deterrence theory.[113] Nevertheless, Møller suggests that deterrence in the Gulf is likely to exhibit a great deal of fragility, since, in a time of crisis, each country has an incentive to strike first in an attempt to weaken its rivals' military capacity. Regional deterrence is also apt to break down if a) 'one of the three states lowers its guard (say, by a partial demobilization)', thereby presenting the others with a 'window of opportunity [which] may prove irresistible'; or b) one of the three states mobilizes its armed forces or initiates large-scale military manoeuvres, thereby prompting one or both of the others 'to fear an impending surprise attack [and] hence strike preemptively'.[114]

Power cycle theory offers an equally promising alternative way to make sense of inter-state interaction in the Gulf. According to this analytical framework, states experience perpetual swings in power relative to one another.[115] Such cycles of rising and falling capabilities accompany fundamental shifts in a country's 'leadership role', that is, in the basic conception that policy-makers have of the state's place, responsibilities and ambitions in the regional order. Certain sorts of role conceptions are appropriate at specific points on the power cycle. If the government adopts a posture or policy that is incongruent with a country's capabilities at that particular moment, then the potential for inter-state conflict jumps. The chances of regional conflict escalate sharply if two or more states simultaneously exhibit a mismatch between their respective positions on the power cycle and the foreign policies that they pursue. This line of argument goes

[109] Ibid., pp. 39–40.
[110] Ibid., p. 51.
[111] Bjørn Møller, *Resolving the Security Dilemma in the Persian Gulf*, Emirates Occasional Papers no. 9 (Abu Dhabi: Emirates Center for Strategic Studies and Research, 1997), pp. 20–27.
[112] Ibid., p. 28.
[113] John Mearsheimer, *Conventional Deterrence* (Ithaca, NY: Cornell University Press, 1985).
[114] Møller, *Resolving the Security Dilemma*, p. 29.
[115] Charles F. Doran, *Systems in Crisis* (Cambridge: Cambridge University Press, 1991).

a long way toward explaining the outbreak of war between Iraq and Iran in 1980 and Baghdad's occupation of Kuwait and the ensuing confrontation with Saudi Arabia a decade later.[116] It also provides insight into trends in relations between Iran and Israel.[117]

Whether or not inter-state interaction in the Gulf can be explained in terms of cultural dynamics remains an open question. Arshin Adib-Moghaddam points to the construction of rival cultural formations in Iran and Iraq as the underlying source of hostility and conflict in regional affairs. The 1970s in particular saw the consolidation of an especially virulent form of Iranianism that posed a profound threat not only to 'genuine communitarian relations in the Gulf' but also to the interests of Iran's Arab neighbours.[118] Iranian 'ultra-nationalism' met its match in the militant Baathist Arabism that took hold in Baghdad around the same time. Under these circumstances, 'parochial debates about the nomenclature of the Gulf and its designation as "Persian" or "Arab" became a symbol for the ideological warfare between two manifestations of nationalism(s), rooted in—and nurtured by—the same exclusionary political philosophy'.[119] The 1978–1979 revolution in Iran added a further complication: a confrontation between, on the one hand, 'Islamic revisionism' and the principle of Westphalian sovereignty combined with both the Baathist Arabism of Iraq and the monarchical Wahhabism of Saudi Arabia on the other. 'Brought to a logical conclusion', Adib-Moghaddam asserts, 'Saddam Hussein's Iraq, as the main agent of Arab nationalism in the region, was a "natural" target of Imam Khomeini's rhetoric, setting the framework for the ensuing process of conflict between the two countries' which led inexorably to the First Gulf War of 1980–1988.[120]

Several key questions remain unresolved in this account. First, as Adib-Moghaddam recognizes, it is hard to explain in cultural terms either the timing or the specific form of the changes that have occurred in the interaction between Iran and Iraq. One might well ask, he remarks, 'why did Iraq not launch an invasion of Iran during the Shah period when there was a more immediate threat of Iranian interference in the country's affairs? Why launch a full-scale invasion of a larger and more resourceful [sic] neighbour?'[121] Rather than offering even a provisional answer to these crucial questions, the text further elaborates the manner in which 'the elite-driven construction of the anti-Iranian norm became a central component of the preferred state identity in Ba'thist Iraq'.[122] By the same token, cultural dynamics shed little light on the intriguing question of why the smaller Arab Gulf states rallied to Iraq's defence. 'It is not suggested that the Gulf states accepted the Iraqi regime's self-perception as the vanguard of pan-Arabism or even shared its anti-Iranian sentiments', the author notes. Arguably, '[t]hey did not.'[123] Rather than addressing the resulting puzzle, however, Adib-Moghaddam turns to a discussion of how support from neighbouring states

[116] Andrew T. Parasiliti, 'The Causes and Timing of Iraq's Wars: A Power Cycle Assessment', *International Political Science Review*, 24 (January 2003).
[117] Trita Parsi, 'Israel-Iranian Relations Assessed: Strategic Competition from the Power Cycle Perspective', *Iranian Studies*, 38 (June 2005).
[118] Arshin Adib-Moghaddam, *The International Politics of the Persian Gulf: A Cultural Genealogy* (London: Routledge, 2006), p. 17.
[119] *Ibid.*, p. 21.
[120] *Ibid.*, p. 31.
[121] *Ibid.*, p. 35.
[122] *Ibid.*, pp. 35–41.
[123] *Ibid.*, p. 41.

boosted Iraqi self-confidence and strengthened Baghdad's commitment to its chosen course of action.[124]

In his analysis of the situation in the region in the aftermath of the 1990–1991 war, Adib-Moghaddam adopts a broader conception of political culture, which incorporates institutions into a country's predominant cultural formation. The years after 1991 saw the emergence throughout the Gulf of 'new modes of public participation' in politics, which dampened earlier religion- and ideology-based antagonisms and laid a foundation for inter-state collaboration.[125] The spread of democratic discourses and practices was epitomized by the rise of the Second Khordad Movement in Iran, the promulgation and ratification of the National Action Charter in Bahrain and increasing activism on the part of elected assemblies in Kuwait and Oman. These developments precipitated a notable reduction in antagonism between Iran and its neighbours, or in Adib-Moghaddam's words, 'the two interdependent concepts, namely the institutionalization of an "Islamic-democratically" legitimated domestic constituency and the projection of dialogue and détente abroad, constituted the meta-narrative for the political disposition of "post-Second Khordad" Iran'.[126] Unfortunately, expanding US military involvement in the region generated friction between the Islamic Republic and the smaller Arab Gulf states, setting the stage for renewed belligerence in the wake of the September 2001 attacks on New York and northern Virginia. Heightened US intervention also sparked widespread anti-imperialist sentiment, which took on a distinctly Islamist coloration.[127] How these trends affected the region's experiments in political liberalization is left unaddressed, but it seems safe to infer that the US-led military campaigns in Afghanistan and Iraq severely undermined the nascent Kantian 'zone of peace' that began to take shape in the mid-1990s.[128]

Conclusion

International relations in the Gulf display a wide range of variation, and pose questions that have sparked heated debate in the academic literature on foreign policy studies, security studies and inter-state interaction. There is thus much that scholarship on the Gulf can contribute not only to knowledge about trends in the region itself, but also to our general understanding of world politics. In addition to the points raised in the preceding sections, evidence from the contemporary Gulf might well illuminate the circumstances under which deterrent threats succeed or fail; the factors that lead some but not other military confrontations to evolve into enduring rivalries; the connection between levels of interdependence and inter-state conflict; the point at which war is most likely to break out during a power transition; and which state—the dominant power or the challenger—is more likely to make the first hostile move in such a transition.

By the same token, scholarship that is framed in terms of theoretical concepts and debates drawn from the three major subfields of international relations can provide new insight into events and processes that continue to exercise specialists

---

[124] *Ibid.*, pp. 41–43.
[125] *Ibid.*, p. 83.
[126] *Ibid.*, p. 86.
[127] *Ibid.*, pp. 111–119.
[128] *Ibid.*, p. 82.

in Gulf affairs. Thanks to the studies examined here, our attention has been drawn to the role that the administrative apparatus plays in foreign policy-making, even in countries that possess highly centralized, autocratic political systems. We will be less likely to formulate questions about regional stability that ignore domestic economic and demographic trends, or that fail to address the complex processes whereby external threats get created, perpetuated or militarized. And we are likely to devote more effort to figuring out exactly why states in this part of the world interact with one another the way they do, instead of simply assuming that episodes of conflict (or instances of co-operation) are inevitable, given the peculiar geography, history and culture of the Gulf.

The Power of Narrative: Saudi Arabia, the United States and the Search for Security

PATRICK CONGE and GWENN OKRUHLIK

ABSTRACT *This article carefully constructs the mainstream narrative that sustains the 'special' relationship between the United States and Saudi Arabia, and demonstrates the persistence and folly of conventional wisdom on security by delineating two normative threads in it. The norm of exceptionality frames the relationship between the states; the norm of dissimilarity frames the relationship between societies. We argue that narrators derive an exceptional quality of the state relationship from the assumed dissimilar quality of each society—state relations work despite vastly different citizenries. The relationship's 'specialness' becomes a euphemism for its lack of transparency and an explanation of authoritarianism as a social preference. The conventional narrative actually portrays an invented Saudi Arabia and hollows out the meaning of stability in the country. A new narrative begins with recognition that both societies share concerns about unbridled state power. We use extensive field research and secondary evidence from the 1943 'original bargain' through the present.*

Narratives are ways to communicate knowledge about how the world works. In the world of foreign policy, narratives matter because they can frame the essential qualities of a state relationship. Narratives also affect how we interpret complex events. Given the complexity of the real world, narratives sometimes obscure more than they illuminate. The strategic relationship between Saudi Arabia and the United States is a case in point. An overarching narrative portrays its logic and worth. We suggest that it structures a more imaginary than concrete point of view.

The power of a narrative is the power to persuade. The most persuasive narratives become 'conventional wisdom'. This makes no claim of validity. Narratives that acquire a dominant pull on public thinking can contain mistaken assumptions and data. Nevertheless, they can stick around long enough that doubt about them simply ceases to exist. Their validity in the public domain, in other words, can derive from their repetition and imitation.

In economics, analysts refer to the cost that individuals bear to make sense of information. It takes time, energy, or financial expenditure to assess the reliability of information, let alone to gather it personally. Since information is scarce and dear in the world of international relations, and the cost thus high, people who must rely on the interpretations of others use the public domain for the dominant reading of events. Political elite, corporate elite, members of the media, scholars, and groups with a vested interest are the entrepreneurs who shape the dominant content of public discussion—and it is they who so often seem to mimic each other when it comes to the matter of Saudi Arabia and the United States.

In the conventional narrative, the security of oil in the Gulf depends on political order in its major producer, Saudi Arabia. This, the *raison d' etat*, defines Saudi Arabia's relationship with its most important protector, the United States. It is the so-called 'original bargain'. President Franklin D. Roosevelt traced its basic outlines in 1943 by combining Saudi Arabia's oil and American companies' interests in exploiting it into 'a vital strategic interest to the United States'.[1]

The strategic features of the relationship are manifest in many ways. Chief among them are the contracting of American corporations to help build military facilities in Saudi Arabia and to train local military personnel and the sales of weaponry to the Saudi state by American industries. Examples of the military logistics and associated costs that accompanied the strategic partnership include Saudi Arabia's financing of the Contra war beginning in 1984, its supply of nationals to fight against the Soviet Union in Afghanistan in the 1980s, the Gulf War of 1990–1991, the basing of American troops in Saudi Arabia in the 1990s, and Saudi Arabia's provision of logistical support for the United States in the war in Iraq that began in 2003. There are continued emphases on military contingency and cooperation in countering terrorist financing.[2]

Protecting the supply of energy, accomplishing military readiness, investing in political stability, and partnering in the war on terrorism all cost money. In the case of the United States and Saudi Arabia, they cost plenty. A July 2007 proposal for an estimated US$20bn worth of military sales over ten years by the United States to countries in the Middle East includes Saudi Arabia as the biggest buyer.[3] Though the sales are new, the story is old. As Secretary of State Condoleezza Rice explained, the selling and buying of weaponry is 'to secure the peace'.[4] Military sales are among the key threads that run through the conventional narrative about the relationship's logic and worth; namely, an exceptionally pragmatic search for security and stability. Secretary of Defense Robert Gates makes this clear in a follow up to Rice's comments: 'We have had ongoing bilateral security relationships with most of the countries in the Gulf for decades. Those assistance programs are tailored to the needs of each of those countries and their perceptions of their own security requirements.'[5]

---

[1] Daryl Champion, *The Paradoxical Kingdom: Saudi Arabia and the Momentum of Reform* (London: Hurst 2003), p. 231.

[2] Remarks made by Daniel Glaser, Deputy Assistant Secretary of the United States Department of the Treasury, during the Senate Judiciary Committee Hearings on Saudi Arabia and the War on Terrorism, 8 November 2005. See also remarks made by Anthony Cordesman during the Senate Judiciary Committee Hearings on Saudi Arabia and the War on Terrorism, 8 November 2005, http://judiciary.senate.gov/resources/transcripts/109_transcripts.cfm

[3] Anthony Cordesman, 'The Gulf Arms Sale: A Background Paper', 17 January 2008, available at www.saudi-us-relations.org. For specific sales, see Defense Security Cooperation Agency (DSCA) New Releases, www.dsca.mil.

[4] Quoted in Donna Miles, 'Military Sales Package Aims to Boost Long-Term Stability in Middle East', *American Forces Information Service*, 1 August 2007.

[5] *Ibid.*

At its core, the conventional narrative places the bargains that Saudi Arabia and the United States strike beyond the reach of normative judgment. It says that the essential quality of the partnership derives genuinely and inextricably from two interrelated needs. The first relates to the supply of energy in the global marketplace and also revolves around a constellation of regional concerns that vary in time or by place.[6] The second is political order in Saudi Arabia.[7]

But a question remains: what *kind* or *level* of political order? This, of course, is a normative question. The conventional effort to downplay normative assessment is ironic because its answer to the question of order—authoritarian rule best fits the political orientation of Saudi Arabian society—is more normatively than empirically inspired. This invented reality flows from powerful, but flawed, norms that remain intact and shape much of the political discussion.

We hold that conventional thinking stands on two longstanding but illusory legs; what we call, first, the norm of exceptionality and, second, the norm of dissimilarity. The power of these norms derives from their juxtaposition. Our purpose is to show how, in the long run, they distort political reality in Saudi Arabia and thereby lay the foundation for political disorder. We concentrate less on a particular policy of security per se and more on the preconceived understandings that shape it. This is a necessary step in trying to appreciate where the relationship might proceed. It is also a call to rethink the validity of prevailing assumptions.

Our analysis is divided into three main parts: first, we identify and describe two interrelated norms that guide conventional thinking and discuss how analysts attempt to depoliticize these norms by representing them as commonsense or theoretical insight; second, we explain why the normative threads that run through the conventional narrative on security offer neither commonsense nor insight and actually hollow out the meaning of political stability in Saudi Arabia; third, we conclude by suggesting a new way to frame the original bargain.

The Norm of Exceptionality and the Norm of Dissimilarity

A narrative that perseveres draws strength from at least some belief in its inherent correctness. It can become so fixed in the imagination that it is difficult to dislodge. International crisis may shake old ways of thinking but habit, familiarity, unawareness, comfort or expediency often work to sustain an undemanding, dominant narrative even in a time of crisis. Various narrators may even attempt to make the crisis a renewed source of instruction for the enduring power of preconceived understandings.

The irony is that as crises compound—fighting between *jihadis* and government in Saudi Arabia, war in Iraq, antagonism with Iran, war between Israel and *Hizballah* in Lebanon, Israel and *Hamas* in Gaza, the advances of the Taliban

---

[6] See 'Strengthening Diplomatic Ties with Saudi Arabia', Statement by the United States reported online by *Business Wire*, 16 May 2008, http://www.businesswire.com. The statement contains references to four 'critical agreements' between the two countries to 'strengthen the protection of energy resources, enhance peaceful nuclear cooperation, broaden the fight against global terrorism, and bolster nonproliferation'. Also see, 'Symposium: Securing US Energy in a Changing World', *Middle East Policy*, 11(4) (Winter 2004), pp. 1–33.

[7] Examples include Jon Alterman, 'Understanding Saudi–US Relations: A Conversation', 21 May 2008, www.saudi-us-relations.org, and 'Hostile Intentions? The Future of US–Saudi Relations', conference sponsored by the Middle East Program of the Center for Strategic and International Studies and by *Asharq al-Awsat*, Washington, DC, 24 May 2005.

in Pakistan—conventional narratives can turn into even more powerful lures. Listening closely to contemporary discussion about Saudi Arabia, the United States, and security in the Gulf makes clear that the old storyline is a compelling one for many analysts. One reason is its ring of authenticity.

The norm of exceptionality frames the relationship between the *states*. The 'special' identity that many superimpose on the relationship between the United States and Saudi Arabia derives from this norm. The norm of dissimilarity frames the relationship between the *societies*. It portrays an invented Saudi Arabia, where societal preferences bring only a single stark choice to national political life: authoritarian rule, of either a royal or religious kind. This supposedly contrasts with the United States, where societal preferences bring an array of political choices.

Both the norm of exceptionality and the norm of dissimilarity embed in language. Below are samples of how the two are merged in the conventional narrative. Notice how the exceptional quality of the state relationship derives from the remarkably dissimilar quality of each society.

We begin with one of the more articulate and succinct versions and follow with renderings that extend in various directions:

> The strong material and political interests that underlie the relationship have overcome the vast political and cultural difference between the two societies.[8]

> There's a centrality and importance to Saudi Arabia that I think most Americans don't really have an appreciation for. ... It's hard [to manage this bilateral relationship] because our systems are extraordinarily different and because there are many things we don't agree on. ... There are a number of people on both sides who do a spectacular job bringing these very different systems and governments together in common purpose to do some really important things in a dazzling array of areas.[9]

> The alternative to Saudi Arabia's royal family today is not some Arabic-speaking version of the Swedish parliament, but a Sunni version of Iran's Shi'ite theocracy. America's 60-year friendship with the Saudi government needs to be nurtured, not censured. Without Saudi Arabia as an ally, the world's oil supplies would be less secure, and peace between Israel and Palestine is improbable.[10]

> One could not come up with two more disparate societies on which to base such a durable bilateral relationship.... Their [Saudi Arabia and the United States] mutual interests in oil, regional security, and in combating global terrorism are too strong.[11]

> Well, Saudi Arabia is important because the United States has a very substantial national security interest in ready access to the energy supplies of the Persian Gulf. Saudi Arabia controls most of those energy supplies. So it has been an ally and friend of the United States for as long as I can remember.... How many Islamic regimes ... are democratic and free markets? I can't think of one.[12]

---

[8] F. Gregory Gause, 'The Approaching Turning Point: The Future of US Relations with the Gulf States', Analysis paper no. 2, Saban Center for Middle East Policy, Brookings Institution, 20 May 2003.
[9] Alterman, 'Understanding Saudi–US Relations'.
[10] Wyche Fowler, Jr. and Mark Weston, *Atlanta Journal Constitution*, 7 January 2008, p. AII.
[11] David E. Long, 'US–Saudi Relations: Evolution, Current Conditions, and Future Prospects', *Mediterranean Quarterly*, 15(25) (2004), pp. 34–35.
[12] James Baker, 'Saudi Time Bomb?', Public Broadcasting Service (PBS) television program *Frontline*, 15 November 2001. For transcripts of the program see http://www.pbs.org

Is it our kind of system [in Saudi Arabia]? No. But it's their kind of system. They are gradually changing. Are they changing the way we would like? I don't think that that ought to be our primary concern.... [A]nd we have great cultural differences with Saudi Arabia.[13]

Even this cursory look at existing interpretations makes clear the patterns in the conventional language on the quality of the bilateral relationship. How has self-interested need been the hallmark of a 'special' kind of relationship? Even if the prevailing narrative frames the relationship to play down normative judgment, why does that matter? Why bring the norm of exceptionality and the norm of dissimilarity into the frame at all? The answers contain less of what people say and more of what they do not. It is especially the case when it comes to the norm of dissimilarity.

Exceptionality and Dissimilarity: Attempting to Depoliticize Politics

In a memo to the President, the National Security Council (NSC) lays out two main reasons for what it calls the rise in danger to the United States from within the Middle East. One is American policy toward Israel. Another, which the NSC gives much greater attention, is the potential 'domestic instability' of various regional states.

The document contains general and specific recommendations to lessen the particular danger of instability. They include: to increase American influence and initiative in the region to help guide social and economic pressures for change into positive channels of economic growth that maintain political stability; to increase military training and strength in the region; to encourage the expansion of private investment; to design better ways to explain American policies toward the area in order to create awareness of our commitment to its welfare; to maximize the impact of American diplomatic, military, economic, and technical assistance to reverse anti-Western trends; to encourage local efforts at self-help; to support or develop local leadership that offers the best prospect of orderly internal, social and economic change; and to strengthen cultural and educational programs sponsored by the United States. As for Saudi Arabia specifically, 'The United States should strengthen its *special* [italics added] position with respect to Saudi Arabia to the extent compatible with general U.S. policies in the area'.

This document might sound as though it is from 2003 or 2004 but it is actually dated 23 July 1954.[14] The recommendations cautiously and purposefully limit their scope to social and economic matters. They downplay distinctly political reform. The larger agenda is political calm. The language is remarkably close to the prevailing narrative today about the strategic arrangements between Saudi Arabia and the United States.[15]

Its tone is set by the so-called original bargain. The bargain rests on two pillars. The first strengthens, or at the least maintains, the ability of the Saudi state to safeguard

---

[13] Brent Scowcroft, 'Saudi Time Bomb?', Public Broadcasting Service (PBS) television program *Frontline*, 15 November 2001. For transcripts of the program see http://www.pbs.org

[14] NSC 5428, 'United States Objectives and Policies with Respect to the Near East', 23 July 1954, see especially pp.1–6 and p. 42. The quote is taken from p. 6

[15] See for example the DSCA News Release on Saudi Arabia, 5 August 2009, available at www.dsca.mil: 'This proposed sale will contribute to the foreign policy and national security of the United States by helping to improve the security of a friendly country which has been and continues to be an important force for political stability and economic progress in the Middle East.'

internal order. The second derives from the unimpeded flow of oil to the international marketplace and the maintenance of stable, reasonable prices for this commodity.[16]

A key by-product of the interest in oil is military cooperation and the security of producers. From this are derived high levels of military procurement and expenditures by Saudi Arabia on arms from the United States.[17] Below the level of the state a range of actors in the elite tier of American society benefit from the relationship. Certainly corporate actors, both past and present, profit from the close military and economic links forged between the two countries, including Standard Oil Company of California, Mobil Oil, Bechtel Corporation, Northrop Grumman Corporation, Vinnell Corporation,[18] and Raytheon Corporation.

Turning political realism on its head

Many who study how security matters for the United States and Saudi Arabia speak and write from the perspective of scholarship on realism. Classical realism places emphases on state interest and need. The realist vision of foreign policy is primarily rooted in the realm of military and material security, with the focus on how distributions of force can structure international political life. Our focus is not on realism per se. Rather, it is to note a particular kind of problem that tends to crop up in studies of the United States and Saudi Arabia: the way analysts stand realism on its head to explain this state relationship.

According to realist logic, international politics is all about expediency, as states seize opportunity to take advantage of each other to satisfy their own selfish needs. States, therefore, fixate on their relative status. In the classic words of Thucydides's *History of the Peloponnesian War*: '[R]ight as the world goes, is only in question between equals in power, while the strong do what they can and the weak suffer what they must.'[19] The selfish need that defines state relations, in other words, is the ordinary stuff of foreign policy.

In this world, the character and the intensity of need vary and, as asymmetry of need marks much of international political life, it fuels worry about commitment. In classic realism, this becomes the fear of a weaker state that must trust a stronger one to meet its need for protection. The intensity of one partner's need for another matters when uncertainty about commitment derives from perceptions of 'little or no alternative' or of 'vulnerability'.[20] It is the kind of world that is ripe for exploitation, both as political leverage and as advantage in bargaining. The point is that shared interest alone may be primarily, perhaps even cynically, the core of a relationship. It may serve to distill and to clarify terms. Yet one can never be entirely certain about things. Even in the best of

---

[16] See the valuable discussion in Simon Bromley, 'Oil and the Middle East: The End of US Hegemony?' *Middle East Report*, 28(208) (1998), pp. 19–22.
[17] Rosemarie Said Zahlan, 'The Impact of US Policy on the Stability of the Gulf States: A Historian's View', in Joseph A. Kechichian (ed.), *Iran, Iraq, and the Arab Gulf States*, (New York: Palgrave, 2001), p. 363. Also see J.E. Peterson, *Saudi Arabia and the Illusion of Security*, Adelphi Paper 348 (Oxford: Oxford University Press for The Institute for Strategic Studies, 2002), pp. 35–39; 'The Arming of Saudi Arabia', *Frontline*, air date 16 February 1993, transcript posted 8 November 2001, see http://www.pbs.org
[18] For example, see the article on Vinnell by William D. Hartung, 'Mercenaries Inc: How a US Company Props up the House of Saud', *The Progressive*, April 1996, pp. 26–28.
[19] Thucydides, *The Peloponnesian War* (New York: Modern Library, 1951), p. 331.
[20] See Albert O. Hirschman, *National Power and the Structure of Foreign Trade: The Politics of the International Economy* (Berkeley, CA: University of California Press, 1981). See also Bahgat Korany, 'Defending the Faith: The Foreign Policy of Saudi Arabia', in Korany and Ali E. Hillal Dessouki (eds), *The Foreign Policy of Arab States* (Boulder, CO: Westview, 1984), especially pp. 248–249.

circumstances, interest is, almost by definition, somewhat coarse and capricious a measure of commitment.

Realism provides little theoretical space for 'exceptionality' in a state relationship that derives its essential quality from self-interested need. This is the *ordinary* business of international political life. So we are left to wonder why, in the end, the strategic partnership that Saudi Arabia and the United States founded in 1943, and continue to manage to this day, merits the Orwellian logic that accompanies its extraordinary designation.

Orwellian logic: standard is special

Reference to the bilateral relationship as something that was, still is, or might be once again 'special' is easy to find. What exactly makes for its special quality is much harder to find. On the surface, there appear four meanings: first, in the prominent version, the special character of the state relationship derives from the continuation of the original bargain, despite occasional and sometimes bitter political disagreements.[21] Each of the next three is more or less a corollary of the first. A second meaning makes reference to the military cooperation between the two states and to Saudi Arabia as the chief military ally of the United States in the region.[22] A third involves the two states' common fear of certain secular movements (e.g., international communism)[23] and a fourth focuses on the common challenge that radical Islamists pose for the two states.[24]

The first and second meanings of security are largely material transactions—energy and arms—that actually reinforce how extraordinarily *ordinary* is the ambition of the venture. It is little surprise, therefore, that the effort to define the exceptional quality of the bilateral relationship drifts toward nonmaterial factors in the last two meanings. We call them shared aversions. Beginning especially in the 1950s, certain negative referents became a critical backdrop for the relationship. An example is the past experience with international communism.

For some observers, the essence of the special relationship was on display during the Cold War. The bond was a shared fear of international communism.

> Saudi Arabia's religiosity, whatever its specific teachings, had served a useful political purpose for the United States for half a century, making the kingdom a reliable Cold War partner and providing its leaders with a perception of global threats similar to the one held by the United States.[25]

---

[21] This is echoed by attendees of two conferences on relations between the United States and Saudi Arabia convened by the Rockefeller Foundation in 2003 and 2004. Participants from both countries, despite mutually bemoaning the plight of the relationship since 11 September 2001, essentially acknowledge that decades of *practical* dealings had 'created a bond that recent strains had not broken. The reality of mutual reliance was still in place'. Clifford Chanin and F. Gregory Gause, 'US–Saudi Relations: A Rocky Road', *Middle East Policy*, 11(4), 2004, p. 34; Chanin and Gause, 'US–Saudi Relations: Bump in the Road or End of the Road?' *Middle East Policy*, 10(4), 2003. See also, David E. Long, 'US–Saudi Relations: Evolution, Current Conditions, and Future Prospects', *Mediterranean Quarterly* 15(3), 2004, pp. 24–37.

[22] An example is Anthony H. Cordesman, *Saudi Arabia Enters the Twenty-First Century: The Political, Foreign Policy, Economic, and Energy Dimensions* (Westport, CT: Praeger, 2003).

[23] Rachel Bronson, *Thicker than Oil: America's Uneasy Partnership with Saudi Arabia* (New York: Oxford University Press, 2006).

[24] See, for example, Judith Kipper, 'Saudi Arabia', 1 April 2002, posted on the Council on Foreign Relations website: www.cfr.org/publication/4500/Saudiarabia. Also see Rachel Bronson, 'Rethinking Religion: The Legacy of the US–Saudi Relationship', *The Washington Quarterly* 28(4) (Autumn 2005), pp. 121–37.

[25] Bronson, 'Rethinking Religion', pp. 121–23, 133. Also see Mohammad al Maddah [Saudi-American Relations are Strategic and Go Beyond Oil] *Okaz*, 1 November 2006.

The example of international communism, however, highlights the normality of the relationship with the United States. The latter part of the twentieth century gave rise to locally inspired pan-Arab and pan-Islamic ideas—ideas that spawned 'indigenous social and national movements'.[26] The United States saw the rise of revolutionary Arab nationalism in the 1950s, against colonialism, the state of Israel, and repressive governments aligned with the West, as a threat to the regimes in oil-producing countries.[27] In the 1960s, the concern was pan-Arab claims, though the ruling family's anxiety outpaced that of policymakers in the Kennedy administration. A particular worry of the Al Saud was the appeal of revolutionary socialism and nationalism to various segments of its own society. The ruling family's attempts to exploit the secular foundations of these ideas and promote Islamic rhetoric were strategies to defend the integrity and legitimacy of its rule 'amidst attacks from opponents and rivals in the Arab world'.[28]

In the 1970s, the ruling family was regularly denounced by some of the secular Arab regimes for its relationship with an imperial power said to sponsor Zionism, the United States. But it was nothing compared to what was to come. Revolution in Iran in 1979 and its message of Islamic republicanism sent shock waves throughout the region. Ayatollah Ruhollah Khomeini possessed great charisma and articulated religious symbols as guides for the revolution. The revolutionaries proceeded to build an Islamic republic referring to his interpretations and aspirations.

From the outset, Khomeini said that the political principles of the revolution transcended geographic borders.[29] His supporters promoted the principle of revolutionary Islam as an exemplar for political action against state oppression and to restore the power of Islam in society. Rhetoric corresponded to events outside Iran. A resurgence of Islamist political movements occurred in the region, including Saudi Arabia, where the Saudi state watched the progress of the revolution in Iran with deepening anxiety. Openly critical of Saudi Arabia's relationship with the United States and keenly aware of Saudi Arabians disaffected by the policies and behaviour of the ruling family, the Iranian leadership represented itself as a pious, moral counterpoint to the Islamic credentials of the Al Saud.

At the same time, the American response to the Soviet Union's invasion of Afghanistan in 1979 laid the groundwork for a contemporary *jihadi* movement, and all its political repercussions. One Saudi Arabian bluntly remarks: 'They took our boys out of school to go to Afghanistan. They came home to no jobs, no respect—they were humiliated.' To another, 'They [the members of the ruling family] were under pressure to support the war but the war is to blame for what happened to our young people.'[30]

Religious and political activism took root underground in Saudi Arabia in the 1970s and 1980s, and then gained strength in the aftermath of the Gulf War

---

[26] Simon Bromley, *American Hegemony and World Oil: The Industry, the State System and the World Economy* (University Park, PA: The Pennsylvania State University Press, 1991), p. 246. For a general look at the United States in the Middle East see Rashid Khalidi, *Resurrecting Empire: Western Footprints and America's Perilous Path in the Middle East* (Boston, MA: Beacon Press, 2005).
[27] Nathan J. Citino, *From Arab Nationalism to OPEC: Eisenhower, King Saud, and the Making of US–Saudi Relations* (Bloomington, IN: Indiana University Press, 2002).
[28] Madawi al-Rasheed, *A History of Saudi Arabia* (Cambridge: Cambridge University Press, 2002), p. 10. Also see pp. 115–134.
[29] Ruhullah Khomeini, *Imam Khomeini's Last Will and Testament* (N.P.: Solna Print, n.d.), p. 16.
[30] Personal interviews, Eastern Province, 22 July 2003; Jeddah, 10 June 2003.

of 1991. Resurgence of religious and political opposition to the royal family was based on important grievances and took shape under the rubric of Islamism. Dissidents both within the country and in exile abroad emerged as symbols of resistance. In addition, a new generation of popular *ulama*, who stridently voiced political opinions in their Friday sermons (*khutba*), called for the removal of American troops from Saudi Arabia and condemned the moral order established under the ruling family.[31]

Another 'specially' shared aversion is radical Islamism that contests both the policies of United States and the policies of the Saudi state. Nevertheless, shared aversions fail as a measure of exceptionality. For Saudi Arabia and the United States, as for many an international relationship, shared aversions constitute business as usual. They may shape the relationship's ebb and flow but do not define its identity. The United States, for its part, seeks to preserve its political entrée into the region and to check the moves by unfriendly actors to control oil in the Gulf. The ruling family, for its part, desires to maintain a grip on power. Thus far it is a grip on highly centralized power. The ruling family uses ideational and symbolic references in this effort.

Symbolism matters here. The United States prefers the Saudi state to play a particular kind of international role: a 'moderating' or stabilizing role, as a contrast with the 'radicalism' of others. The 'authenticity' of the Saudi state is juxtaposed against forces that arise to contest the prevailing order. In the past, the partners' focus was on regional currents of secular nationalism and socialism; now it is on radical Islamism, both within Saudi Arabia and in the vicinity. The special relationship, in turn, becomes the frame through which to view the Saudi state: its political manoeuvrability in the roles of regional stabilizer and leader of the transnational Muslim community,[32] and its ability to counter politically resurgent Shi'a.[33]

Exceptionality and Dissimilarity: Neither Commonsense nor Insight

The conventional narrative about Saudi Arabia and the United States plays up how their partnership is critically different from the ordinary world of interest and need. As a result, any sense of weakness, exposure, encumbrance, resentment, or distrust washes out, as does any worry about indifference or manipulation. It is a realism that is deprived of its starkness even as its language is used.

The reality, though, is that such fears are there, and from very early on. Listen to the words in two cables to the United States Department of State from the American Embassy in Saudi Arabia. The first cable is dated 7 September 1952; the second, 17 November 1953:

> In order [to] avoid offend[ing] Saudi sensibilities ... [USG] believe that in general various projects should be introduced only after ascertaining that they will not (repeat not) be opposed by SAG [Saudi Arabian Government]. ... Goal is emphasis [on] Saudi–American friendship and cooperation as between two *equals* [italics added] in effort

---

[31] Gwenn Okruhlik, 'Networks of Dissent: Islamism and Reform in Saudi Arabia', *Current History*, 101(651) (2002), pp. 22–28.
[32] See Adnan Bariyya, [The King Devotes the Kingdom to Arab and Islamic Issues], *al-Yaum al-Iliktroni*, 30 June 2007.
[33] As noted in Mohamad Bazzi, 'The Saudi Paradox', *The Nation*, 10 April 2007, http://www.thenation.com

to obtain Saudi cooperation internationally and, it seems to us here, of equal importance, protect US oil investment in SA [Saudi Arabia].[34]

As Department aware, Saudis feel they have a special relationship with US because Dhahran Airfield and Aramco and brief visit Vice President [Nixon] to Saudi Arabia would be considered by them as recognition by US of this special relationship. According Department's Circular ... Vice President scheduled to visit Iran and if he does not (repeat not) visit Saudi Arabia, Saudis would ask, as they have in past, if US attaches more importance [in] its relations [with] Iran than [sic] Saudia Arabia.[35]

In the end, the 'special relationship' is language that is meant to register assurance about the 'genuine' need of each for the other; to pledge commitment to the partnership. Why this gesture? The search for military or material security can bring political and symbolic insecurity. Sometimes the tensions between the two are not easily resolved. It is a particularly acute problem for the Saudi state.

For many Saudi Arabians, the Gulf War of 1990–1991 exposed the extent of their country's military dependence on the United States. It was a moment of truth. The Saudi state's enormous expenditures on arms from American suppliers and underwriting of the American military effort led to growing political disenchantment within Saudi Arabia in the 1990s. The stationing of American troops on the same ground as the holy cities, meanwhile, became a flashpoint. Fighting that began in Iraq in 2003, in Lebanon in 2006, and in Gaza in 2008 fuel disillusionment within Saudi Arabia. In short, military dependency on the United States continues to hold politically sensitive ramifications for the Saudi state. A Riyadhi wonders: 'Maybe the question is less about our preferences and more about our needs. Are they transferable elsewhere? Are there substitutes?'[36]

Remember that political calm within Gulf states has long been a key feature of security for American administrations. The 1954 memo by the NSC makes the case clearly. Inventors of the 'special' relationship see it as a device by which to assure American administrations of the correctness of this 'reality': that political calm is only as good as the ability of the Saudi state to safeguard order in its society.

In the conventional narrative, therefore, a key pillar of the original bargain is a political 'order' that sits on potentially shaky ground; namely, public sentiment in Saudi Arabia. *How* to understand public sentiment is beside the point in a narrative that designs it as more culturally than situationally derived. Here is the link between specialness and disparateness. We find ourselves in the only place where the norm of exceptionality can go, left on the doorstep of its normative twin, dissimilarity.

Once we recognize that a narrative works to confine partnerships to the world of selfish need and to keep normative judgment off limits, we can also recognize its purposeful flip side: to make normative discourse 'about particular cases appear to be idle chatter, a mask of noise'.[37] Some level of interest and need keeps any relationship in play. It is certainly the case for Saudi Arabia and the United States.[38] But listen cautiously to the normative admonishment of the conventional

---

[34] US Embassy, Jeddah, Saudi Arabia, Cable to the Department of State, 7 September 1952.
[35] US Embassy, Jeddah, Saudi Arabia, Cable to the Department of State, 17 November 1953.
[36] Personal interview, Riyadh, 3 July 2005.
[37] Michael Walzer, *Just and Unjust Wars: A Moral Argument with Historical Illustrations*, 4th ed. (New York: Basic Books, 2006), p. 4.
[38] See Paul Aarts, 'Events versus Trends: The Role of Energy and Security in Sustaining the US–Saudi Relationship', in Aarts and Gerd Nonneman (eds), *Saudi Arabia in the Balance: Political Economy, Society, Foreign Affairs* (London: C. Hurst & Company, 2005).

narrative, if for no other reason than what the Saudi Arabian voices of the present tell us. The political price that Saudi Arabia's state pays for its need for the United States is steeper still for its society. That is the most glaring omission in many interpretations of the relationship, and it is not merely a product of realist blinders.

Many Saudi Arabians, man or woman, young or old, public servant or private entrepreneur, respond to recent events with a tone of suspicion or ambivalence about American intentions as evidenced in these statements about the relationship with the United States:[39]

> The quality of [American] pressure being applied in Saudi Arabia is tied to United States self-interest. Do you trust a pressure that is not genuine?

> Many of us believe that what American officials say is a smokescreen for what they do, which is the opposite.

> The United States will not promote democracy for the sake of democracy. The United States must have an interest in democracy. Some people do want [American] pressure. They want it out of despair because it is a payback for years of United States support for the regime. Saudi Arabia is just the pumping station to the United States. The United States is not interested in changing Saudi Arabia.

> Change [in Saudi Arabia] led by the United States is nonsense. There is not a single 'value' that a nice fat contract cannot buy.

> The United States is not sincere and we all know that. It only wants to preserve its own interest.

> The way people feel in Saudi Arabia is that the United States made this problem—now it is your job to fix it.

> The United States is not looking for freedom and democracy; it wants oil and stability.

These citizens give contemporary voice to what the US acknowledged in a long-ago cable sent from the American Embassy in Saudi Arabia to the Department of State:

> As previously reported, it is our belief that a propaganda program in this country would be resented by the Saudi Government and would not be tolerated. [The program] has the double objective of promoting and encouraging democratic government on the one hand while presenting the dangers of communism on the other. Since Saudi Arabia is an absolute monarchy its Government cannot be expected to welcome propaganda of the first category.[40]

In the past, the obstacle to political reform was tied directly to the Saudi state. Over the years, the conventional narrative has shifted the spotlight from the state to the people. When public sentiment is even alluded to in mainstream accounts, it is an unchanging reality.[41] It is also typically seen as a risk.[42]

The norm of dissimilarity in the conventional narrative is strikingly inspired by the notion of an enormous gap between the two societies in their political ideals

---

[39] Personal interviews, respectively, Riyadh, 2003; Riyadh, 2005; Safwa, Eastern Province, 2003; Riyadh, 2003; Eastern Province, 22 July 2003; and Jeddah, 2003.
[40] US Embassy, Jeddah, Saudi Arabia, Cable sent to the Department of State, 8 January 1952.
[41] Hamza al Hasan argues that Saudi leaders tout the uniqueness of their society, as one populated by people without political aspiration or ambition and adverse to change. See [Crisis of Reform in a Conservative Country: Amir Abdullah and the Reformists], *Shun'un al-Saudi*, www.saudiaffairs.net.
[42] Chanin and Gause, 'US–Saudi Relations: A Rocky Road'; Chanin and Gause, 'US–Saudi Relations: Bump in the Road or End of the Road?'.

and aspirations. Reference to it is easy to find. Are there dissimilarities? There are indeed and many are fairly easy to see; dress, custom, religious and social differences. It is why after all is said and done most analysts largely internalize the norm of dissimilarity. This distracts them, however, from a broadly shared political concern located within each society: the use and the morality of power wielded by the state.

Listen to four recent portrayals that blur the lines between authoritarian rule and cultural disparity, thereby claiming that absolute power in the state is a social preference.

> Saudi Arabia has a population and mix of clerics that are more conservative than its ruling family ... The stereotype of political development in the West—a progressive people pushing against the resistance of a conservative regime—does not fit this society.[43]

> [D]espite the huge growth of US brands and technology in Saudi Arabia and the modern additions to life such as traffic jams, cell phones, personal computers, and satellite TVs, Saudi society evolved in a manner that had very little in common with US culture. As a result, the staggering Saudi industrial and commercial development, based on US management and technology, did not evolve into a more open, Westernized, liberal society.[44]

> No two countries and no two societies could have been more dissimilar ... [O]ne fundamental, unchanging policy followed by all US administrations since Franklin Roosevelt: The United States does not interfere in Saudi Arabia's internal affairs. How the kingdom treats its citizens is not the business of the United States.

> [I]f our standard is that we wish a government to function with the consent of the governed, I believe Saudi Arabia—the government system in Saudi Arabia generally meets that standard.[45]

The 'special' quality of the relationship that the states forge in the name of security, then, becomes a euphemism for its lack of transparency and an explanation of authoritarian rule as a social preference. The rub is that the simplicity of the equation—order plus oil equals the political *status quo* inside Saudi Arabia—does not reflect empirical reality: it is a much more complicated and nuanced situation, especially beginning in the 1990s. Tensions inside Saudi Arabia over the normative implications of the relationship with the United States and the political orientation of the Saudi state continue to diminish the 'wisdom' of the conventional story. Yet the story remains remarkably resilient over time.

The reality is that some of the most formative issues that any society confronts are where to locate power, to what extent and what to define as the appropriate use or abuse of power. This is a process of contestation that stems from competing ideas about societal rights and state responsibilities. Appropriate rights and responsibilities do not define themselves. Rather, someone must define them. The politics of ideas grow out of their distributive consequences. It begins with power, or the ability of one actor to influence the behavior of another. How each actor prefers to use power may be enhanced or constrained by ideals and

---

[43] See the statement of Anthony Cordesman on 8 November 2005 before the United States Senate Committee on the Judiciary during the Hearing, 'Saudi Arabia: Friend or Foe in the War on Terror?'.

[44] Jean-Francois Seznec, 'Business as Usual: the Saudi–US Relationship', *Harvard International Review*, 26(4) (Winter 2005).

[45] Thomas W. Lippmann, Testimony before the House Committee on Foreign Affairs during the Hearing, 'Is There a Human Rights Double Standard? US Policy toward Saudi Arabia, Iran, and Uzbekistan', 14 June 2007. The first statement is from Prepared Testimony; the second from Oral Remarks.

institutions. Influence always depends on the relative capacity or willingness of different actors to either apply or resist pressure.

The norm of dissimilarity allows analysts to gloss over the concerns of Saudi Arabian citizens about unbridled power and the state under conditions of authoritarian rule. Such concerns cannot be assumed away with passing references to deeply rooted traditional values. Many scholars and policymakers in the United States fixated on the moderate Islamic and Western credentials of the ruling family. They turned a blind eye on crucial matters, willfully or wishfully ignoring powerful forces rooted within Saudi Arabian society. Off of the radar screen for a long time, there was little meaningful debate in the United States on the potency of the ideas critical of authoritarian rule and official Islam. Conventional wisdom fails to capture the complex connections in politics and society that often embed deeply beneath the surface.

In an earlier work, Okruhlik refers to the managers of the relationship between the United States and Saudi Arabia as 'gatekeepers'. They exist in both countries, control key points of access to information by control over commercial contracts, media forays, cultural exchanges and educational missions, and perpetuate the dominant orthodoxy. One unfortunate result was a long-time emphasis on the status quo rather than critiques of it, on states rather than societies, on repressive stability rather than much needed change.[46] The real prize, of course, is access to and information about Saudi Arabia. Access and information are scarce commodities in any system. They remain so in Saudi Arabia even though things are more open than in the past.

In crises, a prevailing narrative about states can become vulnerable on the fictions that it contains. What is interesting is how the shock of 11 September 2001 did prompt discussion about the lacuna of knowledge on socio-political dynamics in Saudi Arabia. Rather than revising the conventional narrative, however, it was ultimately reinforced. Gatekeepers assumed away societal disquiet over unbridled power and the state rather than try and understand it, or they continue to fixate on absolutes rather than notice variations. Saudi Arabia becomes a place devoid of political nuance. For gatekeepers, and those who follow their lead, the problem that matters most is the wide gap that separates each society. What followed was the predictable call for more dialogue aimed at bridging the gap; including, developing programs of exchange. These revolve around academic and military interactions.

As much as things change, they clearly remain the same. Recall, for example, the now decades-old recommendation for greater exchange in NSC 5428. It highlighted military training, strengthening cultural and educational programs, local efforts at self-help, and orderly social and economic change. Exchange may be a worthy proposal. It also continues apace, along with military training, educational reform and orderly social and economic change.[47] What is the anticipated political outcome of these endeavours?

Normative implications of the bilateral relationship abound. Exchange is a prime example. Tens of thousands of Saudi Arabians have studied in the

[46] Okruhlik, 'Bringing the Peninsula in from the Periphery: From Imagined Scholarship to Gendered Discourse', *Middle East Report*, 27(204) (July-September 1997), pp. 36–37

[47] On 25 April 2005, for example, in a joint statement, the two countries declared their intent to increase the number of Saudi Arabian students and military officers who studied and trained in the United States. See Joint Statement by the United States and Saudi Arabia, 25 April 2005.

United States over the years and many disagree with American foreign policy. They also return home to authoritarian governance. How do we factor in the domestic political structure of Saudi Arabia and the deeply held perception within its society of a United States that upholds it? Why do we expect anything to differ as a consequence of exchange if people are not allowed to talk about their experience or to engage in politics? When the two states talk of academic exchange, or educational reform in Saudi Arabia, what do they *want* in an environment of authoritarian rule? When it turns to military exchange, or military sales, how do we account for the deep distrust within Saudi Arabian society over the interdependency and motives of the two states? Many Saudi Arabians voice the scepticism of this man: 'There is a way out of this. But nobody will speak the truth ... Nobody will touch politics!'[48] A Riyadhi says: 'Talk all you want about sending students over to study. But if you don't deal with Israel, nothing will ever change'.[49]

As one analyst rightly remarks, '[societal] differences do not make the relationship less "legitimate" than other international relationships'.[50] What is not asked, however, is how do the broadly shared ideals of each society matter? Even if societies differ on where to place limits on the state's power of coercion, that does not undermine the fundamental fear each shares of absolute power. The relationship between power and the state is not an all or nothing proposition, whether under democratic or authoritarian rule. All polities view state power through the lens of more or less. Ideas about the appropriate power of the state, and certainly innovative ideas, have transnational resonance. Such resonance lies in their attractiveness and in their threat.[51]

Fear of the absolute power of the state is at the core of American political ideals and the political system that Americans created. The same ideal holds promise for those in Saudi Arabia who wish to curb state power; peril for those who seek to advance it. Power is rarely relinquished willingly; absolute power even less so. What many analysts gloss over is that the compelling storyline in Saudi Arabia may not be the battle between the ruling family and the religious extremists for *absolute* authority but rather the contest waged between various other social forces and the Saudi state over its *relative* power. In the words of a Saudi Arabian activist: 'Reform requires concessions. So reform cannot happen here if they [the ruling family] refuse to concede any power.'[52]

Conclusion: Recognizing the Power of Narrative in the Search for Security

[T]he historic meeting between King Abdulaziz Al-Saud and President Franklin D. Roosevelt aboard the USS *Quincy* ... launched the special relationship between the Kingdom of Saudi Arabia and the United States of America.

Two people who work so closely together toward the common goals of security, prosperity, and economic advancement will surely remain friends, and partners, far into the future. In celebrating this friendship, remember its beginnings in our shared

---

[48] Personal interview, Jeddah, 26 May 2003.
[49] Personal interview, Riyadh, 5 July 2005.
[50] Gause, 'The Approaching Turning Point.'
[51] See Patrick J. Conge, *From Revolution to War: State Relations in a World of Change* (Ann Arbor: University of Michigan Press, 2000).
[52] Personal interview, Eastern Province, 20 July 2003.

commitment to open markets, free enterprise, and the pursuit of opportunity to the benefit of both our peoples.'[53]

The usual story about the United States, Saudi Arabia and security in the Gulf illustrates the need for more serious conversation on how to make sense of the complexity that surrounds this relationship and less jockeying to capture constituencies. Self-interested motivations and strategic bargains alone do not separate the United States and Saudi Arabia from ordinary state relationships. Nor is this simply a story about a state relationship that stands outside the typical vicissitudes of international political life. A closer look reveals that it is really about something else. The usual story places the relationship beyond the reach of normative assessment. But the usual story itself rests on a pair of norms. What is particularly troublesome is that the first, the norm of exceptionality, coupled with the second, the norm of dissimilarity, creates a powerful lure. It is the norm of dissimilarity that is actually the stronger of two. Yet there is scant logical or empirical reason to uphold either norm, and they lay bare the illusions in mainstream thinking.

The result is a search for security that leaves hollow its own core. Saudi Arabia may be changing in important ways in its economy and its society but not in its polity. The puzzle in Saudi Arabia concerns *limits* to state power. This is not really a part of the prevailing dialogue about the bilateral relationship; yet Saudi Arabian citizens routinely talk about a future in which the ruling family is subject to the rule of law rather than positioned above it.

The view in the conventional narrative of a United States that prefers to stay out of its partner's internal politics would be incomprehensible to many of Saudi Arabia's citizens. For them, the United States casts a long shadow. Whether some see in that shadow peril, others promise for political consequences in Saudi Arabia, they see one thing in common: a Saudi state that does what it must to preserve the commitment of its protector. People question the political grip of the government and its military dependence on the United States. The idea among citizens of a Saudi state that goes only as far as it must in social or political reform to curry favour with the United States was especially evident in 2002 through early 2004.[54] As several Saudi Arabian women agreed, 'The government is not pro-active. When things calm down, the ruling family will forget their promises; just like what happened after the gulf war [of 1991].'[55]

What matters for many Saudi Arabians is that the United States has never been and is even yet to be neutral in the contest over political reform; a contest that is already somewhat one-sided in favour of royal power. This is not merely a criticism of an America that falls short of its promise abroad. It is about American administrations, whether Republican or Democrat, which many citizens of Saudi Arabia perceive as pillars of an authoritarian edifice in the name of security. For these citizens, the story is less about a United States that engages Saudi Arabia and more about a United States that enables only one choice when it comes to the political possibilities in Saudi Arabia.

---

[53] From an article by former Ambassador of Saudi Arabia to the United States, Bandar bin Sultan, as introduced into the Congressional Record on 12 March 1996: 'The United States—Saudi Economic Partnership.'

[54] Personal interviews, 2003 and 2005.

[55] Personal interviews, Eastern Province, 14 July 2003. For a discussion on the potential ineffectiveness of American pressure see the article by Turki al Hamad, 'The United States and Saudi', *al-Sharq al-Awsat*, 18 August 2002. See Qadaya al Khalij [Gulf Issues], www.gulfissues.net

SECURITY IN THE GULF: HISTORICAL LEGACIES AND FUTURE PROSPECTS

We have argued that much of the conventional narrative is normatively inspired even as it postures itself to be objectively derived. It avoids looking closely at how we arrive at this historical moment and also fails to acknowledge, and therefore to replicate, the illusions of the past. A new narrative on the relationship between Saudi Arabia and the United States begins with the focus on the two societies' shared political concerns about state power.

Nevertheless, many still confine solutions to the problem of 'order' in Saudi Arabia to commercial ties, educational exchange and curricular reform. Recommendations similar to those in 1954 become the 'new' solutions for the 'new' problems. Progress on social and economic fronts may, in the best of circumstances, foster prosperity and reduce stereotypes. It may also lessen concern about the opaque quality of the bilateral relationship. But such progress does not, on the face of it, meaningfully affect the sheer political power of the Saudi state.

Narrative shapes what people think they see and what they do not see when looking at Saudi Arabia. Our purpose was to pull back the narrative curtains to show the precarious health of mainstream debate. The fault lines in the future constitute whether to preserve the essence of the usual story or to proceed toward a meaningful shift in it. Preserving it because we prefer the reassurance of our preconceived ideas will certainly be a problem. If it is to shift, therefore, we must dispel the illusions that keep us from a more sophisticated understanding of the relationship between the United States and Saudi Arabia. Now that would be a really special story.

La Longue Durée and Energy Security in the Gulf

MARY ANN TÉTREAULT

ABSTRACT *Hydrocarbon riches have lifted the states of the Persian-Arabian Gulf out of poverty, but they also attract unwanted attention and external intervention. This essay examines the security goals of Gulf governments over five eras. It suggests that the expansion of state capacity is both cause and effect of foreign investment and other resource transfers, and argues that their hydrocarbon resources have been key assets of Gulf governments in pursuing their national and regional security interests.*

Introduction

The hydrocarbon riches of the Persian-Arabian gulf lifted states and nations out of poverty but also attract unwanted attention and external intervention. In this essay, I examine the changing nature of energy security issues facing Gulf hydrocarbon exporters. I focus on the management of external economic and military threats, and internal challenges to governments and regimes. How well these aims of security can be achieved is a measure of 'stateness': state capacity, national security, and regime stability.[1] In each, hydrocarbons have been prime resources for Gulf governments.

The Aims of Energy Security

Energy security, for states that rely on hydrocarbon export revenues, encompasses more than simply securing supplies for the home market. It includes in addition to the physical integrity of territories and resources, access to markets for imports and exports, and an ability to shelter national economies from naked exposure to market forces.[2] The preponderant weight of markets in this definition of security also points to an expanded concept of vulnerability. It encompasses economic as well as strategic assaults, and the normal cyclical behaviour of commodity markets generally.

Most Gulf states lack conventional strategic depth. Nearly all are small with capital cities, refineries, export facilities, pipelines, and/or production properties lying on or near the coast. Even pipelines located entirely within a sovereign territory are vulnerable to domestic insurgencies. Where they cross national boundaries, oil transit

---

[1] Robert H. Jackson, *Quasi-states: Sovereignty, International Relations and the Third World* (Cambridge: Cambridge University Press, 1990).

[2] Robert O. Keohane and Joseph S. Nye, *Power and Interdependence: World Politics in Transition* (Boston, MA: Little Brown, 1977).

is vulnerable to another sovereign state, its politics, and its capacity to protect. Most Gulf oil exports exit through the Straits of Hormuz, a choke point offering strategic opportunities not only to the states on either side but also to entrepreneurial actors such as terrorists,[3] and pirates operating in adjacent waters.[4] Ever since Gulf exporters assumed the management of their own facilities, strategic redundancy has been their first defence against disruptions of their capacity to produce and export.[5]

Income and income protection are highly salient aspects of security to Gulf-state policy makers. Oil prices are cyclical, as are the prices of most commodities.[6] This reflects an underlying recurrent pattern of demand expansion, scarcity, rapid price rises, supply expansion, glut, and then price collapse. Commodity prices are inherently 'bubblicious': their price cycles reflect oscillations among excesses.[7] Some oil-price cycles are extreme, probably the result of oil's quasi-financial character, particularly when oil-futures speculation takes on the character of currency speculation.[8] Price and income shocks also can be inflicted by formal and informal sanctions such as the UN-mandated sanctions against Iraq initiated during the second Gulf war (1990–1991) and US sanctions imposed at various times, first in 1979 against Iran and later also against Iraq. Producers have used oil to punish rivals and enemies and some resulting disruptions spilled over into the global political economy as a whole. The most notable example is the production cuts instituted by some Arab oil exporters in conjunction with the October 1973 Arab-Israeli war.[9] Efforts to reduce global carbon emissions by reducing consumption of fossil fuels constitute another potential threat to hydrocarbon exporters, but these remain distant concerns to producers. Coal-combustion contributes twice as much to atmospheric carbon than does the burning of natural gas, while carbon from oil combustion falls somewhere in the middle.[10] Policies to combat global climate change will drive investment, production, income distribution, and security across fuels and energy suppliers in the future, but gas and oil will still be in demand as relatively less-polluting fuels compared to coal.

Throughout much of the twentieth century, as oil and gas deposits were discovered around and in the Persian Gulf, external powers played a Janus-faced role as exploiters and protectors. They exercised their influence directly, through relations conventionally classified as 'imperialism', and indirectly through the

[3] Erik Kreil and Matthew Cline, 'The Gulf's Rising Natural Gas Production and Trade', Paper presented at the Gulf & the Globe Conference, Annapolis, Maryland, USA, 28–29 January 2009.

[4] *Ibid.*; Hussein Yusuf, 'What's Next for Somalia?', *Foreign Policy in Focus*, 28 January 2009, http://fpif.org/fpiftxt/5824 (accessed 4 February 2009).

[5] Daniel Moran and James A. Russell, 'The Militarization of Energy Security', *Strategic Insights*, 7(1) (2008), available at http://www.saudi-us-relations.org/articles/2008/ioi/080307-russell-energy.html.

[6] Edward L. Morse, 'After the Fall: The Politics of Oil', *Foreign Affairs*, 64(4) (1986), pp. 792–811.

[7] Mary Ann Tétreault, 'Complex Consequences: Hydrocarbon Production as a Route to Economic Health', In *Rebuilding Devastated Economies in the Middle East*. Ed. Leonard Binder (New York: Palgrave Macmillan, 2007), pp. 77–94; Philip K. Verleger, Jr., 'OPEC's One-way Option: Investors and the Price of Crude Oil', 2005, at www.pkverlegerllc.com/UTexas%20050218.PDF (accessed 1 February 2009).

[8] See Figures 1–3 in Mahmoud Amin El-Gamal and Amy Myers Jaffe, 'Energy, Financial Contagion, and the Dollar', James A. Baker III Working Paper Series: The Global Energy Market: Comprehensive Strategies to Meet Geopolitical and Financial Risks, May 2008, http://www.rice.edu/energy/publications/WorkingPapers/IEEJcontagion-ElGamalJaffe.pdf (accessed 1 February 2009).

[9] Mary Ann Tétreault, *Revolution in the World Petroleum Market* (Westport, CT: Quorum Books, 1985).

[10] United States Energy Information Administration, 'Emissions of Greenhouse Gases in the United States 1985–1990', DOE/EIA-0573, September 1993, p. 16.

activities of private, state-owned, and mixed-ownership firms serving as national champions of their home governments.[11] Oil production is geographically localized. Technology and capital intensity minimize and localize its direct impact on employment and social life.[12] The relative ease with which foreigners could control oil exploitation allowed them to transform local rulers into client partners rather than taking over their territories and ruling directly.[13] Even then, the foreign firms were backed up by governments able to supply cash, diplomatic assistance, and military pressure to keep these partnerships going. In addition, partnerships between home, host, and firm provided outlets for host-country hydrocarbon production through the corporate supply chain, protecting these countries from local enemies and from home-country great-power rivals.[14] These dimensions of energy security might be summed up as issues of sovereignty: the ability of producing states to manage their own resources and to be treated as equals.

A second level of vulnerability embraces issues of autonomy. Most Gulf oil exporters are traditional monarchical regimes[15] whose populations are influenced by familial tribalism[16] as well as religious tribalism organized around national and transnational movements, both of which enjoy a superior—God-given—legitimacy as challengers to the authority of the state.[17] Democratization in this region has empowered these forces,[18] and given them a legitimate voice in determining policies for hydrocarbon exploitation and how hydrocarbon income should be spent. The resulting conflicts among competing demands for investment and consumption constrain the autonomy of producing states.

Security Eras

Energy security before OPEC

The international hydrocarbon industry was the cutting edge of twentieth-century globalization. During the period of initial exploration, development, and production, hydrocarbon operations were conducted primarily by American, British, and Dutch international oil companies (IOCs).[19] Through the establishment of a web of contracts and alliances, they created a global market that gave them and their home governments a greater-than-average influence over the conduct of and

---

[11] Tétreault, *Revolution*.

[12] Adelrahman Munif, *Cities of Salt* (New York: Vintage Books, 1989); Robert Vitalis. *America's Kingdom: Mythmaking on the Saudi Oil Frontier* (Palo Alto CA: Stanford University Press, 2006).

[13] Irvine H. Anderson, *Aramco, the United States, and Saudi Arabia: A Study of the Dynamics of Foreign Oil Policy, 1933-1950* (Princeton, NJ: Princeton University Press, 1981); H.R.P. Dickson, *Kuwait and her Neighbours* (London: Allen and Unwin, 1956); John Foran, *Fragile Resistance: Social Transformation in Iran from 1500 to the Revolution* (Boulder, CO: Westview, 1993); Munif, *Cities*.

[14] Tétreault, *Revolution*.

[15] Michael Herb, *All in the Family: Absolutism, Revolution, and Democracy in the Middle Eastern Monarchies* (Albany, NY: State University of New York Press, 1999); Joseph Kostiner (ed.), *Middle East Monarchies: The Challenge of Modernity* (Boulder, CO: Lynne Rienner, 2000).

[16] Khaldoun Hasan al-Naqeeb, *Society and State in the Gulf and Arab Peninsula: A Different Perspective*, trans. L.M. Kenny (London: Routledge, 1990).

[17] Nazih Ayubi, *Political Islam: Religion and Politics in the Arab World* (London: Routledge, 1991); Olivier Roy, *The Failure of Political Isla.* (London: Verso, 1994).

[18] Marina Ottaway, Nathan J. Brown, Amr Hamzawy, Karm Sadjadpour, and Paul Salem, 'The New Middle East' (Washington DC: Carnegie Endowment for International Peace, 2008). Report available at http://www.carnegieendocument.org/files/new-middle-east-final1.pdf

[19] Anthony Sampson, *The Seven Sisters: The Great Oil Companies and the World They Shaped* (New York: Viking, 1975); Daniel Yergin, *The Prize: The Epic Quest for Oil, Money and Power* (New York: Simon and Schuster, 1991).

rewards going to other market participants. In the process, IOCs generated enormous wealth for their owners, underwrote the strategic and economic security of their home countries, and expanded the state capacity as well as the incomes of host governments. They also, and inadvertently, shifted the balance of power between themselves and exporting states by accumulating sunk costs in production facilities and the integration of particular crudes into refining and distribution systems located abroad.[20]

This energy regime was not without conflict among developed states. The French, for example, were convinced that an Anglo-American cabal controlled oil for the benefit of Anglo-Saxons.[21] Yet what looked from the outside like a dual conspiracy concealed an arena where US and British interests clashed as often as they coincided. Rivalry among oil entrepreneurs allowed each successive Gulf country negotiating concession contracts to learn from other exporters' experiences and take advantage of competition among the nascent IOCs to improve their own positions. Consequently, in spite of British efforts to block it, the Kuwaiti emir succeeded in including an American IOC as an equal partner in the concession he let in 1934, despite Kuwait's status as a British dependency at the time.[22]

The aims and capacities of states are clear on both sides of IOC-mediated petro-political relations. Some see developing areas as sites of primitive politics, but Gulf rulers were skilful managers of late-nineteenth and twentieth-century imperial and IOC intervention.[23] Following the example set by Mubarak al-Sabah, the most ruthless emir in the 250-year history of Sabah family rule in Kuwait, Mubarak's descendants, Abd al-Aziz Ibn Saud, and the al-Thanis in Qatar consolidated their regimes by manipulating the Ottomans, the British and Americans, and the proto-IOCs to support their dynastic ambitions even before they were able to use oil directly as leverage.[24] In some sense they were cheated by the terms of the initial contracts they signed with their IOCs.[25] But when oil income finally arrived, it went directly to these rent-seeking rulers, and most managed to extract additional goods and services from the IOCs and their home governments above what was mandated by concession contracts. During the 1960s, thanks to their growing structural power and what they learned from their peers in the Organization of Petroleum Exporting Countries (OPEC) they were able to induce changes in those contracts that redressed many initial injustices.[26]

The connection between sovereignty and autonomy is also clear: Gulf rulers used their oil incomes to attract domestic allies, maintain their regimes in the face

---

[20] Hans Jacob Bull-Berg, *American International Oil Policy: Causal Factors and Impact* (London: Frances Pinter, 1987); Edith T. Penrose, *The Large International Firm in Developing Countries: The International Petroleum Industry* (Cambridge, MA: MIT Press, 1968); Tétreault, *Revolution*; Mary Ann Tétreault, *The Kuwait Petroleum Corporation and the Economics of the New World Order* (Westport CT: Quorum Books, 1995).

[21] Harvey B. Feigenbaum, *Politics of Public Enterprise: Oil and the French State* (Princeton, NJ: Princeton University Press, 1985).

[22] Archibald H.T. Chisholm, *The First Kuwait Oil Concession Agreement: A Record of the Negotiations, 1911-1934* (London: Frank Cass, 1975).

[23] Frederick F. Anscombe, *The Ottoman Gulf: The Creation of Kuwait, Saudi Arabia, and Qatar* (New York: Columbia University Press, 1997).

[24] Anscombe, *The Ottoman Gulf*; Anderson, *Aramco*; Chisholm, *The First Kuwait*; Jill Crystal, *Oil and Politics in the Gulf: Rulers and Merchants in Kuwait and Qatar* (Cambridge: Cambridge University Press, 1990).

[25] Penrose, *The Large International*; Sampson, *The Seven Sisters*; Tétreault, *Revolution*; Mary Ann Tétreault, 'The Political Economy of Middle Eastern Oil', in Deborah J. Gerner and Jillian Schwedler (eds), *Understanding the Contemporary Middle East*, 2nd ed. (Boulder, CO: Lynne Rienner, 2004), pp. 249–272.

[26] Penrose, *The Large International*; Tétreault, *Revolution*.

of domestic rivals, and fend off external pressures emanating from their neighbours and from the great powers.[27] Although their inexperience may have put them at a disadvantage, they succeeded in protecting their interests as they understood them at the time.

The structure of the market did not always favour them, however. Gulf rulers could adapt the terms of prior contracts to create base lines for new concessions, but they could not counter the political fragmentation that allowed the IOCs to use them against one another once those concessions were signed. For example, when Mohammad Mossadeq's government nationalized Iran's oil, Anglo-Iranian, the forerunner of BP, simply increased its offtake of Kuwaiti crude to keep its operations running thanks to an unusual contract it had made with its partner, Gulf Oil, which excluded Kuwait as a party.[28] The availability of Kuwaiti crude, similar in its physical characteristics to Iranian crude, created space for Britain and the United States to exert pressure on Iran[29] but the flood of revenues made fiscal and political problems for Kuwait.[30] The companies could collude easily—and legally—thanks to their intersecting joint ventures,[31] but host countries were as beset by their rivalries as home countries were by theirs.[32] Until OPEC was formed in 1960, oil-exporter cooperation was hit-or-miss at best.[33]

The rapid development of the first Arab Gulf hydrocarbon industries ran parallel with the unfolding of the Cold War. Both the Soviet Union and the United States were major oil producers at the end of World War II, when the focus of Cold War oil politics was Europe. Europe was pulled and pushed to rebuild economically as an oil-dependent region by the combination of cheap oil from the Middle East and the structure of Marshall Plan assistance; both undermined the dominance of coal as a fuel.[34] The outcome enriched the IOCs, strengthened the dollar as the currency used for most oil (and other international) transactions, and enshrined oil as a linchpin of the Cold War order. After Kremlin policy changed in the 1960s to emphasize foreign sales of oil and natural gas, European fuel-dependency became a superpower battleground whose stakes included both the magnitude of economic returns to owners of hydrocarbon resources and the political alignment of governments.[35]

US foreign policy in the Gulf during this period thus had two chief aims. One was to prevent Soviet penetration and to ensure preferential access to Gulf hydrocarbon resources by Western IOCs; the other was to keep hydrocarbon prices low to encourage the development of an oil-dependent global infrastructure that

---

[27] Madawi Al-Rasheed, *Politics in an Arabian Oasis* (London: I.B. Tauris, 1991); Anderson, *Aramco*; Dickson, *Kuwait and her Neighbours*; Alan De Lacy Rush, *Records of Kuwait, 1899-1961. Vol. 5, Petroleum Affairs* (London: Archive Editions, 1989).

[28] Theodore H. Moran, 'Managing an Oligopoly of Would-Be Sovereigns: The Dynamics of Joint Control and Self-Control in the International Oil Industry Past, Present, and Future', *International Organization*, 41(4) (1987), pp. 676–697.

[29] Sampson, *The Seven Sisters*.

[30] Crystal, *Oil and Politics in the Gulf*, 1990.

[31] Sampson, *The Seven Sisters*.

[32] Tétreault, *Revolution*.

[33] Zuhayr Mikdashi, *The Community of Oil-exporting Countries* (Ithaca, NY: Cornell University Press, 1972).

[34] Richard N. Gardner, *Sterling-Dollar Diplomacy in Current Perspective: The Origins and the Prospects of Our International Economic Order* (New York: Columbia University Press, 1980); David S. Painter, *Oil and the American Century: The Political Economy of US Foreign Oil Policy, 1941-1954* (Baltimore, MD: Johns Hopkins University Press, 1986); Tétreault, *The Kuwait Petroleum Corporation*.

[35] Bruce W. Jentleson, *Pipeline Politics: The Complex Political Economy of East-West Energy Trade* (Ithaca, NY: Cornell University Press, 1986).

would tie the industrialized countries of the 'West'—which included Japan—to US interests.[36] Both were threatened by a gigantic contradiction at the heart of US Middle East policy. On one side were US economic interests exemplified by the role of US firms in the region's oil industry. On the other was US support for Israel, whose rejection by virtually every Middle Eastern state and nation was sustained by Israeli defensive aggressiveness[37] and the bitter politics of the Palestinian diaspora.[38] The United States had difficulty juggling the often incompatible demands arising from its leadership of the Western alliance and the need to manage conflicts in the Middle East to guarantee the continued flow of cheap oil to its major-power allies, and increasingly after 1948, when US oil consumption first exceeded domestic production, to itself. For example, the Eisenhower administration risked NATO integrity to court Arab public opinion by siding with Algerian insurgents in their war against France.[39] This attitude did not extend to most other anti-colonial and revolutionary movements in the Middle East, from the attempt by a democratically elected government in Iran to assert its petroleum sovereignty[40] to the modest efforts of oil workers in Saudi Arabia to improve their political and economic situations.[41]

Energy security in the heyday of OPEC

At the same time, internal development trajectories and the world historical time line left appreciable autonomy with the small, tribally organized Gulf regimes. The relative sufficiency of state capacity rather than its absolute level explains their initial advantage. As previously noted, each potential hydrocarbon producer in the Gulf benefited from what its leaders had observed about a neighbour's contracts and how they had worked out in practice. Both during the early days of the industry[42] and in the years immediately preceding the oil revolution of 1970–1974,[43] several Arab Gulf producers, acting at first individually and then collectively through OPEC, managed without violence to alter contract terms in their own favour. IOCs used that same historical knowledge on their own behalf but, as their fixed capital expanded, they became less able to manoeuvre within the vertically integrated systems they relied on at that time to run the global petroleum regime.[44] Consequently, when they found their astronomical profits inching back to terrestrial levels in response to increased competition from 'independent' companies, contract revisions favouring host governments, and glutted markets, they were prompted to try to regain some of the ground they had lost. US-based

---

[36] Bull-Berg, *American International Oil Policy*.
[37] Uri Bialer, *Oil and the Arab-Israeli Conflict, 1948-63* (Oxford: St Antony's, 1999).
[38] Kathleen Christison, *Perceptions of Palestine: Their Influence on US Middle East Policy* (Berkeley: University of California Press, 1999); Donald L. Losman, 'The Arab Boycott of Israel', *International Journal of Middle East Studies*, 3(2) (1972), pp. 99–122; Benny Morris, *The Birth of the Palestinian Refugee Problem, 1947-1949* (New York: Cambridge University Press, 1987).
[39] Matthew Connelly, 'Rethinking the Cold War and Decolonization: The Grand Strategy of the Algerian War for Independence', *International Journal of Middle East Studies*, 33(2) (2001), pp. 221–245.
[40] Mark J. Gasiorowski, *US Foreign Policy and the Shah: Building a Client State in Iran* (Ithaca, NY: Cornell University Press, 1991).
[41] Vitalis, *America's Kingdom*.
[42] Chisholm, *The First Kuwait*.
[43] Penrose, *The Large International*; Sampson, *The Seven Sisters*; Tétreault, *Revolution*.
[44] Vertical integration refers to company ownership of facilities throughout the supply chain. The multinational structure of the industry allowed IOCs to use transfer pricing between operations to locate profits in a way that minimized their tax liabilities and maximized their profits.

IOCs were able to apply an obscure tax provision allowing them to deduct taxes paid to foreign governments from their US tax obligations. When this was not enough, the IOCs decided to reduce prices paid to producing countries for crude by fiat, first in 1959 and again in 1960. This was the goad producers needed to join formally in an alliance to protect their incomes. OPEC was born in September 1960, shortly after the second price reduction.

The limits of historical knowledge as a guide for the future is demonstrated by the experience of OPEC, which struggled on several fronts against shifts in the distribution of real costs within the industry: from segment to segment in the supply chain, and also across producers, as Latin American exporters increasingly lost out to lower-cost operators in the Gulf. Sharing information and coordinating policies toward the IOCs was a primary goal of OPEC members.[45] The advantages to be gained from collective action were equally clear to the home governments of the IOCs. Consequently, the United States refused to recognize OPEC and ordered its IOCs to deal with OPEC members only as individual countries rather than collectively, via OPEC.[46] There is a certain poetic justice to the oil-exporting countries taking advantage of this US-assisted fragmentation to ratchet up prices in the early 1970s by playing IOC operators in the Gulf off against their counterparts in the Mediterranean.[47] The ratchet ended when an embargo against supporters of Israel in the October 1973 war was imposed by Arab oil exporters and reinforced by production cuts, uncertainty and spot shortages pushed prices up without any need for outside assistance.[48]

This transition constituted a fundamental change in authority over the international energy regime as ownership of equity in oil and gas went from IOCs to host governments. Most oil-exporting countries nationalized their industries or assumed equity control gradually through a process known as 'participation'. Either way, decision-making on production and prices passed from the IOCs to the oil ministries of the host governments, although the transfer of actual operations took a much longer time.[49] Host governments hoped to impose a regime of exporting state-led price regulation via OPEC similar to the old system of administered—posted—prices the IOCs had used, but this turned out to be beyond their capabilities because of the adjustment strategies of other players in energy markets.

The IOCs adjusted so readily to their new roles as operators that critics like M.A. Adelman accused them of being 'tax collectors for OPEC'.[50] Nationalization neither cut off nor reduced the revenues of most IOCs operating in the Middle East.[51] IOC profits generated future problems for OPEC as revenue streams were invested in high-cost exploration, development, and production elsewhere, such as in the very expensive United States and in high-cost regions of Europe like the North Sea. Production from these sources displaced OPEC sales internationally.[52]

[45] Mikdashi, *The Community of Oil-exporting Countries*.
[46] Sampson, *The Seven Sisters*.
[47] Christopher Rand, *Making Democracy Safe for Oil: Oilmen and the Islamic East*. (Boston, MA: Atlantic-Little Brown, 1975); Sampson, *The Seven Sisters*.
[48] Richard Chadbourn Weisberg, 'The Politics of Crude Oil Pricing in the Middle East, 1970-1975: A Study in International Bargaining', Research Series No. 31 (Berkeley CA: Institution of International Studies, 1977).
[49] Valérie Marcel and John V. Mitchell, *Oil Titans: National Oil Companies in the Middle East* (Washington, DC: Brookings, 2006); Tétreault, *The Kuwait Petroleum Corporation*.
[50] M.A. Adelman, 'Is the Oil Shortage Real? Oil Companies as OPEC Tax Collectors,' *Foreign Policy*, 9 (Winter 1972/73), pp. 69–107.
[51] Jonathan Nitzan and Shimshon Bichler, *The Global Political Economy of Israel* (London: Pluto Press, 2002).
[52] Tétreault, *Revolution*.

Strategically vulnerable Gulf exporters also were threatened with sanctions, including threats to cut off food supplies[53] and, in Henry Kissinger's famous January 1974 interview with *Business Week*, with possible military seizure of their oil installations. Arab oil exporters, especially in the Gulf, were treated as malevolent market czars, while OPEC was singled out as *the* cause of the global inflation that had begun prior to the oil revolution, and also of the recession that followed it.[54]

Military intervention was not likely during the Vietnam War; structural responses were preferred. Under the leadership of the United States, oil-importing countries formed an anti-OPEC, the International Energy Agency (IEA). The IEA was designed to ensure a collective response to future oil embargoes and any other disruption in energy markets affecting fuel supplies. One of its most important innovations was to require each IEA member to maintain a 90-day supply of crude oil in a strategic inventory, available for release if such an interruption were to occur.[55] These strategic inventories proved effective in reducing national autonomy and regime stability in the Gulf states.

Inflation was another strategic challenge for acutely oil income-dependent Gulf exporters. Higher oil prices were not the only source of the global inflation that had started in the late 1960s. Indeed, US inflation and the consequent fall in the dollar had forced President Nixon to suspend gold convertibility in 1971.[56] Inflation helped oil importers adjust to the new energy price regime, in much the same way as inflation helped Germany adjust to war reparations after World War I.[57] In both cases, the effects on domestic populations were devastating but from the perspective of the governments whose policies fuelled it, inflation was politically useful.[58] During the 1970s, the United States relied on inflation as well as collective action to diminish the relative impact of higher oil prices on its economy.[59]

The inflation that eroded the value of higher oil prices, like exchange rates earlier in the decade, exposed the vulnerability of oil-exporters and oil-importers to rising levels of international interdependence mediated by trade and investment flows.[60] In the 1970s, Gulf exporters had a low investment capacity so they invested their cash in US treasury bills and, to a lesser extent, foreign equities, and squandered the rest on frivolous consumption. Their populations quickly became accustomed to affluence, both targeted and trickle-down, reducing the none-too-evident impulses of most of their leaders to invest strategically for a comfortable after-oil future. One of the few examples of strategic policy was the discount Saudi Arabia gave its operators. The aim of the 'Aramco advantage' was to put enough lower-cost oil on the market to hold prices at a level that would discourage significant investment in alternative fuels.[61] Yet an experienced observer of the oil industry was able to say truthfully that the period between the price increases associated with the October 1973 war and the second round of massive price

---

[53] William Schneider, *Food, Foreign Policy and Raw Materials Cartels* (New York: Crane, Russak, 1976).
[54] George Tomeh, 'Arab Politics and Priorities in Economic Cooperation with Western Europe', in Edmond Volker (ed.), *Euro-Arab Cooperation* (London: A.W. Sijthoff, 1976).
[55] Tétreault, *Revolution*.
[56] The decline of the dollar triggered the rounds of price ratcheting between Teheran and Tripoli.
[57] Niall Ferguson, *The Pity of War: Explaining World War I* (New York: Basic Books, 1999).
[58] For other examples, see Nitzan and Bichler, *The Global Political Economy of Israel*.
[59] David Deese and Joseph Nye (eds), *Energy and Security* (Cambridge: Ballinger, 1981); Tétreault, *Revolution*.
[60] Keohane and Nye, *Power and Interdependence*.
[61] Tétreault, *Revolution*, p. 61.

increases touched off by the Iranian revolution of 1978–1979 were 'the years that the locust hath eaten', a reflection of how badly the Gulf states in particular had misjudged their ability to manage the oil market to achieve sustainable domestic economies.[62]

Naked in the market

The market for oil was globalized in 1981 when Ronald Reagan decontrolled US crude and product prices, reintegrating the United States into world crude and product markets for the first time since the Great Depression. This looked like a gamble when world oil prices were high, and seems to have been motivated as much by Reagan's 'new Cold War' against the Soviet Union as by his belief that markets would be a better guarantor of US security than the more interventionist policies of his three predecessors.[63] In the event, Reagan's gamble paid off. Crude prices had risen so steeply in 1980 that world demand for petroleum actually remained below 1980 levels for the next seven years.[64] Gains from higher prices were not evenly distributed across producers. African suppliers were able to impose surcharges and quality premiums on top of official OPEC prices, and the high prices of oil from non-OPEC sources were seen as security premiums by buyers willing to pay more not simply for lighter crude but also for 'safer' oil from non-Arab and non-Gulf producers. The new high price level did not last long, either. By 1982, the glutted market routinely pushed realized prices paid for many OPEC crudes below official OPEC prices. Crude oil continually appeared from anticipated new sources, such as North Sea producers Britain and Norway, and unexpected ones, such as cargoes from IEA strategic inventories dumped on the market when demand declined and owners needed less oil to meet the 90-day requirement. The Soviet Union was an aggressive seller throughout most of the decade,[65] along with traditional non-OPEC exporters like Mexico. The constant glut was left entirely to OPEC, and particularly its Gulf members, to manage.

Market fragmentation also continued. Spot price spikes during the revolution in Iran lured governments into abrogating their contracts with IOCs in favour of selling crude directly to other governments or via spot sales. When prices declined, producers did not have these contracts to fall back on, exposing them more directly to market forces, including market manipulation. The disorder of oil markets made often murky spot transactions more important as presumed indicators of the 'real price' of oil. Opacity, uncertainty, and under-the-table dealing amplified price swings throughout the market and, as OPEC proved to have about as much control over the market as the Wizard had over Oz, spot prices also affected official prices.[66]

OPEC did its best to stabilize prices, going so far as to lower the marker[67] price in 1983, the first time official prices had been reduced since the organization was

---

[62] Walter J. Lévy, 'The Years that the Locust Hath Eaten: Oil Policy and OPEC Development Prospects', *Foreign Affairs*, 57(2) (Winter 1978/79), pp. 287–305.

[63] Mary Ann Tétreault, 'Energy Policy and the Reagan Administration', *Forum for Applied Research and Public Policy*, 3(4) (Winter 1988), pp. 70–79.

[64] Demand fell for only two years after 1973. See United States Energy Information Administration, *Annual Energy Review 2007* (Washington, DC: EIA, 2008), p. 319.

[65] Tétreault, *Revolution*; United States Energy Information Administration, *Annual Energy Review 2007*, p. 319.

[66] Tétreault, *Revolution*, appendix.

[67] The 'marker' is the crude used as the product standard. Discounts and surcharges were applied to reflect quality differences between the marker and other traded crudes.

founded. OPEC had few tools to makes its decisions stick, however. Even without the additional fragmentation, OPEC was inherently less able to regulate production than the IOCs. The IOCs had enjoyed the benefit of legally enforceable contracts consciously designed to limit the autonomy of firms most likely to overproduce.[68] OPEC members had no such legal instruments or any institution able to enforce them if they had existed. Preferring sovereignty and autonomy to cooperation and coordination, they resisted attempts to mobilize effective collective action to limit production even though their individual overproduction contributed to lower per-barrel revenues. This jumble of independent policies managed to create the worst of all possible worlds for the Gulf exporters. Demand remained depressed, incomes remained depressed, and the formerly buoyant domestic economies of Gulf states whose national bird once seemed to be the building crane, also remained depressed.[69]

OPEC did try to shore up its price structure, calling first for voluntary and then for mandatory quotas on production, but sovereignty continued to trump market power as a national goal. Saudi Arabia flatly refused to accept a quota on the grounds that it was an infringement on state sovereignty. Instead, it agreed to 'balance' demand by producing only the amount needed to maintain the marker price. Virtually every OPEC member with excess capacity found ways to violate its quota in fruitless attempts to hold its income level in a market where new production and sudden releases of strategic stocks exerted continual downward pressure on prices. By 1985, Saudi crude production had fallen to 3.4 MBD, slightly over one-third of its 1981 level, threatening power cuts because the amount of oil being pumped was not sufficient to supply needed 'associated gas'.[70] Hemmed in by conflicting demands on its production policy, Saudi Arabia increased production by 1.5 MBD in 1986. What was left of the OPEC price structure promptly collapsed, with spot prices falling below $10.00/bbl. that summer.

Lower oil prices were welcomed by consumers but their impact was uneven. Because oil prices were denominated in dollars, Americans experienced the price reductions directly. They revelled in cheap oil, making structural changes in their lifestyles that embedded high and rising fuel use in their daily activities as home owners and commuters. In Europe, lower official prices and even bottom-scraping spot prices had fewer effects on consumption. The higher dollar translated into much smaller price reductions for Europeans than Americans, while the relative weight of crude prices in product prices was far less in Europe than in the United States because of vast differences in product taxes.

The three Gulf wars and security

The first Gulf war (1980–1988), between Iraq and Iran, pitted two military forces fattened by oil revenues against one another, and triggered the expenditure of even more oil revenues for arms.[71] The fighting lasted years longer than its main

---

[68] Moran, 'Managing an Oligopoly'.
[69] Shireen T. Hunter, 'The Gulf Economic Crisis and its Social and Political Consequences', *Middle East Journal*, 40(4) (1986), pp. 593–613.
[70] Tétreault, *Revolution*.
[71] Anthony H. Cordesman and Abraham R. Wagner, *The Lessons of Modern War. Vol. II: The Iran-Iraq War* (Boulder, CO: Westview, 1992), chap. 3; Global Security, *Iran-Iraq War (1980–1988)*, ND. Available online at http://www.globalsecurity.org/military/world/war/iran-iraq.htm

antagonists had ever imagined when it began, bogging down in a war of attrition producing casualties whose exact number remains

> highly uncertain, though estimates suggest more than one and a half million war and war-related casualties—perhaps as many as a million people died, many more were wounded, and millions were made refugees. Iran acknowledged that nearly 300,000 people died in the war; estimates of the Iraqi dead range from 160,000 to 240,000. Iraq suffered an estimated 375,000 casualties, the equivalent of 5.6 million for a population the size of the United States. Another 60,000 were taken prisoner by the Iranians. Iran's losses may have included more than one million people killed or maimed.[72]

Estimates of economic costs were close to $70 billion for Iran and $160 billion for Iraq.[73] In spite of direct attacks on oil installations and shipping, however, the war had little impact on oil prices. Indeed, in the sixth year, after Iranian attacks on tanker traffic had virtually halted, the global price of oil collapsed (see above).

The principal price effects of the war fell squarely on Gulf crudes, whose costs increased due to higher insurance rates for shipping following attacks on tankers. Other installations also were targeted by the belligerents, but had no independent price effects. Exports from other sources replaced a varying portion of Gulf exports throughout the war. Other oil price effects are reflected in the large discrepancy in war cost estimates for Iran and Iraq. Iran is much larger, had a larger military and a larger oil industry. But the United States had imposed sanctions against Iran in November 1979 in response to Iran's capturing and holding hostage US diplomatic personnel, and these sanctions were extended during the Reagan administration in response to the bombing of the Marine barracks in Lebanon in 1983. US directors of international financial institutions were required by an executive order to vote against Iranian loan applications, and in 1986 Iran came under the US Arms Export Control Act, denying it weapons and spare parts.[74] At the same time, the United States was secretly (and illegally) trying to trade arms and spare parts to Iran in exchange for hostages held in Lebanon,[75] but even if this covert operation had not been exposed, it is unlikely to have transferred enough materiel to Iran to compensate for arms going to Iraq. The greater problem for Iran during the war was the effect of sanctions on its ability to borrow. Although both Iran and Iraq saw their oil revenues vary with export levels and per-barrel prices, the effects were felt more by Iran, which depended on current income to finance its war, than Iraq, which was able to borrow from its neighbours and then from banks to replenish its weapons stocks.[76]

Internal security in all the smaller Gulf states suffered from the revenue effects of the oil price collapse in 1986. Those countries diverting oil revenues from domestic needs to finance Iraq's weapons purchases also felt the impact of war costs. Their assistance was delivered as loans and grants to Iraq and, from Saudi Arabia and Kuwait, in the form of a major highway, an oil pipeline through Saudi Arabia from southern Iraq to the Red Sea, and as oil produced in the 'neutral zone'

---

[72] GlobalSecurity, *Iran-Iraq War (1980-1988)*.
[73] Cordesman and Wagner, *The Lessons of Modern War*, p. 3.
[74] Herman Fransen and Elaine Morton, 'A Review of US Unilateral Sanctions Against Iran', *Middle East Economic Survey*, 45(34) (2002), www.mafhoum.com/press3/108E16.htm.
[75] Theodore Draper, *A Very Thin Line: The Iran-Contra Affairs* (New York: Hill and Wang, 1991).
[76] Mary Ann Tétreault, 'Independence, Sovereignty, and Vested Glory: Oil and Politics in the Second Gulf War', *Orient*, 34(1) (1993), p. 96.

and sold 'on Iraq's account'.[77] The domestic economic contraction produced social unrest and communal conflicts.[78] Kuwait's support of Iraq provoked Shi'i dissidents to commit terrorist acts, some directed against oil installations. Terrorists also attempted to assassinate the emir in 1985. Parliamentary opposition to the government's economic policies, coupled with the bouquet of security threats generated by the war led the emir to dismiss the parliament.[79] He subsequently ruled illegally, by decree, until Saddam Hussein launched his invasion of Kuwait in August 1990 and he fled into exile.

The Gulf's dependent economies were products of poor prior choices between investment and consumption, and also within each of those categories. They depended heavily on oil revenues to support rapacious ruling families, subsidize the private sector, and pay for salaries and benefits to workers in a bloated public sector. Contracting oil revenues forced rulers to confront citizens not merely distressed but openly infuriated by cuts in their living standards, and their own family members who wanted to be sure that they would get their cuts of dwindling state income off the top.[80] The only way they could shore up incomes to satisfy these demands was to produce more oil, a perverse strategy that ensured lower prices by adding to the glut, and thereby the need to produce even more just to stay in the same place.

Iraq and Iran were devastated economically by the first Gulf war. Having been prevented by sanctions from borrowing to finance its military, Iran was in a better financial position to rebuild when the war was over. The war itself enabled Iran's new government to consolidate what had been an uncertain regime beset by domestic opponents.[81] Consequently, in spite of the huge cost in blood and treasure, Iran emerged from the war poised to assert its growing strength domestically and in foreign policy.

Iraq had borrowed heavily from its neighbours and from international banks to finance its war effort. When the war was over, these creditors demanded repayment. The Iraqi people also wanted compensation for eight years of privation and slaughter.[82] The government had little to offer them because its war-reduced level of oil exports could not generate enough income to go around given the low price of oil. Iraq blamed its situation on its Gulf neighbours, especially those violating their OPEC quotas, which included everyone with excess production

---

[77] Tétreault, 'Independence, Sovereignty, and Vested Glory', pp. 95–96. The pipeline carried oil for only a year after it was completed in 1989, until Iraq invaded Kuwait. The neutral, now divided zone is a strip of territory straddling the now delineated boundary between Kuwait and Saudi Arabia where sovereignty was left undefined in recognition of its importance as a region of nomadic transit. A similar neutral zone was provided for on the Saudi-Iraqi border.

[78] Hunter, 'The Gulf Economic Crisis', pp. 593–613. This is when Kuwaiti *bidoun* (formally stateless persons) lost their *de facto* rights to jobs, free schooling, health care, and other public services to which Kuwaiti citizens are entitled.

[79] Lori Plotkin Boghardt, *Kuwait Amid War, Peace, and Revolution, 1979-1991 and New Challenges* (New York: Palgrave Macmillan, 2006).

[80] Hunter, 'The Gulf Economic Crisis', pp. 593–613; Tétreault, 'Independence, Sovereignty, and Vested Glory', pp. 87–103.

[81] Maziar Behrooz, 'Trends in the Foreign Policy of the Islamic Republic of Iran, 1979–1988', in N.R. Keddie and M.J. Gasiorowski, *Neither East nor West: Iran, the Soviet Union, and the United States* (New Haven, CT: Yale University Press, 1990), pp. 13–35; Haideh Moghissi, *Populism and Feminism in Iran* (New York: St Martin's, 1994); Gerd Nonneman, 'The Gulf States and the Iran-Iraq War: Pattern Shifts and Continuities', in Lawrence G. Potter and Gary G. Sick (eds), *Iran, Iraq, and the Legacies of War* (New York: Palgrave, 2004), pp. 167–192.

[82] Tétreault, 'Independence, Sovereignty, and Vested Glory', pp. 87–103.

capacity. Kuwait was close enough for Iraq to do something about. Iraq invaded and annexed Kuwait in August 1990, and occupied it for seven months.

The second Gulf war, inaugurated by Saddam's invasion, uncovered more of the impact of post-1980 marketization on intra-regional security. Despite the arms purchases that were part of the Gulf governments' consumption binge following the oil revolution, Kuwaiti security forces were unable to stop the invasion or protect the population.[83] Concerns that Saddam would not stop with Kuwait but would continue into Saudi Arabia, coupled with arm-twisting by the US president, persuaded the Saudi king to invite the United States to defend his country.[84] Unlike the first Gulf war, the second Gulf war had an immediate effect on oil prices, which rose promptly following the invasion and the subsequent UN sanctions against Iraq, which included an oil boycott that also covered oil originating in Kuwait.[85] The price increases were a boon to Saudi Arabia especially, whose production also rose and stabilized at an appreciably higher level than it had been throughout the preceding decade.[86]

External intervention in the second Gulf war was prompted by the feared effects of Saddam Hussein's invasion and occupation of Kuwait on the advantageous energy market position of the United States and its allies. President George H.W. Bush's greatest foreign policy triumph was the 1991 liberation of Kuwait from Iraqi occupation. UN Security Council resolutions to sanction and then bless the military rollback of the invasion were the result of skilful US diplomacy that brought the Soviet Union into the coalition against Saddam, marking the end of Cold War politics in the United Nations. Bush's actions left many unfortunate legacies in the region, however. Whether due to miscalculation or bad faith, his invitation to Iraqi Shi'a to rise up against Saddam was not followed by military or even diplomatic assistance to the insurgents, who were brutally repressed. Post-liberation pressure on Kuwait and the other Gulf states to purchase US arms and permit the maintenance and enlargement of US bases for their future defence undermined regional security strategies, and left these states vulnerable to domestic repercussions, including terrorist attacks, motivated in part by government acquiescence to US demands.[87]

The greatest threat to regime stability came from the ranks of returned mujahidin, soldiers for Islam who had fought in the Afghan, Bosnian, and Chechen wars. After the collapse of the Soviet effort in Afghanistan, they saw themselves as a powerful force. Saudis in the group led by Osama bin Laden felt that their status as divinely intended and tested-in-the-field potential protectors of Saudi Arabia had gone unrecognized when the Saudis surrendered the role of stopping Iraq to the Americans and their coalition.[88] Bin Laden's exile following terrorist attacks in the Middle East and Africa, blamed in part on pressure from the United States, aggravated his hostility toward both countries. Given the widespread interest of other governments in getting rid of someone so ruthless in his politics, he was

---

[83] Interviews in Kuwait, 1992.
[84] Jean Edward Smith, *George Bush's War* (New York: Henry Holt, 1992).
[85] Tétreault, *The Kuwait Petroleum Corporation*.
[86] United States Energy Information Administration, *Annual Energy Review 2007*, p. 309.
[87] Steve Coll, *Ghost Wars: The Secret History of the CIA, Afghanistan, and Bin Laden, from the Soviet Invasion to September 10, 2001* (New York: Penguin, 2004); Ahmed Rashid, *Taliban* (New Haven, CT: Yale Nota Bene, 2000).
[88] Coll, *Ghost*; Rashid, *Taliban*; Olivier Roy, 'Bin Laden et ses Frères', *Politique Internationale*, 93 (2001), pp. 67–81.

forced to find sanctuary in Afghanistan, from which he continued orchestrating terrorist attacks. The most spectacular terrorist attack, on 11 September 2001 against the United States, imposed the edge of a wedge between Saudis and Americans that neoconservatives were eager to push in further.[89]

After the second Gulf war, President Bill Clinton's most extensive intervention in the Gulf was part of a policy of 'dual containment', a package of strategic and economic sanctions intended to neutralize both Iraq and Iran as dangers to US interests.[90] Dual containment also assuaged the fears of the other Gulf states that either of these much larger and more belligerent neighbours would be able to attack them with impunity. Although violations of the borders between Iraq and Kuwait, and Iraq and Saudi Arabia, occurred with some frequency, overall the regional security threats to the smaller Gulf states were indeed contained, while the isolation of Saddam and periodic bombings of Iraq kept oil-production recovery at very low levels until the end of the decade, when the market had other surprises in store.

The ongoing third Gulf war, which began in March 2003, was arguably undertaken in part in pursuit of US global oil interests.[91] The chief among them was that what was expected to be a massive addition to global oil reserves and production capacity from a liberated Iraq would be accomplished with IOC participation.[92] Indeed, after the fall of Baghdad, and in the face of widespread looting, the only buildings in the city guarded by US troops were the Republican Palace and the oil ministry.[93] Few arrangements had been made to deal with 'post-conflict' security issues foreseen by military analysts[94] and the State Department,[95] but the possibility of oil-well fires was anticipated and the few fires that did result were quickly extinguished.[96]

Iraqi oil was not merely a lure for US policymakers envisioning a democratic post-conflict Iraq with a privatized industry that would welcome IOC investment. It drew them directly because it promised that a war to depose Saddam would be cheap. US officials expected to finance the war and postwar reconstruction from revenues derived from oil production and exports.[97] They also expected

[89] James Mann, *Rise of the Vulcans: The History of Bush's War Cabinet* (New York: Viking, 2004).
[90] Rosemary Hollis, 'The US Role: Helpful or Harmful?' in Lawrence G. Potter and Gary G. Sick (eds), *Iran, Iraq, and the Legacies of War* (New York: Palgrave Macmillan, 2004), pp. 193–211.
[91] This is a highly contested view, both because critics take a narrow view of US oil interests, which have focused on market access rather than equity ownership since the Reagan administration, and because it seems to dismiss the myriad other reasons for this over-determined war. On the role of oil as a *casus belli* from a range of ideological and professional perspectives, see Anonymous (Michael Scheuer), *Imperial Hubris: Why the West is Losing the War on Terror* (Dulles, VA: Brassey's, 2004), pp. 12–13; Alan Greenspan, *The Age of Turbulence: Adventures in a New World* (New York: Penguin, 2007), p. 463; Ron Suskind, *The Price of Loyalty: George W. Bush, the White House, and the Education of Paul O'Neill* (New York: Simon and Schuster, 2004), p. 96.
[92] Ali A. Allawi, *The Occupation of Iraq: Winning the War, Losing the Peace* (New Haven, CT: Yale University Press, 2006), pp. 254–257.
[93] Rajiv Chandrasekaran, *Imperial Life in the Emerald City: Inside Iraq's Green Zone* (New York: Knopf, 2006), p. 41.
[94] For example: Conrad C. Crane and W. Andrew Terrill, 'Reconstructing Iraq: Insights, Challenges, and Missions for Military Forces in a Post-Conflict Scenario' (Carlisle, PA: US Army War College, Strategic Studies Institute, 2003). Monograph available online at http://www.strategicstudies/institute.army.mil/pubs/display.cfm?pubID=182
[95] See, for example, David L. Phillips, *Losing Iraq: Inside the Postwar Reconstruction Fiasco* (New York: Basic Books, 2005).
[96] Bob Woodward, *Plan of Attack* (New York: Simon and Schuster, 2004) p. 402; interview in Kuwait with Eisa bu Yabes, formerly chief firefighter with the Kuwait Oil Corporation, June 2006.
[97] George Packer, *The Assassins' Gate: America in Iraq* (New York: Farrar, Straus and Giroux, 2005), p. 116; Woodward, *Plan of Attack*, pp. 322–324.

to use Iraqi resources to award cronies and political allies prestigious jobs and lucrative reconstruction contracts but, while the cronies took Iraqi money and, increasingly, US money, reconstruction results were mixed at best.[98]

Globalization

The high oil prices triggered by the third Gulf war were not simply reactions to the impact of conflict on the security of fuel supplies from the Gulf. Even more, they resulted from fundamental changes in the structure of the global economy—globalization, or 'the closer integration of the countries and peoples of the world which has been brought about by the enormous reduction of costs of transportation and communication, and the breaking down of artificial barriers to the flows of goods, services, capital, knowledge, and (to a lesser extent) people across borders'.[99] Foreshadowed by the global response to the first oil crisis in the early 1970s, globalization accelerated rapidly in response to the collapse of centrally planned economies in Eastern Europe and the opening of East Asian economies, especially China, to foreign investment and international trade. Globalization also expanded trade in oil-based derivatives and the marketing of commodities as an asset class, both of which amplified price movements and contributed heavily to the massive run-up in oil prices during the summer of 2008—for which OPEC was undeservedly blamed.[100]

The fall of the Soviet Union was perhaps the key event speeding globalization on its way at the end of the second Gulf war. The former Soviet republics became 'emerging markets', attracting oil investment and other investors and opportunists, including a huge international criminal class.[101] In the Gulf, the emerging-market mentality attracted drug dealers and human traffickers (many of them locals), arms dealers and money launderers, some licit (e.g. banks in denial) and others working beneath the surface of 'traditional' society.[102] Markets for political and social ideas also broadened and deepened as expectations about the intransigence of particular regimes to democratizing influences changed in response to examples from Eastern Europe, and from Western pressures on Gulf states, particularly Kuwait, which was expected to pay for its liberation by liberalizing its economy and political system. The social pressures generated by constantly increasing influences from abroad provoked greater Islamist mobilization, along with counter movements among women, religious minorities, and others who, like the dominant Islamist groups, received moral and material support from abroad in their pursuit of political aims.[103]

[98] John Cassidy, 'Beneath the Sand', *New Yorker*, 14 July 2003, http://www.newyorker.com/archive/2003/07/14/030714fa_fact3?printable=true (accessed 8 September 2008); Chandrasekaran, *Imperial Life in the Emerald City*; Iraq Revenue Watch, 'Disorder, Negligence and Mismanagement: How the CPA Handled Iraq Reconstruction Funds', Report No. 7, September 2004, at www.iraqrevenuewatch.org/reports/092404.pdf; Jane Mayer, 'Contract Sport', *New Yorker*, 16 February 2004, at www.newyorker.com/fact/content/?040216fa_fact.
[99] Joseph E. Stiglitz, *Globalization and its Discontents* (New York: Norton, 2002), p. 9.
[100] Philip K. Verleger, Jr., 'How Wall Street Controls Oil', *The International Economy*, Winter 2007, pp. 14–17, 60.
[101] Misha Glenny, *McMafia: A Jouney Through the Global Criminal Underworld* (New York: Knopf, 2008); Nitzan and Bichler, *The Global Political Economy of Israel*; Janine R. Wedel, *Collision and Collusion: The Strange Case of Western Aid to Eastern Europe, 1989-1998* (New York: St Martin's, 2008).
[102] Christopher M. Davidson, *Dubai: The Vulnerability of Success* (New York: Columbia University Press, 2008).
[103] Mary Ann Tétreault, Andrzej Kapiszewski, and Gwenn Okruhlik (eds), *Stuck in Transition: Dilemmas of Democratization in the Gulf* (Boulder, CO: Lynne Rienner, forthcoming).

Constraints on state autonomy were countered by the strategic opportunities opened up by globalization. Emerging markets themselves jump-started what had been a sluggish economy since the oil revolution. Outsourcing boosted the economies of large developing states, many of which were eager to regularize relationships with oil-producing countries. Investments by Gulf states in India and China promised not only conventional returns but also, as Iran's experience under decades of US sanctions showed, alternative markets for oil and gas.[104] Diversification of investment in oil development in the Gulf states is also taking place, most notably in Iraq which, in August 2008 announced a $3 billion deal with China.

The market narrative depicts an open system where decisions are made on the basis of efficiency, but Gulf state planners are well aware of the impact of conventions and punitive policies on ostensibly free investment and consumption choices.[105] The downstream integration that had been a strategy for market expansion and protection since the early 1980s moved eastward as opportunities opened to diversify investment and reduce Gulf dependency on the US-dominated West.[106] Sanctions and political pressures increase the attractiveness of partnerships with Asian states and firms. Such partnerships are more complicated at the contracting stage but far less so once these terms are agreed upon.

A second front in the war to protect populations from sanctions is the relatively new trend in investment by Gulf countries in agricultural operations in Asia and Africa.[107] Food insecurity was a primary impetus for the widely criticized investment of Saudi Arabia in domestic wheat production, which yielded wheat for $28 a bushel when world prices hovered around $3, and also produced a bumper crop of subsidy recipients that proved highly resistant to state attempts to curb these newly vested interests.[108] The need to trade autonomy for security is sidestepped by the foreign investment route. Costs are lower overseas than at home because the state partners chosen, such as Sudan, actually have good soil and abundant water to produce food crops, while agricultural investment does not generate the domestic entitlements that growing food at home has done.[109]

The market narrative also discounts the role of speculators in major world markets but an investigation of the massive instability in oil prices in 2008 told a different story. If spot markets became the key arena for trading at the time of the Iranian revolution, futures markets and hedge fund trading have taken over that role.[110] Futures trading in itself might be reasonably transparent but the main

[104] Meena Janardhan, 'In the Race for Renewables', *IPS News*, 22 August 2008, at www.ipsterraviva.net/europe/article.aspx?id=6439.
[105] Tétreault, *Revolution*; Tétreault, *The Kuwait Petroleum Corporation*.
[106] Marcel and Mitchell, *Oil Titans*; Tétreault, *The Kuwait Petroleum Corporation*.
[107] Meena Janardhan, 'Development: Gulf Eyes "Oil-for-food" Deal with Neighbours', IPS, 19 June 2009. Available at http://www.ipsnews.net/news.asp?idnews=42877; Ali Khalil, 'Gulf States Look to Harvest Food from Foreign Investment', *Middle East Times*, 20 July 2008, at www.metimes.com/Politics/2008/07/20/gulf_states_look_to_harvest_food_from_foreign_investment/afp/; KUNA (Kuwait News Agency), 'GCC Leaders Keen on Guaranteeing Food Security for Citizens, Expats: Attiyah', 8 September 2008, at www.kuna.net.kw/NewsAgenciesPublicSite/ArticleDetails.aspx?id=1936273&Language=en&searchtext=food%20security.
[108] Kirin Aziz Chaudhry, *The Price of Wealth: Economics and Institutions in the Middle East* (Ithaca, NY: Cornell University Press, 1997).
[109] But there are other demands that the Gulf states have been quite ready to meet in the Sudanese case, chiefly shielding it from sanctions imposed in retaliation for the ongoing genocide in Darfur. Any offshore reliance exposes the investor to the results of unrest and war, both of which are endemic in Sudan and threatening to spread back to the south, where Khartoum's reneging on power-sharing arrangements could reignite civil war.
[110] Verleger, 'How Wall Street Controls Oil', pp. 14–17, 60.

futures traders, most of them speculators, and their activities—speculation—are not. In August 2008 reporter David Cho looked at the results of an investigation by the US Commodity Futures Trading Commission (CFTC) which found that a large corporation that had billed itself as a trader matching firm's needs for oil with what was available in the market was, in reality, speculative venture that, 'at one point in July [2008] ... held 11 per cent of all the contracts traded on the New York Mercantile Exchange'.[111] Prior to a specific request for information from the CFTC, this regulatory agency had no idea how much trading on the exchange was in the hands of a tiny group of speculators. The CFTC subsequently estimated that these speculators held at least 81 per cent of the total of futures contracts. The speculating firm is a Swiss company, Vitol, which traded in swaps, requiring little money down thereby increasing its leverage. Almost as if by magic, astronomical crude futures prices began to fall in August, perhaps in response to the focus on traders but more likely in anticipation of the financial collapse, although US regulators insisted that the sharp decline, like the rapid rise, was simply the result of supply and demand.[112]

Currency fluctuations have presented severe problems to Gulf state governments for some years as their economies have been rocked by the inflationary effects of a depressed dollar. Kuwait ended the peg of the dinar to the dollar in June 2007 although, at this writing, the dollar has recovered some of its value and other Gulf states with dollar pegs are keeping them. Besides exchange rates, inflation in Gulf states also is affected by highly speculative domestic real estate markets, demands on governments to subsidize politically powerful population groups, and higher capital costs for investments intended to increase productivity. Real estate and capital costs are already declining, however, and the severe global economic downturn, itself the product of fraud and speculation, may prove to have blessings as well as curses for alert governments and investors.

Conclusion

Autonomy, capacity, and sovereignty

A wild card in the Gulf energy security game is Russia. Its new assertion of primacy in its self-defined 'sphere of influence' seems to include interdiction of pipelines that bypass its own extensive network; and the spread of Russian-protected criminal organizations in the Crimea.[113] As during the Cold War, the main Russian focus is Europe[114] but Russia's foreign policy assertions offer opportunities to Gulf energy exporters and to the United States. Under the Obama administration, US policy toward Russia has become fluid and even conciliatory. Arguably, engaging simultaneously with Russia and Iran would increase US policy autonomy and improve energy security for Europe. The dependence

---

[111] David Cho, 'A Few Speculators Dominate Vast Market for Oil Trading', *Washington Post*, 21 August 2008, p. A01.
[112] *Ibid.*
[113] Michael Bronner, 'When the War Ends, Start to Worry', *New York Times*, 15 August 2008, at www.nytimes.com/2008/08/16/opinion/16bronner.html?_r=1&scp=2&sq=op%20ed%20Georgia%20Ossetia%20organized%20crime&st=cse&oref=slogin; Andrew E. Kramer, 'Putin's Grasp of Energy Drives Russian Agenda', *New York Times*, 29 January 2009, pp. A1, 10.
[114] Kramer, 'Putin's Grasp of Energy Drives Russian Agenda'.

of Western Europe on Russian transit facilities is a direct outgrowth of home-country insistence that US-based IOCs abandon plans to route pipelines from Central Asia through Iran. Because the drawbacks of European reliance on hydrocarbon transit through Russia have not changed since the 1980s,[115] and because Georgia seems unlikely to become an independent transit state any time soon—if at all[116]—a pipeline through Iran offers one way out of the impasse. Iran would like more than investment; recognition of its importance in its region and the world are equally desirable, as its 2003 offers to negotiate with the United States demonstrate. The moment for diplomatic breakthroughs on this front has probably passed, however, blown away by the questionable results of the June 2009 Iranian presidential election and the ferocity of state repression of dissenters from the official line.

Energy security in the Gulf has never been simply a matter of fuel production and sales. The concentration of natural resource endowments in a relatively compact and highly accessible location has always made the Gulf states vulnerable to external efforts to control fuel supplies and access to them. Internally, the wealth produced by even highly unequal contract terms generated competing domestic demands to distribute that income to particular groups, including rulers and their families. Yet even though the literature on the *rentier* state assumes that distribution of oil revenues smothers politics,[117] it is equally plausible to argue that politics gave rise to that distribution—the best example is Kuwait and the *majlis* movement of the late 1930s[118]—and that social contracts between rulers and those demanding their share of national resources have operated more in the breach than otherwise, and on both sides.[119] Indeed, oil revenues contributed directly to the development of sovereignty in the UAE, where they underpinned the pact establishing the federation,[120] and to state capacity wherever significant proportions of revenues were invested in human capital.[121]

Globalization has added new dimensions to security issues since the end of the Second World War, when oil sales became instruments of wealth redistribution among oil exporters, and between them and their customers. As globalization accelerated and OPEC members cut themselves loose from the constraining mediating structures imposed by IOCs, the Gulf states have come to view energy security in broader frames and devise policies to spread their risks. Market diversification, downstream investment, and even investment in food supplies from outside the region are now deeply embedded in the security of energy supplies, markets, and the populations they support. Rising domestic energy

---

[115] Jentleson, *Pipeline Politics*; Kramer, 'Putin's Grasp of Energy Drives Russian Agenda'.

[116] George Friedman, 'Georgia and the Balance of Power', *New York Review of Books*, 25 September 2008, pp. 24, 26.

[117] Hazem Beblawi, 'The Rentier State in the Arab World', in G. Luciani (ed.), *The Arab State* (Berkeley, CA: University of California Press, 1990), pp. 85–98; also Michael L. Ross, 'Does Oil Hinder Democracy?', *World Politics*, 53(3) (2001), pp. 325–361.

[118] Mary Ann Tétreault, *Stories of Democracy: Politics and Society in Contemporary Kuwait* (New York: Columbia Universiy Press, 2000).

[119] Crystal, *Oil and Politics in the Gulf*, 1990.

[120] Mary Ann Tétreault, 'The Economics of National Autonomy in the UAE', in Joseph A. Kechichian (ed.), *A Century in Thirty Years: Shaykh Zayed and the United Arab Emirates* (Washington DC: Middle East Policy Council, 2000), pp. 107–148; for an example of an oil-revenue-greased pact in Latin America see Terry Lynn Karl, 'Petroleum and Political Pacts: The Transition to Democracy in Venezuela', *Latin American Research Review*, 22(1) (1987), pp. 63–94.

[121] Tétreault, *Stories of Democracy*.

demand and the desire to maximize hydrocarbons available for export are moving Gulf governments to investigate alternative energy sources for domestic power generation. In spite of the alarm it raises, interest in nuclear power as an alternative energy source has been expressed by several Gulf states in addition to Iran, and climate and terrain make investment in research and development of solar and wind systems economically as well as strategically attractive. Iran's investments in wind energy make it the Germany of the Gulf. Despite shrunken balances in their sovereign wealth funds, several Gulf states have more than enough tucked away for domestic equity investment in renewable energy, a better bet for a long-lived payout than real-estate bailouts.[122] Such domestic infrastructure investments, especially if they take the form of public-private partnerships, also justify limiting direct distribution to citizens out of funds that could fulfil widely shared aspirations to provide for future generations.

Current world economic difficulties offer opportunities for extensive restructuring of domestic and foreign investment in the Gulf. The Gulf states are well positioned to take advantage of them if their strategic situations remain relatively stable and they are skilful managers of their political and economic resources. Security in the Gulf, as always, depends on external forces its governments cannot control. Even so, their increasingly active efforts to assert themselves in the international arena suggest that they are better able to hold their own than they were in the crises of the past.

---

[122] Brad Setser and Rachel Ziemba, 'GCC Sovereign Funds: Reversal of Fortune', Working Paper, Council on Foreign Relations, New York, January 2009.

Jihad, Yes, But Not Revolution: Explaining the Extraversion of Islamist Violence in Saudi Arabia

THOMAS HEGGHAMMER

ABSTRACT *Patterns of Islamist violence in Saudi Arabia suggest that it has been much easier to mobilize Saudis for extreme pan-Islamist activism than for revolutionary activism. This is unlike most Arab republics which show the opposite pattern. This article empirically documents the curious extraversion of Saudi militancy, contrasts it with patterns of Islamist violence in Algeria and Egypt, and presents four explanations to account for it: first, that the typical grievances of revolutionary Islamism are less pronounced in Saudi Arabia; second, that structural characteristics of Saudi state and society inhibit anti-regime mobilization; third, that Wahhabism or socio-cultural isolation make Saudi Islamists particularly hostile to non-Muslims; and fourth, and most important, that the Saudi regime has promoted pan-Islamism to divert challenges to its own legitimacy.*

Introduction

Saudi Arabia is often perceived as a regime on the brink of collapse. Many studies of Saudi politics have assumed the existence of a deep undercurrent of political discontent just waiting to be unleashed to flush away the House of Saud.[1] In the aftermath of dramatic episodes such as the 1979 Mecca rebellion or the 2003 terrorism campaign, commentators often have explained the violence as the near-inevitable outcome of the many alleged tensions and contradictions in Saudi society. In this paper I turn the issue of violent contestation on its head and ask: If the regime is so unpopular and the radicals so numerous, why has there not been more violence in the Kingdom, especially against the government?

In a region where several regimes have fought large Islamist insurgencies and at least one president has been assassinated, Saudi Arabia stands out as an exception by virtue of having experienced remarkably low levels of anti-regime violence.[2] This absence would perhaps not have been so remarkable were it not for the fact that Saudi Arabia is home to a large community of militant Islamists. These

---

[1] See e.g. Helen Lackner, *A House Built on Sand: A Political Economy of Saudi Arabia* (London: Ithaca Press, 1978); Peter W. Wilson and Douglas Graham, *Saudi Arabia: The Coming Storm* (Armonk, NY: M.E. Sharpe, 1994); Saïd K. Aburish, *The Rise, Corruption, and Coming Fall of the House of Saud* (New York: St Martin's Press, 1995) and Robert Baer, 'The Fall of the House of Saud', *Atlantic Monthly*, 291 (2003), pp. 53–62.

[2] In this article, the term 'Islamist' is defined broadly as *Islamic activist*, while 'jihadist' is defined as *violent Sunni Islamist*.

activists have attacked Westerners in the Kingdom and travelled in the thousands to fight in Afghanistan, Bosnia and elsewhere, but as of 2008 they have never assassinated a senior prince or attacked a royal palace.

The principal aim of the article is to document and explain the 'outward orientation' of Islamist violence in Saudi Arabia.[3] By contrasting the Saudi case to that of Egypt and Algeria at appropriate stages in the analysis, I also hope to contribute to the study of the comparative politics of the Middle East. The analysis will proceed in two steps. I start by examining the record of internal violence in Saudi Arabia since the 1960s before proposing four explanations for the extraversion of Islamist militancy in Saudi Arabia: lack of local grievances, structural obstacles to revolutionary mobilisation, xenophobia, and political diversion.

Patterns of Violence in Saudi Arabia

Before the age of satellite TV and the Internet, information on Saudi domestic security incidents was scarce and tightly controlled by the Saudi government. In recent years, more details of past and recent events have become available as documents have been declassified and the Kingdom has opened up to field research. What, then, do we know about the patterns of political violence in Saudi Arabia from the 1960s until today?

First of all, the overall level of political violence has been relatively low. The three main existing databases for terrorism incidents, the Global Terrorism Database,[4] the RAND/MIPT database[5] and the ITERATE database,[6] each of which use slightly different counting criteria, all suggest that there has been markedly less terrorism in Saudi Arabia than in Egypt and Algeria, except for the 1998–2004 period (see Table 1). Given that all these datasets underreport domestic terrorism (where attackers and victims are from the same country), and that Islamist militancy in Saudi Arabia has had a more transnational character than that of Algeria and Egypt, as we shall see below, it is reasonable to assume that the relative level of terrorism in Saudi Arabia has been even lower than these figures suggest.

There are numerous methodological problems associated with counting terrorist incidents, many stemming from the difficulty of defining terrorism.[7] We should therefore not attach too much importance to these numbers beyond what they tell us about the overall relative level of internal violence. To get a better sense of the scope and nature of the violence in the Kingdom, we must take a closer look at specific cases. Generally speaking, violent political activism in the Kingdom has been of three kinds: leftist, Shiite and Sunni Islamist. While this article is primarily

---

[3] The same puzzle was observed and addressed in Madawi al-Rasheed, 'The Minaret and the Palace: Obedience at Home and Rebellion Abroad', in Madawi al-Rasheed (ed.), *Kingdom without Borders* (New York: Columbia University Press, 2008), pp. 199–220.

[4] Gary LaFree and Laura Dugan, *Global Terrorism Database 1.1, 1970-1997* [Computer file]. ICPSR22541-v1 (College Park: University of Maryland, 2006 and Ann Arbor: Inter-university Consortium for Political and Social Research, 2008), www.start.umd.edu/data/gtd/ (accessed 14 September 2008).

[5] *RAND-MIPT Terrorism Incident Database*, www.terrorisminfo.mipt.org/incidentcalendar.asp (accessed 14 September 2008).

[6] Edward F. Mickolus *et al.*, *International Terrorism: Attributes of Terrorist Events (ITERATE), 1968-2007* (Dunn Loring: Vinyard Software, 2008).

[7] For more on the weaknesses of terrorism incident data, see e.g. Alex P. Schmid and Albert J. Jongman, *Political Terrorism: A New Guide to Actors, Authors, Concepts, Data Bases, Theories & Literature* (New Brunswick, NJ: Transaction, 1988), pp. 137–175; Andrew Silke, 'The Devil You Know: Continuing Problems with Research on Terrorism', *Terrorism and Political Violence*, 13(4) (2001), pp. 1–14; Leonard Weinberg and William Eubank, 'Data Daze', *Criminology and Public Policy*, 8(3) (2009), pp. 601–606.

Table 1. Number of International Terrorist Attacks in Algeria, Egypt and Saudi Arabia According to Major Terrorism Databases

	GTD 1970–1997	GTD 1998–2004	RAND/MIPT (1930–2007)	ITERATE (1968–2002)
Algeria	1159	426	234	83
Egypt	459	6	41	161
Saudi Arabia	19	32	11	38

concerned with the latter, a brief review of other forms of militancy helps contextualise Sunni Islamist violence.

Leftist and Shiite militancy

In the 1950s and 1960s, the organised opposition consisted primarily of leftist and Arab nationalist movements.[8] In 1953, a massive strike among Aramco workers famously prompted the intervention of the Army.[9] Throughout the 1960s, the authorities reportedly foiled a number of alleged plots and 'subversive acts'. In late 1962, police pre-emptively arrested and deported large numbers of Yemenis suspected of communist sympathies. The most serious violence to take place was a series of bomb blasts in Riyadh in late 1966 and early 1967. The bombings, which caused no known casualties, were claimed by the North Yemen-based Nasserite organisation Union of the People of the Arabian Peninsula [*ittihad sha'b al-jazira al-'arabiyya*] (UPAP).[10] After the attacks, Saudi authorities arrested several hundred Yemenis, executed 17 of them and expelled the rest.

The most serious development occurred in the summer of 1969, when intelligence services arrested hundreds of individuals in a crackdown on what was described as two separate conspiracies to topple the government. One network allegedly consisted of Hijaz-based civilian reformers linked to Prince Talal. The other, allegedly much more serious, conspiracy included officers in the Air Force and the Army.[11] This may have been the closest Saudi Arabia ever came to a military coup.

The 1970s were quieter, although the 1977 trial of 17 officers and a group of civilians charged with plotting another coup showed the regime was still wary of leftist opposition.[12] It is difficult to judge how serious the threat from the Arab nationalists really was, because most of the available information stems from government sources or from the unreliable statements of the UPAP. There was no doubt a certain paranoia in the government about the leftist threat, and the authorities are known to have made extensive use of torture in their interrogation

---

[8] For more details on leftist activism, see Alexei Vassiliev, *The History of Saudi Arabia* (London: Saqi Books, 2000), pp. 368–372; John E. Peterson, *Historical Dictionary of Saudi Arabia* (Lanham, MD: Scarecrow Press, 2003), pp. 108–110; Fred Halliday, *Arabia Without Sultans*, 2nd ed. (London: Saqi, 2002), pp. 66–69; James Buchan, 'Secular and Religious Opposition in Saudi Arabia', in Tim Niblock (ed.), *State, Society and Economy in Saudi Arabia* (London: Croom Helm, 1982), pp. 106–124.
[9] Robert Vitalis, *America's Kingdom: Mythmaking on the Saudi Oil Frontier* (Stanford: Stanford University Press, 2006), p. 149.
[10] Halliday, *Arabia Without Sultans*, p. 68.
[11] Anita L.P. Burdett (ed.), *Records of Saudi Arabia, 1966-1971*, Vol. IV (Slough: Archive Editions, 2004), pp. 3–91; Halliday, *Arabia Without Sultans*, p. 68; Vassiliev, *The History of Saudi Arabia*, p. 371.
[12] Adeed Dawisha, 'Saudi Arabia's Search for Security', Adelphi Paper 158 (London: International Institute for Strategic Studies, 1979), p. 7.

of suspects. What is certain is that by the 1980s the threat from leftist groups had practically disappeared.[13]

Meanwhile, discontent grew in another part of Saudi society, namely the minority Shiite community.[14] Several of the most significant security incidents in Saudi Arabia in recent decades have been instigated by Shiite militants. In the late 1970s, tensions between the regime and the marginalised Shiite population increased, culminating in the seven-day riots in the Eastern Province in November 1979, which left at least two dozen people dead and hundreds wounded.[15] The 1979 clashes, combined with the Saudi–Iranian rivalry in the 1980s, fuelled an organised Shiite Islamist movement that remained very active throughout the 1980s and beyond.

Most Shiite Islamists followed the relatively moderate 'Organisation of the Islamic Revolution' [*munazzamat al-thawra al-islamiyya*] (OIR) led by Hassan al-Saffar. A relatively large organization with branches in several countries, including Iran, Syria and Britain, the OIR sought concessions from Riyadh on issues such as the right to observe Shiite rituals, an end to discrimination on the labour market, and a greater share in oil income. The OIR did not engage in terrorist activities and would enter into a reconciliation agreement with the Saudi government in the autumn of 1993.

However, the late 1980s had seen the emergence of a smaller and much more radical organisation, 'Hizbollah of the Hijaz' [*Hizballah al-Hijaz*]. Pro-Khomeini (as opposed to the pro-Shirazi OIR[16]), the Saudi Hizbollah is believed to have been responsible for a number of serious attacks in Saudi Arabia in the second half of the 1980s, including the August 1987 bombing of an Eastern Province gas plant and the March 1988 bombing of oil installations at Ras Tanura and Jubayl, as well as a series of bombings in Riyadh in 1985 and 1989.[17] Some have also suspected organised domestic Shiite involvement in the Hajj riots Mecca in July 1987 in which more than 400 people died after Saudi police cracked down on demonstrating Iranian pilgrims.[18] Questions also shroud the June 1996 Khobar bombing, which was officially blamed on the Hizbollah of the Hijaz. The group may have wanted to assert its disapproval of the 1993 reconciliation between the Saudi Government and the OIR, and may have received operational assistance from the Lebanese Hizballah. Some observers have disputed this assessment and argued that the operation was carried out by al-Qaida, but this author considers that on balance, the available evidence suggests Shiite responsibility.[19]

---

[13] One of the last signs of life from radical Saudi leftists came in November 1979, when Nasir al-Sa'id, head of the UPAP, curiously claimed responsibility for the Mecca uprising. Shortly afterward, al-Said mysteriously disappeared; liquidated, some believe, by an intelligence agency. Although Kuwait-based leftists had printed Juhayman al-Utaybi's letters, the UPAP had nothing to do with the Mecca events. Soviet media took al-Sa'id at his word and reported a working-class uprising in the Hijaz in November 1979; this, incidentally, is the source of the misrepresentation of the Juhayman incident in Alexey Vassiliev's otherwise reliable *History of Saudi Arabia*.

[14] For more on Shiites in Saudi Arabia, see Fouad Ibrahim, *The Shi'is of Saudi Arabia* (London: Saqi, 2007); Toby Jones, 'The Shiite Question in Saudi Arabia', in *Middle East Report* (Brussels: International Crisis Group, 2005) and Laurence Louër, *Transnational Shia Politics. Political and Religious Networks in the Gulf* (London and New York: Hurst and Columbia University Press, 2008).

[15] Toby Jones, 'Rebellion on the Saudi Periphery: Modernity, Marginalization, and the Shi'a Uprising of 1979', *International Journal of Middle East Studies*, 38(2) (2006), pp. 213–233.

[16] Followers of the 'Shirazi marja' considered Grand Ayatollah Muhammad ibn Mahdi al-Hussayni al-Shirazi (1928–2001) as their main religious authority.

[17] Peterson, *Historical Dictionary of Saudi Arabia*, p. 110.

[18] Martin Kramer, *Arab Awakening and Islamic Revival* (New Brunswick: Transaction, 1996), pp. 161–187.

[19] Thomas Hegghammer, 'Deconstructing the Myth about al-Qa'ida and Khobar', *The Sentinel*, 1(3) (2008), pp. 20–22. Thus far, the strongest case for al-Qaida responsibility for Khobar has been made by Gareth Porter in a five-part article series in *Inter Press Service* (www.ips.org), 22–26 June 2009.

In April 2000, the southern city of Najran experienced violent unrest in the local Ismaili community.[20] The Ismailis, who follow their own calendar, had prepared to celebrate Id a few days earlier than the Sunni majority when the Wahhabi establishment ordered the closure of Ismaili mosques, sparking a small two-day riot that left two Ismailis dead and two wounded. The events were followed by a massive police crackdown on the Ismaili community.

Despite these occasional outbursts of violence, Shiite Islamists never represented an existential threat to the Saudi government, if only because the Shiite population is so small (an estimated 10 to 15 per cent of the overall population, though no reliable figures exist). Rebellion in Sunni quarters, on the other hand, was potentially much more dangerous.

Sunni Islamist violence

Prior to 1979, modern Saudi Arabia experienced very few cases of Sunni Islamist violence. The late 1920s had seen the famous 'Ikhwan revolt' in which Ibn Saud's army of religiously indoctrinated tribal fighters refused to heed the King's order to stop their raids at international borders.[21] Following the Ikhwan revolt, the Kingdom experienced five decades with virtually no organised Islamist militancy. There were instances of low-level vigilante violence, such as skirmishes in early 1960s Medina between local residents and pietistic activists acting as self-appointed religious police.[22] There were also a few cases of spontaneous violent protests against social or technological innovations, such as the August 1965 demonstrations in Riyadh in response to the introduction of the television.[23] The introduction of girls' education in 1961 allegedly also prompted demonstrations in Burayda, but it is not clear whether these were particularly violent.[24] There were also demonstrations in response to international events; during the six-day war in June 1967, anti-Israeli demonstrators allegedly marched on the US consulate in Dhahran and threw an explosive device at the US consulate in Jeddah.[25]

The history of organized Sunni militancy in the Kingdom thus begins in the late 1970s. How much violence has there been since then, and where has it been directed? Before answering this question, it is necessary to clarify the analytical concepts I use to determine the patterns of Sunni Islamist violence. A central premise in my analysis is that there are different types of Islamist violence,

---

[20] Human Rights Watch, *The Ismailis of Najran: Second-class Saudi Citizens* (New York: Human Rights Watch, 2008), pp. 19–28.

[21] For more on the Ikhwan, see John Habib, *Ibn Saud's Warriors of Islam: The Ikhwan of Najd and Their Role in the Creation of the Sa'udi Kingdom, 1910-1930* (Leiden: Brill, 1978); Christine Moss Helms, *The Cohesion of Saudi Arabia: Evolution of Political Identity* (Baltimore, MD: John Hopkins University Press, 1981), pp. 127–150, 225–274; Joseph Kostiner, *The Making of Saudi Arabia: From Chieftaincy to Monarchical State* (New York: Oxford University Press, 1993), pp. 72–79.

[22] Thomas Hegghammer and Stéphane Lacroix, 'Rejectionist Islamism in Saudi Arabia: The Story of Juhayman al-Utaybi Revisited', *International Journal of Middle East Studies*, 39(1) (2007), p. 106.

[23] Mufid al-Zaydi, *al-tayyarat al-fikriyya fi'l-khalij al-'arabi, 1938-1971* [Ideological Currents in the Arab Gulf, 1938-1971] (Beirut: Markaz Dirasat al-Wihda al-Arabiyya, 2000), p. 268. See also William A. Rugh, 'Saudi Mass Media and Society in the Faisal Era', in Willard Beling (ed.), *King Faisal and the Modernisation of Saudi Arabia* (London: Croom Helm, 1980), p. 30.

[24] Haya Saad Al Rawaf and Cyril Simmons, 'The Education of Women in Saudi-Arabia', *Comparative Education*, 27(3) (1991), pp. 287–295.

[25] Eric Schmitt, 'FBI Agents Join Search In Saudi Blast', *New York Times*, 15 November 1995, p. 7; Vassiliev, *The History of Saudi Arabia*, p. 370.

because Islamists fight for different things.[26] Islamist violence may be classified according to its direction, i.e. the nature of the target, and its rationale, i.e. the immediate agenda of the perpetrator. I further posit that Sunni Islamist violence presents itself in five ideal-types:

- *revolutionary violence:* usually directed against government targets and rationalised as a struggle to depose the Muslim ruler
- *pan-Islamist violence:* usually directed against Western or non-Muslim targets and rationalised as defence of the Muslim nation
- *vigilantist violence:* usually directed against symbols of moral corruption and rationalised as a means to correct the moral behaviour of Muslims
- *sectarian violence:* directed against Shiites, rationalised as intimidation of the competing sect.
- *irredentist violence:* directed against the local non-Muslim occupier, rationalised as a struggle for national liberation. This type only occurs in territories contested or occupied by non-Muslim forces (such as in Palestine, Chechnya, Kashmir, etc.) and hence does not apply in the Saudi context.

How much violence of each type has taken place in Saudi Arabia since 1979? To answer this question, I compiled a detailed chronology of violent incidents in Saudi Arabia, taking John E. Peterson's data as a starting point and adding further news reports and relevant primary sources.[27]

There have been, broadly speaking, seven major episodes (defined as attacks or waves of attacks) in the modern history of Sunni Islamist violence in Saudi Arabia. First was the 1979 Mecca incident in which several hundred militants led by Juhayman al-Utaybi seized the Great Mosque in Mecca, claiming that one of their companions was the Mahdi, an Islamic messianic figure.[28] The precise intentions behind this unique incident are difficult to ascertain, because Juhayman was never able to publicly explain them in detail after the operation (he was executed within weeks). However, the writings of Juhayman combined with the nature of the target—which indicates an utter lack of concern for his political legacy—suggest that the attack had an important apocalyptic dimension and may have been intended as an act of collective moral purification.[29] As such, the Mecca incident is closest to the vigilantist type of violence described above. This is consistent with the fact that the movement from which most rebels emerged had previously engaged in private moral policing in Medina. The militants were certainly not pure revolutionaries, for they envisaged no alternative government, explicitly refused to excommunicate the King, and chose to attack the main sanctity of Islam when they had the firepower to strike at a government target.

[26] For a more detailed explanation of this typology, see Thomas Hegghammer, 'Jihadi Salafis or Revolutionaries? On Theology and Politics in the Study of Militant Islamism', in Roel Meijer (ed.), *Global Salafism* (London and New York: Hurst and Columbia University Press, 2009), pp. 244–266.
[27] J.E. Peterson, 'Saudi Arabia: Internal Security Incidents Since 1979', *Arabian Peninsula Background Note*, 3 (2005); available at www.jepeterson.net/source_material.html.
[28] Florian Peil, 'Die Besetzung der Großen Moschee von Mekka 1979', *Orient*, 47(3) (2006), pp. 387–408; Hegghammer and Lacroix, 'Rejectionist Islamism in Saudi Arabia'; Yaroslav Trofimov, *The Siege of Mecca: The Forgotten Uprising in Islam's Holiest Shrine and the Birth of al Qaeda* (New York: Doubleday, 2007).
[29] For more on Juhayman's apocalypticism, see Jean-Pierre Filiu, *L'apocalypse dans l'islam* (Paris: Fayard, 2008), pp. 112–118.

The 1980s saw virtually no Sunni Islamist violence in the kingdom. This quiet was broken during the Gulf War in early 1991, when the Kingdom witnessed at least three minor attacks on US targets. On 3 February 1991, unknown persons fired shots at a US military bus in Jeddah, injuring three US soldiers and a Saudi guard. The same day, unidentified individuals doused a US transport bus in Jeddah with kerosene. On 28 March at least six shots were fired at a US Marine vehicle, injuring three marines.[30] The perpetrators were never identified, but they were most likely independent groups of low-level activists expressing their hostility to the foreign military presence.

The third wave of incidents is much less well known and occurred in the Riyadh and Burayda areas around 1991, in the form of around ten attacks against video stores, women's centres and empty cars of people suspected of leading 'sinful lives'.[31] There were no casualties. The perpetrators, some of whom were interviewed by this author in 2005, said that they had wanted to exact *isba* or moral policing. They explicitly said they were not, at the time, interested in politics, neither domestic nor international. These incidents can therefore be considered acts of vigilantist violence. It is worth noting that in November 1994, Abdallah al-Hudhayf, one of the 1991 vigilantists, threw acid in the face of a police officer whom he suspected of torturing imprisoned Islamists.[32] This isolated attack, the first in modern Saudi history to explicitly target a policeman, may be considered an early act of revolutionary violence.

The fourth major development was the November 1995 bombing of the American training mission to the Saudi National Guard (APM/SANG building) in Riyadh.[33] This operation, which killed five Americans and two Indians, was the first major terrorist attack on a US target in Saudi Arabia. It was carried out by four Saudi veterans of the Afghan and Bosnian jihad who acted independently on the call to expel the US military from the Kingdom, a message that had been repeated by Saudi Islamist leaders throughout the early 1990s. The perpetrators had allegedly radicalised after the September 1994 crackdown on the non-violent opposition (the Sahwa movement), and decided to take action after the August 1995 execution, behind closed prison doors, of the abovementioned Abdallah al-Hudhayf, who was a close friend of the attackers.[34]

The available evidence suggests that Osama Bin Laden was not directly involved in neither the 1995 Riyadh bombing nor the 1996 Khobar bombing, but in early 1998 al-Qaida did try to mount an attack against a US target (most likely the US consulate in Jeddah) with anti-tank missiles. The plot fell apart when the missiles were seized and the operatives arrested on the Yemeni border in January 1998.[35] The crackdowns following the Riyadh and Khobar bombings as well as the 1998 missile plot crippled the Saudi jihadist community, which partly explains the near-absence of Islamist violence in the Kingdom in the second half of the 1990s.

[30] *Report to the President and Congress on the Protection of US Forces Deployed Abroad* (Washington DC: US Department of Defense, 1996), p. 29.
[31] Interviews with Nasir al-Barrak, Dammam, December 2005, and Mansur al-Nuqaydan, Riyadh, April 2004.
[32] 'Urgent Action 200/95', Amnesty International, 15 August 1995; *Statement 38* (London: Committee for the Defence of Legitimate Rights, 1995).
[33] Joshua Teitelbaum, *Holier Than Thou: Saudi Arabia's Islamic Opposition* (Washington, DC: Washington Institute for Near East Studies, 2000), pp. 73–82.
[34] Interview with unidentified Islamist, Jeddaah, April 2004, and Nasir al-Barrak, Dammam, December 2005.
[35] *The 9/11 Commission Report* (New York: W.W. Norton, 2004), pp. 152, 491.

The fifth major wave of Islamist violence occurred between 2000 and 2003 and consisted of a series of low-level attacks against Western targets, primarily individual expatriates. These attacks, which took the form of drive-by shootings, booby traps and letter bombs, killed a total six Westerners and wounded at least 13 in the course of two and a half years.[36] Some of the incidents were blamed by Saudi authorities on Western alcohol traders, but these allegations have never been substantiated by forensic evidence and are most likely fabricated. Although the precise identity and motivations of the perpetrators have never been established, circumstantial evidence strongly suggests the attacks were carried out by scattered groups of amateur anti-Western jihadists.[37]

The sixth development was a series of five drive-by shootings of policemen and judges in the city of Sakaka in the northern Jawf region in late 2002 and early 2003.[38] Two policemen were killed, as was a court judge and the deputy governor of the Jawf region. Another policeman was wounded. These assassinations were perpetrated by a small and independent group of militants who had returned from Afghanistan in the spring of 2002. This violence was clearly revolutionary in nature. Moreover, the two killings of the judge and the deputy governor are very interesting, because they represent the only cases, in modern Saudi history, of Islamist violence against civilian representatives of the government. There have been unconfirmed reports of foiled assassination attempts on the royal family, but all actual instances of anti-regime violence have targeted the security establishment.[39]

The seventh, final, and by far the most significant wave of violence was, of course, the campaign launched in 2003 by al-Qaida on the Arabian Peninsula (QAP). The scope, duration, and complexity of the violence call for a closer analysis, not least to answer the question of whether the QAP had a revolutionary or a pan-Islamist agenda.

The QAP campaign

The QAP campaign began in May 2003, reached a high point (in terms of attack frequency) in the spring of 2004, only to peter out from late 2004 onward as a result of blows to the organisation. By 2007, the QAP organisation had effectively been crushed by the security services, although scattered cells of activists continued to plot minor attacks across the kingdom.

The QAP executed between 20 and 25 operations between 2003 and 2007—not counting planned attacks foiled before execution stage and not counting shootouts or sieges initiated by police (most of the shootouts during the QAP campaign were in fact initiated by police, not militants). The operations included five suicide car

---

[36] Thomas Hegghammer, 'Violent Islamism in Saudi Arabia, 1979–2006: The Power and Perils of Pan-Islamic Nationalism' (PhD thesis, Sciences-Po Paris, 2007), pp. 128–132, 134–135.

[37] The size and overall activity of the jihadist community in the Kingdom increased dramatically in the 2000–2003 period. Moreover, an assassination manual published by a Saudi writer on jihadi websites in 2004 included several of the same tactics employed in the 2000–2003 period; see Abu Jandal al-Azdi, 'tahrid al-mujahidin al-abtal ala ihya sunnat al-ightiyal [Encouraging the Heroic Mujahidin to Revive the Practice of Assassinations]', www.tawhed.ws, 2004.

[38] Hegghammer, 'Violent Islamism', pp. 132–133.

[39] In November 2001, the *Washington Times* reported an attempted assassination attempt on King Fahd that had allegedly occurred in the form of an attack on his motorcade. These reports were vehemently denied by Saudi authorities; See 'Al-Riyadh Denied Assassination Attempt at King Fahd', *ArabicNews.com*, 24 November 2001.

Table 2. Major Premeditated Operations Executed by Sunni Militants in Saudi Arabia, 2003–2008

	DATE	LOCATION	TARGET	DEAD	TACTICS
Suicide car operations					
East Riyadh operation	12 May 2003	Riyadh	Western compounds	35	3 suicide car bombs
Muhayya operation	9 Nov 2003	Riyadh	Western compound	17	suicide car bomb
Al-Washm operation	21 Apr 2004	Riyadh	Police building	5	suicide car bomb
Interior ministry operation	29 Dec 2004	Riyadh	Interior Ministry, National Guard facility	10	2 suicide car bombs, premature explosion
Abqaiq operation	24 Feb 2006	Abqaiq	Oil refinery	4	suicide car bomb, premature explosion
Coordinated shooting sprees					
Yanbu operation	1 May 2004	Yanbu	Office buildings of Western companies	7	
Khobar operation	30 May 2004	Khobar	Office buildings of Western companies	22	
US consulate operation	6 Dec 2004	Jidda	US consulate	9	
Burayda police operation	27 Dec 2005	Burayda	Saudi police officers	5	
Mada'in Salih operation	26 Feb 2007	Medina	French tour group	4	
Assassinations					
Abd al-Aziz al-Huwayrini	4 Dec 2003	Riyadh	Saudi intelligence officer	0	Shooting
Jonathan Bengler (Germany)	22 May 2004	Riyadh	Western expatriate	1	Shooting
Unidentified American	2 Jun 2004	Riyadh	Western expatriate	0	Shooting
Simon Cumbers (Ireland) and Frank Gardner (UK)	6 Jun 2004	Riyadh	Western expatriate	1	Shooting
Robert Jacobs (US)	8 Jun 2004	Riyadh	Western expatriate	1	Shooting
Kenneth Scroggs (US)	12 Jun 2004	Riyadh	Western expatriate	1	Shooting
Paul Johnston (US)	mid-June 2004	Riyadh	Western expatriate	1	Kidnapping, decapitation
Anthony Higgins (UK)	3 Aug 2004	Riyadh	Western expatriate	1	Shooting
Edward Muirhead-Smith (UK)	15 Sep 2004	Riyadh	Western expatriate	1	Shooting
Laurent Barbot (France)	23 Sep 2004	Jidda	Western expatriate	1	Shooting
Mubarak al-Sawwat	19 Jun 2005	Riyadh	Saudi police officer	1	Shooting
Unidentified Saudi	March 2007	Burayda	Saudi police officer	1	Kidnapping, decapitation

operations (involving altogether eight vehicles), five coordinated shooting sprees, and 12 individual assassinations.

The QAP displayed a consistent preference for Western targets. A clear majority of the premeditated attacks by QAP militants were directed against Westerners: three of five suicide car operations; four of five shooting sprees; and nine of 12 assassinations.

The QAP started targeting security forces relatively late in the campaign, only after the police had cracked down hard on the organisation. The first few small attacks on police took place in December 2003, but the first serious bombing of a security target did not occur until April 2004, nearly a year after the outbreak of the campaign. This suggests that the group originally preferred Western targets, but that vengeance factors drew the militants into a spiral of tit-for-tat violence with the police.

It is noteworthy that the militants never actually attacked a government target outside of the security establishment. There were no assassination attempts on the King, ministers or senior princes, with the exception of Deputy Minister of Interior Prince Muhammad bin Nayef, who was lightly wounded in an attack on his office in August 2009.[40] No royal palace or ministry (except the Interior Ministry) nor any Saudi embassies abroad were attacked. US and Saudi authorities have claimed that the militants had been planning large-scale attacks on government targets since 2002, but these allegations have never been substantiated and there are no indications of such plans in the QAP's own texts.[41] Until substantial evidence to the contrary is presented, we have rely on the positive evidence, which clearly indicate that the QAP chose to spend most of their precious military resources on attacking Western targets, not the government.

These political preferences also manifest themselves in the group's ideological production. The QAP's 'manifesto', a book entitled *This is How We View the Jihad and How We Want It*, placed the 'Jews and the Crusaders' on the top of its hierarchy of enemies and stated that 'this is the enemy against which we must act at this stage'.[42] Statements to the same effect are found throughout the QAP literature, not least in their bimonthly journals *Sawt al-Jihad* and *Mu'askar al-Battar*. The QAP explicitly dismissed accusations that they wanted to attack Muslims. Keen to rid himself of the 'takfiri' label, QAP leader Yusuf al-Uyayri stated in May 2003: 'How logical is it that we should sacrifice our blood and our throats for those far away, and then decide to terrorize and shed the blood of our own people?'[43]

In the early part of the campaign, the militants explicitly said they would not target the security forces unless the latter interfered to protect the Crusaders. As the campaign proceeded, the discourse grew more hostile to the regime and the militants began carrying out premeditated offensives against Saudi security forces.

[40] 'Saudi Royal Survives Attack Claimed By Qaeda', *Reuters*, 28 August 2009. Since the late 1990s, Muhammad bin Nayif has been the main contact point for militants wishing to surrender. The 2009 assassination attempt occurred when a wanted militant pretending to surrender slipped through security and blew himself up.

[41] See e.g. Alan Sipress and Peter Finn, 'Terror Cell Had Recent Gun Battle With Police', *Washington Post*, 14 May 2003.

[42] Hazim al-Madani, '*hakadha nara al-jihad wa nuriduhu* [This is How We View the Jihad and How We Want It]', www.qa3edoon.com, 2002.

[43] Anonymous, '*ghazwat al-hadi 'ashar min rabi' al-awwal: 'amaliyyat sharq al-riyadh wa-harbuna ma' amrika wa 'umala'iha* [The 12 May Raid: The East Riyadh Operation and Our War with America and its Agents]', www.qa3edoon.com, 2003.

After the 20 April 2004 bombing of a police building in the al-Washm district of Riyadh, the QAP published a book called *The Prophet's Guidance on Targeting Emergency Forces*.[44] The book blamed the police for provoking the violence and explained that the aggression of the security forces had prompted another organisation, the 'Haramain Brigades', to step in and defend the mujahidin. The QAP literature from early 2004 onward is full of verbal attacks against the Saudi regime in general and the security establishment in particular. No strangers to humour and irony, QAP leaders used terms such as *kha'in al-haramayn* (the Traitor of the Two Holy Mosques) instead of *khadim al-haramayn* (Custodian of the Two Holy Mosques) and *hay'at kibar al-umala* (The Council of Collaborators) instead of *hay'at kibar al-ulama* (The Council of Senior Scholars).

Nevertheless, the declared main purpose of the QAP campaign was still to evict the Crusaders, not to topple the Saudi regime. Moreover, the main accusation levelled against the government was collaboration with the Crusaders, not corruption or oppression of the people. Finally, the overall discursive theme of the QAP's propaganda texts and videos was more pan-Islamist than revolutionary.

To understand the relationship between pan-Islamist and revolutionary motivations it is useful to distinguish between short- and long-term strategies and between low and top levels of the organisation. There are indeed indications that the top al-Qaida leadership ultimately wanted to topple the Saudi regime. Khalid Sheikh Muhammad allegedly told interrogators that Bin Laden's highest priority was to spur a revolution in Saudi Arabia and overthrow the government.[45] Captured QAP militants have allegedly said that QAP leaders envisaged a two-stage campaign; a first phase aimed at mobilising the Saudi people for jihad against the crusaders, and a second stage in which the enthusiastic masses would turn against the Al Saud.[46]

However, even if we suppose that such a secret long-term plan existed, it had few operational consequences. For a start it did not inform the QAP's short-term operational priorities, which was clearly geared toward attacking Westerners. Moreover, the revolutionary agenda was by all accounts not known to low-level operatives. The QAP leadership went to great lengths to conceal its revolutionary agenda both from its own constituency and from the broader Saudi public. For example, when the QAP began the controversial task of attacking Saudi police targets, it claimed these operations in the name of a fictitious entity called the 'Haramain Brigades'. This was to preserve the clarity of the QAP's 'Americans first' strategy and to avoid staining the QAP's reputation with Muslim blood.[47] Why would the QAP leadership keep its revolutionary agenda secret when other militants, such as the GIA or Egyptian Islamic Jihad, have been explicit about it? The most likely reason is that the QAP realised that revolutionary discourse and violence would not draw sufficient followers in Saudi Arabia.

We have seen that most of the Islamist violence in the Kingdom has been of the pan-Islamist kind, to a lesser extent, of the vigilantist type (see Table 3). Interestingly, there has been no anti-Shiite violence and very little anti-regime

---

[44] Abu Bakr al-Husni, '*hidayat al-sari fi hukm istihdaf al-tawari*' [The Prophet's Guidance on Targeting Emergency Forces]', www.qa3edoon.com, 2004.
[45] George Tenet, *At the Center of the Storm: My Years at the CIA* (New York: HarperCollins, 2007), p. 248.
[46] Rawya Rageh, 'Ex-Militants: al-Qaida Preys on Young Men', *Associated Press*, 22 September 2004.
[47] Interview with Saudi security source, Riyadh, November 2005; Mahmoud Ahmad, 'Al-Qaeda Operatives Are an Ignorant Lot, Say Former Members', *Arab News*, 3 October 2003.

violence. Apart from two assassinations in Sakaka in 2002, there have been no confirmed attacks on civilian representatives of the government or on government buildings unrelated to the security establishment. The semi-successful attack on the Ministry of Interior in December 2004 could be seen as an attack on the civilian government, but this operation was one of the last carried out by the QAP, which underscores the fact that the group's primary focus was on Western targets.

One might of course argue that this is merely a series of historical accidents, and that the total number of incidents is too low to establish a pattern. One might also argue that the pattern reflects not the intentions of Islamists but the capabilities of the Saudi security services; perhaps the latter simply did a better job at protecting the royal family than Westerners. Both these hypotheses are theoretically possible, but unlikely. Not even the best security services would have been able to keep a clean record for decades in the face of a serious intention to attack the government. Moreover, the pattern of attacks is mirrored by the declared intentions of the militant Islamists: there are more explicitly anti-Western texts than there are explicitly anti-government texts in the corpus of post-1980 Saudi jihadist literature. In any case, even if we assume that anti-regime violence is somewhat underreported, the figures are such that the balance would most likely still tilt toward anti-Western violence.

More importantly, if we contrast this pattern with the record of Islamist violence in Arab republics such as Algeria and Egypt the difference is striking. These countries have not only seen more violence in absolute terms, but also a very different pattern of attacks. Until 2002, these countries saw considerably more revolutionary activism than anti-Western violence.[48] Unlike Saudi Arabia, they have experienced several assassination attempts on government ministers, and in Egypt's case, even on the head of state.[49]

Saudi Arabia does not seem to have had a strong revolutionary movement of the Egyptian or Algerian type. On the other hand the Kingdom does seem to have had a large community of extreme pan-Islamists. It has in other words been relatively difficult to mobilize for revolutionary activism and relatively easy to mobilize for pan-Islamist militancy. Why?

Explanations

In the following I shall consider four possible explanations; two of which address the absence of revolutionary violence and two of which concern the high levels of pan-Islamist violence.

[48] See for example *Terrorism in Egypt—A Timeline*, gemsofislamism.tripod.com/timeline_egypt.html (accessed 26 October 2008); and Salah-Eddine Sidhoum, *Chronologie des Massacres en Algerie 1992-2005*, www.algeria-watch.org/francais.htm (accessed 26 October 2008).
[49] For example, Egyptian militants have attacked high-level officials on numerous occasions: Awqaf Minister Muhammad al-Dhahabi abducted and killed, July 1977; President Anwar Sadat killed, October 1981; Interior Minister Zaki Badr almost killed, December 1989; Speaker of the Parliament Rifaat al-Mahgoub killed and Interior Minister Abdel Halim Moussa almost killed, October 1990; Information Minister Safwat Sharif almost killed, April 1993; Interior Minister Hasan al-Alfi badly injured, August 1993; Prime Minister Atef Sidqi almost killed, November 1993; Deputy Chief of the Security Service Rawf Khayrat killed, April 1994; and President Mubarak almost assassinated in June 1995.

Table 3. Patterns of Sunni Islamist Violence in Saudi Arabia, 1979–2007

EPISODE	DOMINANT RATIONALE	ATTACKS AGAINST NON-MUSLIMS?	ATTACKS AGAINST SECURITY ESTABLISHMENT?	ATTACKS AGAINST CIVILIAN GOVERNMENT?
1979 Mecca event	Messianic/vigilantist	No	No	No
1991 Gulf war attacks	Pan-Islamist	Yes	No	No
1991 moral policing	Vigilantist	No	No	No
1995 Riyadh bombing	Pan-Islamist	Yes	No	No
2002 Jawf incidents	Revolutionary	No	Yes	Yes
2000-2003 assassinations	Pan-Islamist	Yes	No	No
QAP campaign	Pan-Islamist	Yes	Yes, late in campaign	No

Lack of grievances

It is natural to start our analysis by looking for the presence or absence of factors that are known to have contributed to the production of revolutionary Islamist violence in other countries. Studies of the Egyptian and Algerian experience have identified two sets of factors that may be considered the principal—although certainly not the only—causes of revolutionary Islamist violence. First are economic deprivation (relative and absolute) and social mobility closure. The violence in late 1970s Egypt and early 1990s Algeria was in each case preceded by 3–5 years of severe economic hardship experienced by large parts of the population.[50] Reduced state income combined with population increases led to unemployment and social mobility closure for talented and entrepreneurial university graduates, who would form the backbone of militant Islamist groups, particularly in Egypt.[51] Second are political factors such as violent state repression and political exclusion. Although the level of repression varied over time in both Egypt and Algeria, both countries have remained police states with pervasive security services that make extensive use of torture. In both countries, moderate Islamists have been systematically excluded from meaningful official politics, despite enjoying considerable popular support. In each country, early manifestations of revolutionary activism were met with draconian measures and collective punishment of entire communities. Nasser's brutal crackdown of the Muslim Brotherhood in the 1960s was a major factor in the radicalisation of the Islamist community in Egypt.[52] The brutal and indiscriminate counterterrorism tactics employed by the Algerian regime in the early 1990s—in the form of mass arrests,

---

[50] See e.g. Rodney Wilson, 'Whither the Egyptian Economy?', *British Journal of Middle Eastern Studies*, 20(2) (1993), p. 205; Miriam L. Lowi, 'Algeria, 1992–2002: Anatomy of a Civil War', in Paul Collier (ed.), *Understanding Civil War: Evidence and Analysis* (Herndon, VA: World Bank, 2005), pp. 224–225.

[51] Saad Eddin Ibrahim, 'Anatomy of Egypt's Militant Islamic Groups: Methodological Notes and Preliminary Findings', *International Journal of Middle East Studies*, 12(4) (1981), pp. 423–453.

[52] See e.g. Gilles Kepel, *Muslim Extremism in Egypt* (Berkeley: University of California Press, 2003), pp. 26–35.

torture camps, and arming of unaccountable paramilitaries—are widely considered to have fuelled the insurgency.[53]

Both these sets of factors have been less pronounced in Saudi Arabia than in Egypt and Algeria. For a start, the post-1970 standard of living (measured in GDP per capita) has been many times higher in Saudi Arabia than in Egypt and Algeria.[54] Moreover, although the Kingdom experienced economic downturns in the mid-1980s and the late 1990s, the Saudi population was shielded from the worst consequences of the crisis by the government's upholding of food subsidies and a public sector employment regime.[55] Although the state eventually had to end its jobs-for-all policy in the late 1980s and unemployment rose again in the late 1990s, unemployed Saudis generally did not face a life in poverty as might be the case of young men in the suburbs of Cairo and Algiers.[56] Relative deprivation may have been a factor in the increased Islamist mobilisation in the late 1980s and early 1990s (to Afghanistan and to the so-called Sahwa movement) as well as in the increased recruitment to al-Qaida training camps at the end of the 1990s. However, the Sahwa movement never turned violent, and the late 1990s al-Qaida recruits did not fight the regime, which suggests that relative deprivation on its own is not a sufficient cause for revolutionary activism.

The level of violent state repression has also been lower in Saudi Arabia than in Egypt and Algeria. Of course, Saudi Arabia is no liberal democracy: it is an authoritarian state with record of detention without trial and torture of security suspects. Nevertheless, on most available measures for state repression such as Gibney and Dalton's *Political Terror Scale*[57] and the *Cingranelli-Richards Human Rights Dataset*,[58] Saudi Arabia compares favourably to Algeria and Egypt (see Table 4).

Moreover, by all available historical accounts, the level of physical violence used by the state to repress Islamists has been considerably lower in Saudi Arabia than in Egypt and Algeria. One might of course argue that Saudi Arabia never needed to be heavy-handed because other factors prevented a revolutionary mobilisation in the first place; in other words that the Saudi relative softness toward Islamists is a consequence, not a cause, of the lack of anti-regime militancy. However, this is unconvincing. For a start, ever since the 1950s, the state handling of *non-violent* Islamist activism has consistently been much more heavy-handed in the republics than in Saudi Arabia. Moreover, if we look at the three countries' counterterrorism policies in the *initial* stages of their respective insurgencies (1991–1992 in the case of Egypt and Algeria, 2003 in the case of Saudi Arabia)—at points in time when the full potential of the insurgencies was not known—the republics used considerably more brutal and less discriminate methods than did Saudi Arabia.

---

[53] See e.g. Luis Martinez, *The Algerian Civil War: 1990-1998* (London: Hurst, 2000), p. 147ff.
[54] Average GDP per capita (in constant 2000 USD) for Saudi Arabia, Algeria and Egypt in the period 1970–2007 was $10,850, $1,805 and $1,123 respectively; *World Development Indicators* (Washington DC: World Bank, 2007).
[55] Email correspondence with Steffen Hertog, 25 November 2007.
[56] Steffen Hertog, 'Segmented Clientelism: The Politics of Economic Reform in Saudi Arabia' (Oxford University, 2006), p. 218.
[57] M. Gibney, L. Cornett, and R. Wood, *Political Terror Scale 1976–2006* (2008), at www.political terrorscale.org/ (accessed 14 September 2008).
[58] David L. Cingranelli and David L. Richards, The Cingranelli-Richards (CIRI) Human Rights Dataset (12 March 2008 version), at www.humanrightsdata.org (accessed 14 September 2008).

Table 4. Indicators of Political Repression in Algeria, Egypt and Saudi Arabia

	POLITICAL TERROR SCALE, 1976–2006 (1–5, 5 IS WORST)	PHYSICAL INTEGRITY RIGHTS INDEX, 1981–2004 (0–8, 0 IS WORST)
Algeria	3.36	3.77
Egypt	3.15	3.73
Saudi Arabia	2.69	4.28

On the issue of political exclusion it is more difficult to make comparisons. On the one hand the Saudi state has provided ample space for religious activity and has given the religious establishment considerable power to influence the education and judicial sectors. On the other hand, the royal family has never allowed clerical interference in core matters of state policy, and never authorised organised opposition activism of any kind.[59] However, one might speculate that the political exclusion in the Arab republics produces more resentment among Islamists because it is uneven—it treats religious and secular actors differently. In both Saudi Arabia and the Arab republics, Islamist reformists are excluded from official politics, but in the republics, non-Islamist forms of organised political activity *are* allowed, at least on paper.

The relatively low levels of socio-economic hardship and violent regime repression may help explain the absence of revolutionary violence in the Kingdom. Put very simply, Saudi Islamists have had fewer material reasons to complain about their regime than have their Algerian and Egyptian counterparts. However, violent contestation is of course not a linear expression of the level of objective suffering or discontent in a population. Opportunities and resources for contestation are also highly important. At the same time, as shown above, pervasive security has not constituted such a restraint, nor has access to militant resources. Unlike in police states such as Syria or pre-2003 Iraq, it has not been particularly difficult, from a purely operational point of view, to mount violent attacks in Saudi Arabia. Could there be other structural obstacles to revolutionary mobilisation in the Kingdom?

Obstacles to mobilisation

Another possible explanation for the extroversion of Islamist violence in the Kingdom is that the Saudi state and society has certain structural or cultural characteristics that make it relatively difficult to mobilize significant numbers of people for revolutionary activism. Four such inhibiting factors seem particularly plausible.

First is the charismatic legitimacy of the regime. Saudi Arabia was not colonised and has been ruled by the same family on and off since the eighteenth century, longer than most countries in the region. While this does not automatically translate into government legitimacy, the charismatic legitimacy of the Al Saud is arguably often underestimated. Saudi Arabia has also avoided the militarisation of the government apparatus that eroded the legitimacy of the post-colonial Arab republics. There may also be a self-perpetuating dimension

---

[59] Ayman al-Yassini, *Religion and State in the Kingdom of Saudi Arabia* (Boulder, CO: Westview Press, 1985).

to Saudi regime stability, as the absence of a revolutionary precedent in recent Saudi history arguably makes the task of Saudi revolutionaries harder.

Second is the rentier economy. While too big a subject to be analysed in detail here, it may be argued that the rent constitutes an additional instrument of political control which most of the Arab republics do not have. It essentially adds a spectrum of leverage above that of physical coercion. While Egyptian militants had little to lose and the state little to offer, Saudi Islamists often have jobs and money to lose and the state is wealthy. The Saudi regime thus has more 'power of cooptation', which it can use to demobilize aspiring Islamist entrepreneurs and divide nascent social movements. There are many examples in Saudi history of the government combining soft coercion with financial incentives to rein in dissidents or rebels. The imprisonment, liberation and eventual cooptation of the Sahwa leaders in the late 1990s is a prominent example. The current rehabilitation programmes for imprisoned jihadists, in which detainees are given lump sums of money for education and marriage, is another.[60] Such measures require a very high 'GDP per militant capita', which countries such as Egypt do not enjoy.

A third factor may be the relative strength of traditional social structures such as tribes and extended families. The so-called 'tribal factor' is often seen by Western observers as a destabilising force in Saudi Arabia. In fact, however, it is very difficult to empirically document such a factor.[61] If anything, tribes seem to play a politically stabilising role, as tribal identity cuts across interest groups and prevent class identity formation. Even more significant for political stability are family structures, which are arguably stronger in Saudi Arabia than in the Arab republics, where they are more rapidly dismembered by economic migration and underdeveloped communication infrastructure. The extended family seems to play a very important role in limiting political activism in the Kingdom, because family structures add a significant social cost—in the form of family dishonour and possibly severed family links—to individual revolutionary activism. It is no coincidence that the rehabilitation programs for imprisoned jihadist in post-2003 Saudi Arabia systematically involve prisoners' families in the process.[62]

The fourth possible obstacle to revolutionary Islamist mobilisation is the role of religion in Saudi society. The Saudi state puts a much greater emphasis on the observance and promotion of religious conservatism than do the Arab republics. This probably affords the Saudi state a higher degree of protection against accusations of apostasy than the secular Arab republics. The Saudi state emphasis on religion has also produced a political culture in which all political arguments, including those of the opposition, have to be carefully couched in religious terms.[63] Political legitimacy has thus become very closely connected with religious legitimacy and scriptural proficiency. Because the most able scholars are employed by the state, and because official ulema still enjoy considerable legitimacy, revolutionaries may have

[60] Christopher Boucek, *Saudi Arabia's 'Soft' Counterterrorism Strategy* (Washington, DC: Carnegie Endowment for International Peace, 2008).
[61] Most assumptions on the role of tribes have been based on the profiles of the Saudi 9/11 hijackers, which included several southern tribesmen. More recent research has shown that the composition of the 9/11 attack team was not representative of Saudi al-Qaida members. Moreover, in the absence of overall figures on the size of Saudi tribes, it is impossible to know whether certain tribes are over-represented. See Thomas Hegghammer, 'Terrorist Recruitment and Radicalisation in Saudi Arabia', *Middle East Policy*, 13(4) (2006), pp. 39–60.
[62] Boucek, *Saudi Arabia's 'Soft' Counterterrorism Strategy*, p. 13.
[63] Madawi al-Rasheed, 'God, the King and the Nation: Political Rhetoric in Saudi Arabia in the 1990s', *Middle East Journal*, 50(3) (1996), pp. 359–371.

found it more difficult to articulate religiously credible calls for regime change. This tendency may have been strengthened by the content of the state ideology; the Wahhabi doctrine as promoted by the state places a particularly strong emphasis on obedience to political authority. As Madawi al-Rasheed has demonstrated, a Saudi 'theology of obedience at home' has served to depoliticize the population.[64]

The inhibiting effect of these four factors on anti-regime violence remains hypothetical, as it is very difficult to measure empirically. Further research into each of these four dynamics is required before their precise role can be established.

So far we have seen that the absence of grievances and presence of obstacles to anti-government mobilisation may help explain the low levels of revolutionary violence in the Kingdom. However, these factors only explain one half of the puzzle; they do not account for the high levels of pan-Islamist violence. How could it be so easy to mobilise for pan-Islamist activism when it was so difficult to mobilise for revolutionary activism?

Xenophobia

The third proposed explanation is that a peculiar Saudi xenophobia has made Saudi Islamists are more hostile to non-Muslims than are other Islamists from other countries. It is of course difficult to measure the level of xenophobia in a given society, but in the case of Saudi Arabia the anecdotal evidence of hostility to outsiders is so overwhelming that this hypothesis deserves to be taken seriously. This presumed Saudi xenophobia is likely to have two possible sources, one ideological, the other sociological.

One possibility is that the Wahhabi religious tradition promotes stronger hostility to non-Muslims than do other religious traditions.[65] While one must be careful in ascribing a doctrinal essence to a living religious tradition such as Wahhabism, it is fair to say that a distinguishing feature of Wahhabi doctrine as articulated by Najdi theologians since the eighteenth century is the emphasis on the purity of Islamic doctrine and practice.[66] A central tenet in the Wahhabi tradition is the notion of 'loyalty and disassociation' [al-wala' wa'l-bara] which encourages believers to actively distance themselves from and publicly declare their hostility toward infidels, and, conversely, to declare their loyalty to good Muslims.[67] This is one of the main sources for the strong emphasis in Saudi religious education on the distinction between Muslims and non-Muslims and the superiority of the former. Critics may object that the Wahhabi concern for purity was historically directed more at sinful Muslims than at outsiders. From the eighteenth to the early twentieth century, Wahhabi zealots fought mainly other nominal Muslims, not infidels. However, this may have had more to do with the geopolitics of the day, notably the sheer absence of non-Muslim populations

---

[64] Al-Rasheed, 'The Minaret and the Palace', pp. 204–206; Madawi al-Rasheed, *Contesting the Saudi State: Islamic Voices from a New Generation* (Cambridge: University Press, 2007) p. 22ff.

[65] In a related argument, Madawi al-Rasheed has maintained that the Wahhabi religious establishment has developed and promoted a peculiar 'theology of rebellion abroad'. Since the 1940s, she argues, the state systematically allowed and promoted the glorification of jihad in certain conflict zones abroad, notably in Palestine and Afghanistan; Al-Rasheed, 'The Minaret and the Palace', pp. 206–208.

[66] See e.g. David Commins, *The Wahhabi Mission and Saudi Arabia* (London: I.B. Tauris, 2006) and Guido Steinberg, *Religion und Staat in Saudi-Arabien* (Wurzburg: Egon, 2002).

[67] David Cook, *Understanding Jihad* (Berkeley: University of California Press, 2005), pp. 141–142; Joas Wagemakers, 'Framing the 'Threat to Islam': al-wala' wa al-bara' in Salafi Discourse', *Arab Studies Quarterly*, 30(4) (2008), pp. 1–22.

in the vicinity of the Najd. When Wahhabi scholars and Islamists came into regular contact with non-Muslims in the twentieth century, they were hardly at the forefront of inter-religious dialogue. Another possible source is social distance. Ordinary Saudis' lack of exposure to and knowledge of non-Muslims and non-Muslim cultures may have fuelled a certain xenophobia which in turn has made Saudi Islamists particularly hostile to non-Muslims. Scholars such as Senechal de la Roche have written about the link between 'social distance' and conflict, suggesting that long cultural and relational distance between two collectivities increases the likelihood of inter-group violence.[68] This seems intuitively applicable to Saudi Arabia, which, unlike other countries in the region, receives virtually no Western tourists and encourages expatriate workers to stay in isolated compounds. Saudi Arabia is also religiously extremely homogenous, lacking a significant Christian Arab population. While difficult to prove empirically, anecdotal evidence suggests that until recently, the majority of Saudis had minimal normal social interaction with non-Muslims in Saudi Arabia. Some Saudis study abroad and interact with Westerners in the Kingdom, but they represent a small minority of the overall Saudi population. In the Islamist community such interaction has been particularly rare. This author has studied the biographies of 800 Saudi jihadists active between 1980 and 2006; only a tiny minority had studied in the West and the vast majority seem to have had little or no personal contact with Westerners, or non-Muslims for that matter, in their lives.[69]

The Saudi education system has also come under heavy criticism, from both inside and outside Saudi Arabia, for emphasizing the superiority of Muslims over non-Muslims and for providing Saudi pupils with an ethnocentric understanding of history and limited knowledge about other cultures.[70] Others will point out that all education systems are ethnocentric and that the number of Saudi militants is too small to blame the education system as a whole. However, the degree of ethnocentrism in the Saudi education system has until recently been so high that it cannot be disregarded. We can thus not exclude the possibility that the level of social interaction with and knowledge about non-Muslims has been particularly low in Saudi Arabia and that this has stimulated xenophobia and anti-Westernism.

Of course, in the absence of good polls, this hypothesis is difficult to test. The few quantitative studies on Saudi political and religious attitudes show mixed evidence. On the one hand, available polls show that Saudis are considerably more socially conservative than for example Egyptians and Iranians.[71] On the other hand a 2002 poll placed Saudi Arabia in the middle of the list of Muslim states in terms of declared anti-Americanism.[72]

---

[68] Roberta Senechal de la Roche, 'Collective Violence as Social Control', *Sociological Forum*, 11 (1) (1996), pp. 118–122; Donald Black, 'The Geometry of Terrorism', *Sociological Theory*, 22 (1) (2004), pp. 14–25.
[69] Hegghammer, 'Violent Islamism', pp. 635–721.
[70] For a good treatment of the subject of Saudi education, see Michaela Prokop, 'Saudi Arabia: The Politics of Education', *International Affairs*, 79(1) (2003), pp. 77–89. For more critical treatments, see e.g. Nina Shea, *Saudi Arabia's Curriculum of Intolerance* (Washington DC: Hudson Institute, 2008) and *Excerpts from Saudi Ministry of Education Textbooks for Islamic Studies: Arabic with English Translation* (Washington DC: Freedom House, 2006). Criticism of Saudi curricula has also been voiced publicly by Saudi intellectuals, notably by the Islamist lawyer Abd al-Aziz al-Qasim. For a Wahhabi response to the criticism, see *Does Saudi Arabia Preach Intolerance and Hatred in the UK and US? An Independent Study of the Neo-Con and Sufi Partnership*, www.SalafiManhaj.com, 2007.
[71] Mansoor Moaddel, 'The Saudi Public Speaks: Religion, Gender and Politics', *International Journal of Middle East Studies*, 38(1) (2006), pp. 79–108.
[72] Zogby International, 'The Ten Nations 'Impressions of America' Poll Report' (2002).

Either way, the problem with these explanations, as with all essentialist paradigms, is that they do not explain chronological variation. If Saudis are so hostile to non-Muslims, why did they not fight them until the 1980s Afghan jihad? And why was there not more violence against Westerners in the Kingdom before the year 2000? To account for these variations we will probably need to look at politics.

Political diversion

The last explanation we shall consider is that the Saudi regime, at particular times in recent decades, has encouraged or allowed extreme pan-Islamist activism in order to divert Islamist challenges to its own legitimacy.

Over the years, many have accused the Saudi state for having a double standard toward Islamist militancy, i.e. for leaving Saudi militants alone so long as their violence did not take place on Saudi territory.[73] This suspicion is not unfounded. Saudi Arabia long treated its jihadists relatively softly. In the 1980s, the state encouraged and supported Saudi volunteers who wanted to fight in Afghanistan. In the early 1990s, the government did little if anything to prevent volunteers from heading off to fight in Bosnia. In 1993, as a result of the controversial activities of Arab Afghans around the world, the government began imposing mild restrictions on recruitment for the jihad in Bosnia, but it was not until after the 1995 Riyadh bombing that the regime ended its policy of tacit support for Saudi participation in jihad fronts abroad.[74] However, when the second Chechen war and the second Palestinian intifada broke out in 1999 and 2000 and caused a massive increase in recruitment and fundraising to jihadist groups abroad, the authorities did not interfere much in this kind of support activity. Even in 2002, foreign fighters were treated relatively softly, at least compared to veteran jihadists in other countries. Most of the hundreds of Saudi fighters who returned to the Kingdom from al-Qaida training camps in Afghanistan in 2002 were not detained by Saudi police for more than a few weeks upon arrival, if at all. In the early 2000s, al-Qaida leaders rightly considered Saudi Arabia as its most important source of recruits, money and clerical opinions.[75] It was only after the outbreak of the QAP campaign in 2003 that support structures for militants abroad were being systematically dismantled by the state. Yet even today, Interior Ministry officials are open about the fact that returnees from Iraq are treated more softly than captured members of the QAP.[76]

In contrast, government responses to large-scale terrorist activity on Saudi soil have been merciless.[77] In the aftermath of the 1995 Riyadh bombing and the 1996 Khobar bombing, police arrested and tortured hundreds of suspects. After the foiled al-Qaida missile plot in early 1998, an alleged 800 people were rounded up

---

[73] Some analysts have even suggested that the government had secretly paid al-Qaida not to conduct terrorist attacks in Saudi Arabia. This, however, is a conspiracy theory. The absence of al-Qaida operations in the Kingdom in the late 1990s was due, first, to lack of capability, and subsequently to a lack of intention; see Thomas Hegghammer, 'Islamist Violence and Regime Stability in Saudi Arabia', *International Affairs*, 84(4) (2008), pp. 701–715.
[74] Hegghammer, 'Violent Islamism', p. 298.
[75] *Sawt al-Jihad*, 2 (2003), p. 24.
[76] Interview with unidentified Interior Ministry official, Riyadh, May 2008.
[77] I specify 'large-scale terrorism' because small-scale violence was largely ignored by the authorities. A large number of small but lethal attacks on individual Westerners in the Kingdom between 2000 and 2003 were never properly investigated by Saudi police. Instead, some of the attacks were even blamed on Western alcohol traders in what most outside observers view as gross miscarriage of justice. See Hegghammer, 'Violent Islamism', pp. 128–135.

by the security services.[78] When the terrorism campaign broke out in May 2003, the state threw its full weight behind the fight against the QAP, albeit with less brutal methods than in 1996 and 1998.

At the heart of this systematic differential treatment is of course an issue of legitimacy. There is a difference between guerrilla warfare against the Russian military in Chechnya and suicide car bombs on civilians in Saudi cities. The Saudi regime no doubt considered 'classical jihadism'—private military involvement in other Muslims' struggles of national liberation—as less reprehensible than global jihadist or revolutionary violence. This, of course, is a view they share with most Muslims (and probably by many non-Muslims, for that matter). However, why would the Saudi regime be more positively inclined to pan-Islamist activism than other regimes in the region?

Part of the answer to this question lies in the religious basis for the Saudi state and the role of pan-Islamism in Saudi state discourse since King Faisal. In the 1960s and 1970s, Saudi Arabia had invested considerable prestige and money in promoting the notion of Muslim solidarity. When, from the 1980s onward, when the pan-Islamist movement gained momentum—primarily as a result of the communications revolution and the real increase in the number of conflicts pitting Muslims versus non-Muslims—it was politically difficult for the Saudi regime to prevent mobilisation for jihad in the name of Muslim solidarity.

This path dependency might have sufficed as an explanation, were it not for the fact that the variations in Saudi support or tolerance for pan-Islamist militancy since the 1980s correlate so closely with domestic political challenges to the State. For example, the massive increase in state support for the Afghan jihad in the 1980s occurred at a time when oil income was plummeting, Saudi unemployment was soaring, and the so-called Sahwa movement was gaining momentum. Similarly, the massive Saudi state support for the Bosnian jihad—which was higher (measured in financial support per annum) than for any other foreign cause in Saudi history—occurred at a time when the confrontation between the Sahwa and the regime was at its most fierce.[79] After the Sahwa was neutralised in the mid-1990s, it became much more difficult for Saudi volunteers to reach foreign jihad fronts. This suggests that in the 1985–1995 period at least, the Saudi regime was not just tolerating, but actively promoting pan-Islamism, most likely to undermine regime-oriented political contestation. Put somewhat crudely, the regime may have promoted pan-Islamism as Saudi Arabia's 'opium for the people'. This type of 'diversionary politics' is well known from other contexts. For example, in the 1970s and 1980s, government religious spending in Algeria increased as GDP per capita went down.[80]

However, despite the end of direct official support for jihadist causes in the mid-1990s, private support would continue. Pan-Islamism could not be ruled out by decree—it would remain a very strong force in Saudi political culture for years to come. The state's ability to crack down on support networks in the Kingdom thus remained restricted. Authorities could not easily arrest people involved

---

[78] Hegghammer, 'Violent Islamism', pp. 298–302.
[79] See Ziyad Salih al-Hadhlul and Muhammad Abdallah al-Humaydhi, *al-qissa al-kamila li'l-dawr al-sa'udi fi al-busna wa'l-harsak* [*The Full Story of the Saudi Role in Bosnia-Herzegovina*] (Riyadh: Al-Homaidhi Printing Press, 1998) and Hegghammer, 'Islamist Violence and Regime Stability in Saudi Arabia', p. 704.
[80] Abdelaziz Testas, 'The Roots of Algeria's Ethnic and Religious Violence', *Studies in Conflict and Terrorism*, 25 (2002), pp. 161–183.

in fundraising to Chechnya in the late 1990s, for example, because most Saudis viewed this sort of activity as charity and altruism, not terrorism. It was not until after the outbreak of the QAP campaign that the Saudi regime dared take measures that ran counter to pan-Islamist sentiment and publicly admitted that its previous soft stance on jihadism abroad was problematic.

The regime's crackdowns on violence at home and tolerance of militancy abroad in the 1980s and 1990s created a skewed incentive structure which may be considered the principal cause of the extraversion of Saudi Islamist violence. Without entering into counterfactual speculation, it seems reasonable to assume that the Kingdom would have seen more revolutionary activism had it pursued a zero tolerance policy for radical pan-Islamist activism in this period. It is telling that when such a zero-tolerance policy was finally implemented in 2003, anti-regime violence in the form of attacks on security forces increased considerably.

Conclusion

This article has attempted to document and explain the curious outward orientation of Islamist violence in Saudi Arabia. Unlike several of the Arab republics, Saudi Arabia has seen very little violence directed against the government and a large number of attacks against non-Muslims, primarily Westerners. The absence of revolutionary violence in the Kingdom seems to be due to two main sets of factors: first are the low levels of socio-economic hardship and violent regime oppression; second are the structural characteristics of Saudi state and society, notably the charismatic legitimacy of the regime, the rentier economy, the tribes, and the state's religious profile, all of which make revolutionary Islamist mobilisation difficult. The Saudi Islamist propensity for violence against non-Muslims may have been facilitated by a certain Saudi xenophobia, rooted in the Wahhabi hostility to non-Muslims and the social distance between Saudis and non-Muslim societies. Most important, however, was the Saudi state's ambiguous policy toward Islamist militancy, in particular its tolerance of extreme pan-Islamism and intolerance of revolutionary activism. The government set an incentive structure for aspiring Saudi Islamists that implicitly said 'jihad, yes, but not revolution'. Since 2003, the regime seems to have implemented a zero-tolerance policy toward all forms of militancy, including so-called 'classical jihadism' abroad. If the current analysis is correct, and if the new Saudi policies are maintained, we should expect to see a somewhat more inward-oriented pattern of Islamist activism—though probably no revolution—in the Kingdom in the years to come.

The analysis has provided useful insights into the dynamics of Islamist violence and on the comparative politics of the Middle East. The findings support the hypothesis that there are different types of Islamist violence and that the causal dynamics differ somewhat from one type to another. Moreover, differences in structure and political culture between states in the Middle East seem to affect the patterns of Islamist violence in the same countries. It would seem, for example, that poor, secular and repressive Arab republics are much more likely to see revolutionary activism than a relatively rich, religious and consensus-based kingdom such as Saudi Arabia. The distinction between the ideal types of Islamist activism should not be exaggerated, as extreme pan-Islamists and revolutionary Islamists have partially overlapping agendas. Nor should we overemphasize the analytical distinction between religious kingdoms and secular republics in the

Middle East. Nevertheless, the comparative politics of Islamist contestation seems to constitute a fruitful avenue for further research.

Acknowledgements

The author is grateful to Dr Steffen Hertog for useful comments to an early version of the manuscript. The paper was first presented at the annual meeting of the Middle East Studies Association in Montreal in November 2007, and later at the University of Ottawa in December 2008; the author thanks the participants at these discussions for useful comments.

Saudi Arabia and the Arab–Israeli Peace Process: The Fluctuation of Regional Coordination

JOSEPH KOSTINER

ABSTRACT *This article aims to demonstrate that since the 1970s Saudi Arabia had exercised a policy of regional coordination among Middle Eastern states, and between them and the United States. This policy stems from Saudi leaders' understanding that regional conflict mediation has been, and still is, the best strategy to achieve the Saudi Kingdom's security. This strategy developed into an all embracing perception of playing the role of regional coordinator among the various actors in the Middle East, including the United States. This paper stresses how this policy was shaped in the 1970s, and then came to fruition in the next decade. The analysis revolves around the Saudi initiative for peace between Arab parties and Israel in the 1980s ("The Fahd Plan" leading up to "The Fez resolutions" – 1981–1982) and in the beginning of the twenty-first century ("The Abdullah initiative" leading up to "The Arab peace initiative", 2002–2007).*

Introduction

The special position that Saudi Arabia has occupied over the last few decades in Arab-Israeli affairs reflects the Saudi kingdom's role as regional coordinator. In seeking an appropriate role in the region, Saudi leaders opted against playing the part of a regional 'ringleader', similar to the one played by Gamal 'Abd al-Nasir's Egypt in the 1950s and 1960s. Saudi Arabia, however, lacked the historical and cultural heritage, and military prowess for this sort of role. States vying for such a position should also have notable military experience, large standing armies, and recognition as leaders of military campaigns.[1] Moreover, it is important that such states have the self-confidence to take on a leadership role. Saudi Arabia has had none of these paramount qualities. Rather, it was more suited to play the role of a regional mediator, while making use of its financial capacities and experience in tribal politics. Furthermore, this role bestowed on the Saudis an image of performing an indispensable conciliatory role in the region, which added a layer of assurance against regional attacks to the Kingdom's security. However, in the dynamics of Middle Eastern diplomacy, Saudi leaders further developed a role of regional coordinator, going above and beyond simple mediation.

Tel Aviv, Israel. Email: kostiner@post.tau.ac.il
[1] On regional roles see Michael Barnett, 'Institutions, Roles and Disorder: The Case of the Arab State System', *International Studies Quarterly*, 37(3) (1993), pp. 271–296.

The Formative Stage

In can be argued that attempts made by Saudi leaders to establish a role for Saudi Arabia as mediator were impressive, but did not give the Saudis all the functions and instruments that enabled them to develop the broader role of regional coordinator. A paramount job of mediation was carried out by Saudi Arabia during the era of King Khalid, primarily spear-headed by Crown Prince Fahd. In October 1976, the Saudis brought the leaders of Egypt and Syria to Riyadh, brokering a trade-off that might end the ongoing tension between them: his own presence at the meeting On one hand, the Egyptians would stop criticizing the Syrian invasion of Lebanon earlier that year, which included serious violence and fighting with Palestinians; The Syrians, on the other, agreed to stop criticizing the Egyptian separation of forces agreement with Israel, known as 'Sinai II', in which the Israelis withdrew from the Suez Canal. In the perspective of many Arab countries, including Syria, the Egyptians should not have reached an agreement with Israel before Israel agreed to give back all territories it occupied in 1967.

The Saudis' success in improving relations between the leaders of these two countries in effect thawed Egyptian-Syrian tensions, and encouraged the Saudis to devise a plan to form a unified Arab position vis-à-vis Israel that would hinge on an agreement between Egypt, Syria and Saudi Arabia. This agreement would focus on a peace proposal that the leaders of these states would present to the American president, Jimmy Carter, in April 1977. However, Saudi efforts were thwarted by regional events. The government of Israel, led by Menachem Begin, engaged in a peace process with Egypt's President Anwar al-Sadat, which became the central agenda for both Egypt and Israel, making the Saudi role redundant.[2]

Egypt headed towards bilateral peace with Israel, an entente finally signed as 'The Camp David Accords' on 26 March 1979. Saudi Arabia attempted to discourage the Arab parties that were critical of Egypt's role in the peace process—Iraq, Syria and the Palestinian Liberation Organization (PLO)—from punishing and boycotting Egypt for signing the peace treaty. The Saudis met with this coalition of Arab states in Baghdad at the time of the signing of the peace agreement, in hopes of thwarting punitive Arab action against Egypt, by arguing that diplomatic relations are a matter of bilateral consideration and cannot result from the collective action of the Arab League. However, pressures from the host, Saddam Hussein, and other Arab leaders pushed King Khalid to order his foreign minister, Saud al-Faisal, to join other Arab states in boycotting Egypt and breaking diplomatic relations with Cairo. Saudi leaders were forced to join the anti-Egyptian bloc, which they had not favoured, putting them in conflict with the United States, which had strongly supported the peace process.

The Saudis then started looking for a new peace initiative that would, at the same time, focus on the Palestinians and involve all of the Arab states. Through such an initiative, they hoped to introduce a new level of Arab solidarity, which would hinge on cooperation among all the Arab states. It could cure the Arab world of the inter-Arab schisms that had resulted from the Camp David Accords. Saudi leaders also sought to prevent a situation that would allow the Soviet Union to come to the aid of radical Arab states, thereby possibly sparking tension with Israel and

---

[2] Middle East News Agency, 19 May 1977, via FBIS, 20 May 1977; Radio Riyadh, 24 May 1977, via FBIS, 24 May 1977; Nadav Safran, *Saudi Arabia: The Ceaseless Quest for Security* (Cambridge, MA: Harvard University Press, 1985), pp. 229–230, 241–244.

disrupting Saudi oil exports to the West. Hence, Crown Prince Fahd developed a new plan, which he first published in August 1981 in various media outlets. The plan contained eight points, six of which were quite common, having already been made public by other Arab countries. Key among these was the demand that Israel withdraw from all the territories that it occupied from Arab countries in 1967.

Two points of the plan were, however, unusual and innovative. Point number seven stipulated that all Middle Eastern states have the right to live in peace, and point number eight guaranteed the implementation of the former seven points by the United Nations. Thus, for the first time, a new element was brought onto the agenda of Arab politics: If Israel did, in fact, withdraw from the occupied territories, the Jewish state, like the Arab states of the region, would have the right to exist in peace. With the exception of Egypt in its bilateral agreement with Israel, no Arab state had hitherto acknowledged Israel's right to exist. Furthermore, most of them vehemently opposed any political engagement with Israel.[3]

Considering Arab politics at the time, this proposal was extremely innovative and progressive. This plan was not merely conciliation or mediation of a regional conflict; it was an attempt to pacify the entire Arab-Israeli conflict. The plan also extended an olive branch to the West by proving that the Saudis were proponents of peace. Earlier, in January 1981, Saudis had purchased advanced AWACS airplanes from the United States, used for intelligence gathering. The purchase proved to be very difficult to broker. The acquisition of this sensitive technology was met by staunch objection from the Israeli lobby in the US, and was only made possible after President Ronald Reagan directly intervened with the Senate. Following the AWACS sale, the American administration showed that it believed the Saudis to be a beacon of peace in the region.[4]

These elements showed that Saudi Arabia was attempting to bring the entire Middle East into a stable order, hoping to position itself as the conductor of this concert, and thus link itself to US policies in the region.[5] The Fahd plan did not, however, generate sufficient support after its first month of publication. The US was preoccupied with other interests and did not pay close attention to Prince Fahd's aspirations. More intransigent states still dominated the Arab parties, and Syria—the leading force among them—rejected the Fahd plan. It argued that the plan, while it was forthcoming towards Israel, did not give sufficient rights to the Palestinians and did not stipulate a timetable for Israeli withdrawal from the occupied territories. The hard liners also felt that the Fahd plan did not give sufficient verbal support to Arab objections to the Camp David accords.

The Saudi attempt to obtain formal Arab League recognition for the Fahd Plan was foiled by Syria at the onset of the Arab summit meeting in Fez, Morocco, in November 1981. Syrian opposition to the plan was, however, softened in the summer of 1982 due to the Lebanese–Israeli war. Israeli forces managed to shoot down several Syrian aircraft, greatly embarrassing the Syrian regime. The Palestinians were also defeated, and the PLO was forced to leave Beirut, first for Tripoli in northern

---

[3] Jacob Goldberg, 'Saudi Arabia and the Egyptian Israeli Peace Process, 1977–1981', *Middle East Review*, 18 (4) (1986), pp. 25–33.

[4] Radio Riyadh, 4 January 1982, via FBIS, 5 January 1982; *Time*, 3 March 1982; Adeed Dawisha, 'Saudi Arabia and the Arab-Israeli Conflict: The Ups and Downs of Pragmatic Moderation', *International Journal*, 38(4) (1983), pp. 674–689.

[5] Herman Eilts, 'Raegan's Middle East Initiative', *American Arab Affairs*, 1(2) (1982), pp. 1–5; Munther Dajani and Mohammad Daoudi, 'New Frontiers in the Search for Peace: The Saudi Initiative', *International Studies*, 23 (1) (1986), pp. 63–74.

Lebanon and later to Tunis. Hence, the Saudis were able to exercise greater leverage over the two relatively weakened parties.

Iraq, which had been a major opponent to the Camp David accords, was engaged in war with Iran and was far less concerned with events in the Arab–Israeli arena. However, American interest in the Fahd Plan was increasing. There is no convincing explanation for this, other than the fact that the Reagan administration had sought to calm rivalries in the Middle East and develop a peace plan for the Israeli–Palestinian conflict, based on Israeli withdrawal from Palestinian territories on the one hand, and the re-inclusion of these lands into Jordan as autonomous regions, on the other. The Reagan Plan differed substantially from the Saudi initiative, but nevertheless hinged on a common denominator, namely the achievement of peace and stability. In addition, the Fahd Plan had the potential to help Washington enlist a coalition of Arab states that would side with the US and oppose the Soviet Union.

The Saudis learned their lesson from 1981, when they had not consulted the Syrians sufficiently before attempting to implement the plan. In preparing for a second round, they properly consulted the Syrians with regards to the details. To receive Syrian support, they were even ready to alter the plan. The changes to the Fahd Plan revolved around shrinking the scope of the legitimacy that would be accorded to the existence and recognition of the State of Israel.

The plan was reintroduced by Saudi Arabia at another Fez Conference of the Arab League in September 1982. This time, the unusual point stressing that all states in the region have a right to exist was eliminated. In its place was put a new point number seven, which stipulated that the UN Security Council would provide guarantees of peace among all states in the region, including an independent Palestinian state. Israel's legitimate existence was reduced to a hint. Both Syrians and Palestinians, who felt that they now had more of a stake in the arrangement, accepted this plan. In another point, the PLO was described as the 'sole legitimate representative of the Palestinian people', pleasing the PLO to the point that they expressed general acceptance of the reworked language. Under these circumstances, with the new formulation, the Fahd Plan was accepted as an Arab program for peace by the Arab League.[6]

Meanings and Observations

Saudi Arabia presented an approach to settling the Arab–Israeli conflict that was very different from the Egyptian–Israeli approach, manifested in the Camp David Accords. The Egyptian–Israeli approach hinged on a bilateral agreement achieved in tedious negotiations, where the end result had not been decided until the final signing of the agreement. The Saudis believed that this kind of bilateral approach was in fact destructive and isolated the agreement from the Arab state system, thereby causing a rift between Egypt and the rest of the Arab world.

The Saudis considered the concept of a separate, bilateral peace to be unacceptable. King Khalid himself noted the kingdom's rejection of a 'unilateral stand' with regard to a peace settlement.[7] Rather, the Saudis came up with a plan that was comprehensive and included all of the Arab states. The Saudis felt that

---

[6] *Al-Qabas* (Kuwait), 15 September 1982; see also Daniel Dishon, Bruce Maddy-Weitzman, 'Inter-Arab Relations', in Colin Legum, Haim Shaked and Dishon (eds), *Middle East Contemporary Survey* (MECS), Vol. 6 (1981–82), pp. 253–258.

[7] Quoted in *al-Jumhurriya* (Cairo), 2 April 1976.

this arrangement would provide a sufficient incentive to each Arab state to sign on, bringing the Arab world together behind the proposed accords. Peace with Israel was the instrument for achieving political cooperation amongst Arab states. The Saudi leadership thereby hoped to bridge inter-Arab schisms, like those that had developed after the signing of the Camp David Accords in 1979. This was the first priority for Saudi leaders.

The Saudis were also ready to set down the final shape of the accords in advance, namely the formation of an independent Palestinian state with Jerusalem as its capital, as well the return of Jordanian and Syrian lands that were lost in the war of 1967. The reason for which the Saudis were willing to map out the specifics of the final arrangement before the deal had been signed, was to show Arab leaders, as well as the US and Israel, what the tangible terms of a settlement might be, so that other Arab leaders could adjust to the idea.[8]

Unlike the first time the Saudis attempted to enact the Fahd Plan, the second attempt took into account the perspectives of more intransigent Arab parties. Although the alterations to the plan, most notably the seventh point, made the proposal less attractive to Israel and the West, they provided the ability to rally Arab support for the proposal, which was ultimately the most important objective of the Saudi leaders.[9] The element of introducing a plan, which could be altered as a result of consultation with other Arab parties, became a crucial tenet of future Saudi attempts at brokering peace between Israel and the Arabs.

For example, in late 1994, following previously achieved peace agreements, most notably the Oslo Accords between Israel and the PLO in September 1993, and the October 1994 agreement with Jordan, Saudi Arabia joined Egypt and Syria in what is known as the 'Alexandria Agreement'. Syria had feared exclusion from peace agreements with Israel, which, in the Saudi view, simply demonstrated that the agreements of 1993 and 1994 suffered from not being comprehensive. They were essentially bilateral agreements that mirrored the Camp David accords. Syria's complaint was actually an attempt to initiate a new agreement with the Saudis and the Egyptians to bring back the Fez accords. The Egyptians did not want to reawaken the 1979 schism and prepared to join the camp in 1994. It was agreed that no Arab party would sign a peace agreement with Israel without these three states' consent, thus protecting Syria's interests not to be excluded from any future peace agreement with Israel. This was yet another case where the Saudis were willing to cooperate with radical Arab elements and support a radical Arab state that was far more apprehensive in accepting an Arab–Israeli peace in the first place. The Saudis once again demonstrated their belief that if a peace agreement were to be mutually beneficial to all Arab states and contribute to the sustainability of a greater Arab political calm – it would be supported by Saudi leaders.[10]

While the Saudis were ready to cooperate with other Arab states, even radical parties, they also saw cooperation with the US as paramount to achieving their ultimate goals. The Saudis did not forget their interests in cultivating a close relationship with the US, their primary protector during the Iran–Iraq War and

---

[8] Dajani and Daoudi, 'New Frontiers in the Search for Peace'; Tamar Yegnes, 'Saudi Arabia and the Peace Process', *The Jerusalem Quarterly*, 18 (1981), p. 104.

[9] Compare with Eli Podeh, *From Fahd to Abdullah: The Origins of the Peace Initiatives and Their Impact on the Arab State System and Israel*, Gitelson Peace Publication, No. 24 (Jerusalem: The Harry S. Truman Research Institute for the Advancement of Peace, 2003).

[10] *Al-Hayat* (London), 27 December 1994; *Al-Sharq al-Awsat* (London), 30 December 1994.

their main supplier of advanced weapons. They likewise understood that the US had the strongest influence over Israel and knew that including Washington in the process would help to ensure Israeli cooperation. This made US involvement essential. Therefore, the Saudis fervently pushed their agenda in Washington, trying to prove to the Americans that they had a serious resolution that could alleviate a great deal of tension in the Middle East and which was also conducive to the formation of an anti-Soviet camp.

The Saudis and the Reagan administration found common cause. The Reagan administration's idea was that the Arab states, in tandem with Israel, could form an anti-Soviet coalition. The Saudi leaders' anti-Soviet attitude was reawakened after the Soviet invasion of Afghanistan in December 1978. In the end, regional cooperation did not come to fruition; the Arab states remained divided and Israel was unwilling to accept the terms of the Saudi initiative. However, the effort demonstrated to the US that it had a partner in the Middle East, despite Saudi Arabia's expressed disapproval of Camp David. Furthermore, by linking all the Arab states and the US in a common peace initiative, Saudi efforts were not merely acts of conciliation, or mediation, but rather a form of regional coordination, bringing together local states and a superpower, and aspiring to set the regional agenda for the future.

Abdullah's Peace Initiative 2002

In late March 2002, the Arab League summit in Beirut officially endorsed the peace initiative presented by Crown Prince Abdullah on 13 February 2002. This plan became known as the Arab Peace Initiative.[11] The background of this plan can be understood by examining two different arenas in which the Saudis had been involved.

The first was the Palestinian intifada in the West Bank and the Gaza Strip. The intifada, which began in the fall of 2002, became a bloody and violent process. It did not, however, produce a clear road to Palestinian statehood or improve the Palestinian population's political or economic conditions. Within the Arab world, there was growing support among the masses for the Palestinian cause. This support seemed to fuel opposition to the governments of Arab states, specifically the more moderate ones, such as Egypt, Jordan, Morocco and Saudi Arabia, who had maintained good relations with the West. These states, at the very least, had also been known to support peace with Israel, while Jordan and Egypt had already made peace with the latter. The Arab public's protests against these states acted as a catalyst towards Saudi action. It caused restiveness in these moderate regimes and Arab public in general, urging the Saudis to fear that the situation in the Arab world, particularly in the pro-Western monarchies, would develop into a shaky and turbulent situation. In turn, Crown Prince Abdullah wanted to demonstrate to both the Palestinians and the Arab public in general that unlike most Arab states, which remained passive in responding to the Palestinian plight, a Saudi initiative would assist the Palestinians in achieving an independent state.

Several observations are required in order to explain the nature of the points that the Saudis raised in their peace initiative. The linkage between the motivation

---

[11] *Al-Zamman* (London), 19 February 2002; See also 'Special Policy Forum Report on the Arab-Israeli Peace Process', Policy Watch No. 372, The Washington Institute for Near East Policy, 8 April 2002.

to pacify the Arab masses and Palestinians, on the one hand, and pacify American leaders, on the other, was in this case far stronger than the link that the Saudis had conceived in 1982. In 2002, the Saudis had burning and immediate concerns. Therefore, this was not just a peace initiative that could be released to the Arab world without looking to the US, but rather had to impact both arenas in tandem.

Another interesting point is that once again the Saudis did not just focus on the Palestinians. They were working to satisfy all the concerned Arab parties participating in the summit in Beirut, especially Arab states that had territorial claims to Israel, particularly Syria and Lebanon. Kuwait and Iraq were also supposed to participate in the conference despite their remote link to Israeli–Palestinian issues; the Saudis wanted to use this initiative as a chance to mediate sour relations between these two countries who had been split since the Iraqi invasion of Kuwait in 1990. Thus, the Saudis saw another opportunity to cultivate their role as regional mediator.[12]

The actual peace initiative, which consisted of eight points, can be divided into three main parts. First, Israel should fully withdraw from all territories occupied in 1967, in addition to all the territories that Israel re-entered in attempts to suppress the Palestinian intifada in 2001 and early 2002. Consequently, the Palestinians would be able to strengthen central authority, en route to establishing a fully independent state. The Saudis hoped that this initiative would allay the demonstrations and angry voices in the Arab world and would be well received by both the Palestinians and Arab public opinion, most notably in the states regarded as moderate. The call that aimed at achieving a full Israeli withdrawal from all occupied territories showed the Syrians that their concerns had not been forgotten, and, therefore, Israel would have to withdraw from the Golan Heights and some areas of southern Lebanon. Even Iraqi interests to mend burnt bridges with its neighbours were taken into account.[13]

Second, after the ultimate Israeli withdrawal, and the subsequent establishment of a Palestinian state, the conflict would end, leading to the normalization (*tatbi'*) of relations between Israel and the rest of the Arab world. This was apparently the contribution of the National Security Advisor of Saudi Arabia, Adil al-Jubair, who had collaborated in forging the peace initiative. He used the vast knowledge that he had acquired during his service in the US as a senior diplomat for the Saudi embassy, where he served for several years. Much like in 1982, this initiative advanced the idea that all Arab states should end the Arab–Israeli conflict and enter the peace process with Israel; in other words, it would be a collective effort. In the final statement of the Beirut conference, the term 'normal relations' ('*alaqat tabi'iyya*), replaced the term normalization.

The Saudi initiative received immediate positive recognition in the US, Western Europe and the Arab world.[14] It was the most positive expression concerning Israel

[12] On Saudi Arabia's regional standing, See Gerd Nonneman, 'Determinants and Patterns of Saudi Foreign Policy: Omnibalancing and "Relative Autonomy" in Multiple Environments', in Paul Aarts and Gerd Nonneman, *Saudi Arabia in the Balance: Political Economy, Society, Foreign Affairs* (London: Hurst & Company, 2005), pp. 315–351; Gawdat Bahgat 'The New Middle East: The Gulf Monarchies and Israel', *Journal of Social Political and Economics Studies*, 28(2) (2003); Khalid al-Dakhil, 'Buruz al-Dawr al- Saudi fi Al-Nizam al-Arabi al-Rahin', *Majallat al-Dirasat Filastiniyya*, 72 (2007), pp. 5–15.

[13] See Nimrod Rafaeli, 'Iraq-Saudi Arabia Rapprochement', *Middle East Media Research (MEMRI) Economic Studies*, no. 31, 17 June 2002, online at http://www.memri.org/bin/articles.cgi?Page=subjects&Area=economic&ID = EA3102.

[14] *New York Times*, 13 February 2002, 22 February 2002; *Agence France Presse*, 25 and 26 February 2002.

that had ever been stated in an Arab League resolution. However, the 2002 initiative also demonstrates a certain twist in the Saudi attitude toward the US. The initiative reflects the Saudi understanding that while the US has been the main defender of Saudi Arabia in terms of offsetting military threats, as well as being the Kingdom's main supplier of weapons, the US would not be able to help with other threats, such as terrorism, and might in fact become a liability.

This became evident in November 1995 and June 1996, when American bases in Saudi Arabia were targets of major terrorist attacks. Moreover, in various Arab quarters, the US military presence in the Kingdom provoked high levels of propaganda against the Saudi regime. The Kingdom's close ties with Washington were a main focus of the campaign. Saudi leaders reached the conclusion that while they would want to keep the US as their main military defender and arms supplier, they would not want the US as a defender against terrorism and political propaganda campaigns launched by other regional powers.[15]

Saudi leaders would have preferred a security strategy that capitalized on both of these two different areas: reliance on the US for military defence and reliance on the Arab world for coping with legitimacy and propaganda challenges. In fact, in 2002, the Abdullah Plan was established to achieve precisely this type of coordination: allowing Saudi Arabia to reap benefits from both the US and the Arab world. To demonstrate Saudi willingness to defer to the interests of other Arab parties in an attempt to win them over and turn them into supporters of their plan, Saudi leaders agreed to introduce two adjustments to the original plan. In preparation for the Beirut Summit of 2002, it was stipulated that Israel must withdraw from, in addition to Palestinian territories, the Golan Heights and land in Southern Lebanon. An Israeli withdrawal from only one territory would not exclude withdrawal from others. Thus, it was made clear that any future peace negotiations would relate to all of the relevant parties and would not simply focus on the Palestinian front.

Another important issue was the inclusion of the resolution of the Palestinian refugee problem, which had been excluded from the original Saudi initiative. Under Syrian and Palestinian pressure, this issue was brought into the Beirut text. It was stated that the refugee problem would be settled according to UN Resolution 194 of 1949, which mandated the return of Palestinian refugees to their homes. The Beirut resolution stated that the parties would decide the final number of the Palestinian refugees who would be permitted to return. This was supposed to be a certain opening for Israel, to enlist its acceptance of the initiative. However, the inclusion of UN Resolution 194 was a non-starter for Israeli leaders.[16]

These two adjustments demonstrate Saudi readiness to make compromises in their original peace initiative in order to make room for various Arab states' interests. Crown Prince Abdullah was even able to bring about a meeting between the Kuwaiti prime minister and the Iraqi vice-president to demonstrate reconciliation after Iraq had conceded Kuwait's right to exist within the new borders that had been demarcated

---

[15] On Gulf states' security options, with some references to the US shortcomings, see Michael Collins Dunn, 'Five Years After Desert Storm: Gulf Security, Stability and the US Presence', *Middle East Policy*, 4 (March 1996), pp. 30–38; cf. Anthony Cordesman, 'Saudi Arabia and the Struggle Against Terrorism', Saudi–US Relations Information Service, 11 April 2005; Anthony Cordesman and Khalid R. al-Rodhan, 'The Gulf Military Forces in an Era of Asymmetric War: Qatar and Saudi Arabia', Working Draft, Revised 28 June 2006, Center for Strategic and International Studies (CSIS), http://csis.org/files/media/csis/pubs/060728_gulf_iran.pdf

[16] On Israel's response to the Arab peace initiative see Podeh, *From Fahd to Abdullah*; and Joshua Teitelbaum, *The Arab Peace Initiative: A Primer and Future Prospects* (Jerusalem: The Jerusalem Center for Public Affairs, 2009).

after the 1991 war. The Saudis thus facilitated another step of reconciliation between formerly hostile parties.

Saudi success was marked by the wide recognition that the Kingdom received as peace initiators. President George W. Bush included the Abdullah peace initiative as a basis for his US peace policy for the Middle East in a June 2002 speech. The Quartet's peace plan also drew on the Beirut Plan. Saudi leaders, in their turn, understood that they would receive credit even without direct involvement in the mediation process. They did not see themselves taking over direct mediation from the US.

Coping with Iranian Ascendancy

Iran's wide reach in the Middle East was revealed in the course of the 2006 Israel–Lebanon war. It became evident that a militant and aggressive Shi'i force, Hizbullah, was even more potent and active in Lebanon than the one the Saudis had come to know as the Mahdi Army in southern Iraq. A militarily strong state like Israel was proven unable to contain this party. Furthermore, the uprising in Lebanon proved that pro-Western regimes friendly to Saudi Arabia, such as the Fuad Sinyura government in Lebanon, were not immune to terrorist activities, which could check the legal government. Saud al-Faysal called this the 'hijacking' of the government of Lebanon by a non-state organization.[17]

The situation, from a Saudi viewpoint, could have become much worse. The Saudis were worried about developments in the war in Iraq. They objected to the idea that Iraq would be ruled by Shi'is and did not trust the Shi'i-led government of Nuri al-Maliki. The situation in Iraq was very volatile, and the strengthening of the Mahdi Army, led by Muqtada al-Sadr and aided by Iran, would be devastating.[18] The Saudis also understood that Hamas, the Sunni fundamentalist organization active in both Gaza and the West Bank, could develop into a pro-Iranian client, overpowering what was perceived in the Arab world to be the legal representative of the Palestinians, the Palestinian Authority (PA), led by Fatah.[19] Thus the Saudis had concerns about the growing power of a nascent pro-Iranian, Shi'i axis, which might affect various arenas such as Lebanon, Iraq and the Palestinian territories. In addition, Iran's systematic development of a nuclear capability, although declared to be purely peaceful, was worrisome.[20]

Saudi leaders faced a dilemma concerning how to meet these various challenges. One option was to help foster an anti-Iranian coalition comprised of pro-Western states, which would effectively contain Iran. The Bush administration was in favour of such a program, and the Saudi Adviser for National Security Bandar bin Sultan, a former ambassador to the US, seemed to be the key Saudi figure in its promotion. On 6 September 2006, he met with an Israeli

---

[17] *Gulf States Newsletter*, 23 (823), 18 February 2008.
[18] See Joseph McMillan, 'Saudi Arabia and Iraq', *United States Institute of Peace*, Special Report No. 157, January 2006; John Alterman, 'Iraq and the Gulf States: The Balance of Power,' *United States Institute for Peace*, Special Report No. 189, August 2007.
[19] Martin Valbjorn, Andre Bank, 'Signs of a new Arab Cold War', *Middle East Report* (2007).
[20] Simon Henderson, 'The Elephant in the Gulf: Arab States and the Iran Nuclear Program', *Policy Watch*, The Washington Institute for Near East Policy, 21 December 2005; Ambassador Turki al-Faisal, Speech to the Phoenix Committee on Foreign Relations, SUSRIS, 8 February 2006, www.Saudi-us-relations.org/fact-book/speeches2006/060207-turki-cfr.html; Seymour Hersch, 'Last Stand', *The New Yorker*, 9 July 2006.

cabinet minister, Avi Dichter, in Amman.[21] However, there were no clear indications that the Saudis favoured advancing further in this direction. During the fall of 2006, the Saudis preferred to set up high-level contacts with Iranian diplomats, in meetings that took place in Riyadh, Baghdad and Beirut. This was an attempt to calm the Iraqi and Lebanese arenas, with Iranian help. Moreover, in October 2006, the Saudis convened a meeting of senior Iraqi clerics in order to promote a thaw in tensions among Iraq's major religious groups.[22] Hence, one can conclude that the Saudis resorted to the practice they have known best: an attempt to coordinate regional events.

The components of this Saudi coordination policy in 2006–2007 were not officially announced, and the Kingdom did not turn back to the policy of participating in an anti-Iranian camp. Washington believed that Riyadh would continue to support an anti-Iranian coalition. However, it seems that Riyadh understood that it would be useless to object openly to and resist the Iranian nuclear initiative, whether its goals were peaceful or aggressive, especially after Saudi leaders realized that US and European governments had failed to convince Tehran to stop its nuclear program. In addition, it seems that the Saudi leaders, King Abdullah himself among them, feared an Iranian backlash against Saudi and other Gulf Cooperation Council (GCC) targets. In a later interview, King Abdullah explained the policy of publicly avoiding criticism of Iran's nuclear initiative. He stated,

> We have advised the Iranians not to expose the Gulf region to dangers that would affect this or that country... any country that would carry out unwise actions will be held accountable for them by countries of the region. Iran is a Muslim neighbour. I explained to the Iranian emissary, Ali Larijani, that the Saudi policies are not to interfere in anyone's affairs and not to assist anyone who behaves in a hostile manner, be it Iran or any other country. Saudi Arabia does not want anyone to display hostility towards it, or its brethren in the GCC or towards the other countries of the Arab world who have mutual defence agreements with it.[23]

The message that Abdullah was trying to convey was that Saudi Arabia would not press Iran to change its policies or initiatives. Abdullah's only expectation was that the Kingdom, or any other GCC states, should not be attacked. This was the first principle of Saudi policy.

The other component of Saudi policy was limiting Iranian influence in various Middle Eastern arenas. The Kingdom was willing to cooperate with Iran to settle regional conflicts, but made it clear that it would not tolerate an Iranian takeover. This policy was also raised in the discussions that King Abdullah had with Iranian President Mahmud Ahmadinejad in Mecca in March 2007. Both leaders agreed to curb tensions between Sunnis and Shi'is in Iraq, and discussed Palestinian issues as well as ways to end the stand-off in Lebanon between Hizbullah and the Lebanese government. The Saudi press agency also stated that Abdullah had secured support from Ahmadinejad for the 2002 Arab Peace Initiative, which, in

---

[21] Seymour Hersh, 'The Redirection', *The New Yorker*, 3 March 2007; see also Raghida Dergham, 'The Arab Moderates Locked between Two Options: the US and Iran', *Dar Al-Hayat* (Lebanon), 18 January 2008.
[22] Habib Trabolsi, 'Iraq Clerics Convene in Mecca in Bid to Halt Bloodshed', *Agence France Presse,* 18 October 2006.
[23] Y. Carmon, H. Varulkar, Y. Mansharof and Y. Yehoshua, 'The Middle East on a Collision Course (2): The Saudi Position', MEMRI Inquiry and Analysis, no. 319, 31 January 2007. Available at http://www.memri.org/bin/articles.cgi?Area = ia&ID = IA31907&Page = archives.

one way or another, recognizes Israel. An Iranian official, however, contradicted these statements by saying that Iran had not in fact agreed to such a policy.[24]

The Saudis then embarked on several initiatives regarding other Middle Eastern arenas that will only be mentioned briefly here. In Lebanon, the Saudis dispatched an ambassador to engage in contacts with both Hizbullah and the Sinyura government, in an attempt to calm tensions, but with little effect. The Sunni radical group known as the 'Islamic army' or '*Fatah al-Islam*' might have been instigated by the Saudis in an attempt to strengthen the Sunni side of the Lebanese political sphere, but the exact nature of their contacts is unclear.[25] The main arena for Saudi intervention was Israeli–Arab affairs. The Saudis were ready to reintroduce the 2002 initiative for reconfirmation in the inter-Arab summit that convened in Riyadh in March 2007. However, a new policy component of this plan was a readiness to mediate the inter-Palestinian dispute between the radical Islamic Hamas and the secular Fatah group, a dispute in which Hamas seemed to be gaining strength. In 2006, it won a majority of seats in the Palestinian National Council, with its leader Ismail Haniyyah becoming the Palestinian Authority's prime minister. Its political and military branches gained overwhelming amounts of support, allowing it to overpower Fatah at the street level. Moreover, it was supported both financially and ideologically by Iran, despite the fact that it was Sunni. It was, therefore, important for the Saudis to calm the situation, limit Hamas's growing influence and create a new balance between Hamas and Fatah.

The Saudis hoped that they would be able to ease the tension by adopting a policy of mediation. They did not, however, have a clear plan for such mediation. Moreover, they did not seem to have sufficient knowledge about the dispute or sufficient intelligence about Hamas's real strength or political ambitions. However, King Abdullah, who initiated this mediation, hoped that the holy atmosphere in Mecca coupled with his own presence there, would be enough stimulus to aid the two parties in mending the fences between them in the meeting, which was held late February 2007.

After several days of negotiation, the two parties agreed to establish a unity government. Ismail Haniyyah of Hamas would remain as the prime minister, with a deputy from Fatah. There would also be an officially mandated division of power within the government, with eight ministers from Hamas and six ministers from Fatah. The important ministries of Finance and Foreign Affairs would be handed over to outside specialists, so that the appointment of ministers would not be an issue of contention. King Abdullah also promised three quarters of a billion dollars in foreign aid to the unity government, which was far more than the Iranians had offered to Hamas. One more point was the demand that Hamas recognize and accept the Palestinian Authorities' agreements with the international communities and Israel. Hamas's downfall was that it could not accept such an agreement. In the discussion, certain formulations had been agreed on, stating that Hamas would 'honour' what the PA had committed itself to fulfil vis-à-vis Israel at an earlier stage of the Palestinian–Israeli peace process. In interviews, however, Hamas insisted that it had not been forced to recognize Israel and, furthermore, never would. Despite the signing of the Mecca agreement, this issue remained disputed.[26]

---

[24] Saudi–US Relations Information Service, 5 March 2007.
[25] Fida Aytami, *al-Jihadiyyun Fi Lubnan* (London: Dar al-Saqi, 2008).
[26] 'The Text of the Palestinian-Mecca Agreement', *Khaleej Times*, 9 February 2007; *Haaretz*, 13 March 2007; *Haaretz*, 30 March 2007.

When the agreement was concluded, it seemed that it would hold water. The Saudis met with Ahmadinejad on 4 March 2007, and held the inter-Arab summit of the Arab League in Riyadh at the end of the same month. At this summit, the participants reconfirmed the 2002 Arab initiative. No changes were introduced to the plan itself, but the conference agreed that Egyptian and Jordanian emissaries would visit Israel and urge it to accept the initiative. Thus, the Saudis included a new element, namely inter-Palestinian mediation, as a means of strengthening the grounds for an Israeli–Arab thaw. The question then arises, to what extent was this renewed initiative with the inter-Palestinian thaw really a drive for a new Arab–Israeli peace process? The Saudis were ready to intervene in local, specific arenas, but not in the broader contours of the Arab–Israeli conflict. Israel was still not invited and was not brought into the discussion, and it seemed that the Saudis were still adhering to the policy of using the Arab–Israeli peace process as a means of improving relations among Arab parties. The Saudis hoped that this would lead to the reconvening of an Arab comprehensive attitude, aligning Arab states along a unified policy line, including Fatah and Hamas. This seemed to be their main interest in this case as well. Moreover, while the Saudis were still interested in military and political cooperation with the US, as in the case of the Iraqi arena, they were, however, ready to disregard US objections to the inclusion of Hamas in Arab–Israeli discussions.

During his meeting with Ahmadinejad in March 2007, King Abdullah commented that the US occupation of Iraq was illegal. It was clearly a signal to Iranian ears that the Saudis were ready to get closer to an Iranian view that the US's extended stay in Iraq was illegal and that US forces should be withdrawn. This view was contradictory to their messages urging the US to reinforce their presence in Iraq. However, this policy was aimed at indicating Riyadh's interest in cooperation with Tehran and that Saudi Arabia did not see itself as a member of an anti-Iranian coalition. During these weeks, Washington learned Saudi Arabia's actual position, including both their criticism of the US presence in Iraq and of their attempt to bring Hamas in the game. Thus, a certain disappointment developed in Washington in regards to Riyadh. Martin Indyk, a former high official in the Clinton administration, wrote in the *Washington Post* that the US policy of isolating Iran, which had been promoted by the Saudi National Security Adviser, apparently had not been successful. He then wrote, 'We seem to have backed the wrong Saudi', indicating that King Abdullah was not ready to pursue Bandar's line.[27] Moreover, the fact that Hamas had been brought into the negotiations, while Israel remained officially excluded, coupled with the fact that the initiative did not present a practical plan for negotiations, led Israeli leaders to be apprehensive in accepting the initiative. The initiative did receive some encouraging words from Prime Minister Ehud Olmert and Foreign Minister Tzipi Livni to the effect that it had interesting components and should be examined. However, this was simply lip service to the possibility that Israel would still be included in a peace initiative with the Saudis.[28]

The Saudis apparently thought that preventing US involvement in the Arab–Israeli arena at that point would help achieve Saudi interests. As it became clear, the assessment of the leaders, notably King Abdullah, proved unrealistic.

---

[27] Martin Indyk, 'The Honeymoon's Over for Bush and the Saudis', *Washington Post*, 29 April 2007.
[28] *San Francisco Chronicle*, 27 March 2007; *Haaretz*, 30 March 2007.

Moreover, their assets as mediators did not impress their radical interlocutors. Thus, the Saudis failed in the inter-Palestinian arena; In June 2007, Hamas captured power in the Gaza Strip, ousting Fatah from its positions there, nullifying the unity government that had been loosely agreed upon in the Mecca meeting. Thereon, the Palestinian territories experienced a deep split between Fatah and Hamas. Fatah, in its capacity as leader of the PA, ruled over the West Bank, while Hamas ruled over Gaza. Saudi disappointment with regards to the Palestinians was made evident in June 2007 in the words of Foreign Minister Saud al-Faisal, who stated, 'the Palestinians have come close to putting by themselves the last nail in the coffin of the Palestinian cause'.[29] In Lebanon, the Saudis also failed in suppressing Hizbullah, who kept growing. In 2008, it was in fact Qatar who negotiated between Hizbullah and the Lebanese government, coming to an agreement, making it possible for Hizbullah to strengthen its position in the Lebanese government, giving it a further opportunity to secure its perceived victory in the 2009 Lebanese elections.[30] From a Saudi viewpoint, it was a fruitless attempt to mediate problems in Lebanon. Only in Iraq, thanks to the ongoing activities of the US army, together with factions who had turned in favour of the al-Maliki government, did the situation stabilize. The Saudi policy of encouraging the US surge in Iraq had a fruitful outcome.

In summation, the Saudis' coordination efforts were hardly successful in 2007. The fact that they were merely passive spectators in the December 2007 US-initiated talks in Annapolis between the Palestinians and Israelis is, in itself, very telling. It demonstrates that the Saudis had nothing to offer at this point, and that the US could not replace the vacuum that the Saudi failure of coordination had left.

Having said that, the fact remains that Saudi leaders managed to create the posture of regional coordinator; a status that has the ability to link Arab states and superpowers together in a coordinated attempt to bring stability to the Middle East. Moreover, from a Saudi viewpoint, failure was only temporary. The Saudis tried to re-awaken the 2002 peace initiative against the backdrop of the Israeli–Hamas wars of September 2008 and January 2009. Apparently, Riyadh's inclination to use coordination as its primary regional strategy did not cease. Every few years, the Saudis renew this attempt.

Acknowledgements

The author would like to extend his greatest thanks to Dr Paul Marcus for his invaluable assistance, which made it possible to carry out the research for this article. He would also like extend his thanks to Eli Sperling for his assistance in preparing this manuscript and bringing it the present standard.

---

[29] 'A "Nail in Palestinian Coffin"', GulfNews.com, 16 July 2007, http://archive.gulfnews.com/articles/07/06/16/10132824.html (accessed 9 April 2008).

[30] On Qatar's Initiatives see Robert F. Worth, 'Qatar, Playing All Sides, Is a Nonstop Mediator', *New York Times*, 9 July 2008.

Dubai and the United Arab Emirates: Security Threats

CHRISTOPHER M. DAVIDSON

ABSTRACT *The United Arab Emirates' (UAE) wealthiest emirate, Abu Dhabi, has built up the UAE Armed Forces in recent decades by procuring some of the finest military hardware available. This has provided the UAE with a strong defence shield and has undoubtedly reduced the threat of foreign invasion. However, the UAE's hard security capabilities are either insufficient or inappropriate for countering remaining regional threats from Iran or, to a lesser extent, other Arab states. As such, the UAE has had little option but to remain under a Western military umbrella. Moreover, as an unfortunate but perhaps inescapable hidden cost of its emergence as the region's premier free port, for many years the UAE's second wealthiest emirate of Dubai has attracted the attention of both international criminal and terrorist organisations, many of which have exploited the emirate's laissez-faire attitudes and impressive physical infrastructure to set up various smuggling, gun-running, human-trafficking, and money-laundering operations. Despite Dubai's undoubted usefulness to such groups, the final section of this article will reveal that the UAE has been unable to remain completely in the eye of the storm and has suffered from a number of terrorist attacks on its own soil*

Introduction

The federation of United Arab Emirates (UAE) has emerged as one of the Arab Gulf's most successful post-oil states. With political stability guaranteed by highly resilient, dynamic, and popular traditional monarchies,[1] the UAE has been able to press forward with developing a diverse economic base that up until the global credit crunch enjoyed strong rates of growth and boasted an impressive track record in attracting foreign direct investment. By 2008, the UAE's second largest constituent emirate, Dubai, was drawing over 97 per cent of its GDP from non-oil sectors,[2] including a real estate industry, a world class luxury tourism industry, an international financial centre, and a range of re-exporting and other commercial activities based out of international 'free zones'.[3] While the real

---

[1] For a discussion of monarchical survival in the UAE and the 'ruling bargain' that exists between the ruling families and regular citizens see Christopher M. Davidson, *The United Arab Emirates: A Study in Survival* (Boulder, CO: Lynne Rienner, 2005), pp. 65–119. For a more specific discussion of monarchical survival in the emirate of Dubai see Christopher M. Davidson, *Dubai: The Vulnerability of Success* (New York: Columbia University Press, 2008), pp. 137–177.
[2] Estimate based on data supplied by the UAE Ministry of Economy, 2008. Also see Davidson, *Dubai*, p. 135.
[3] For a discussion of Dubai's development model see Martin Hvidt, 'Public-Private Ties and their Contribution to Development: The Case of Dubai', *Middle Eastern Studies*, 43(4) (2007); pp. 48–49; Davidson, *Dubai*, pp. 113–135.

estate bubble has now burst and there has been an overextension of leisure and tourism megaprojects, Dubai and its neighbouring emirates have historically confounded their critics, and are likely to rebound when the international conditions improve. However, long-term investor confidence in these strategies remains in question given the UAE's awkward geographic location close to regional hot spots, and given the rising level of other security concerns, both external and internal. Should such threats escalate, and ever directly or indirectly involve the UAE, then the federation's carefully cultivated reputation for political and economic stability would likely decline, thereby severely impacting upon its fragile foreign investment-dependent development trajectory.

As the first section of this article will demonstrate, the UAE's wealthiest emirate, Abu Dhabi, has built up the UAE Armed Forces in recent decades by procuring some of the finest military hardware available. This has placed the UAE in a much stronger position, especially with the menace of Iraq having subsided since Saddam Hussein's fall in 2003. Nevertheless, the UAE's defensive capabilities are either insufficient or inappropriate for countering remaining regional threats from Iran or, to a lesser extent, other Arab states. As such, the federation has had little option but to remain under a Western military umbrella. This not only undermines the UAE's current preference for neutrality, but also may weaken the legitimacy of a federal government that has traditionally sought close relations with the Arab nationalist republics and the Arab League.

Moreover, as an unfortunate but perhaps inescapable hidden cost of its emergence as the region's premier free port, for many years Dubai has attracted the attention of both international criminal and terrorist organisations, many of which have exploited the emirate's laissez-faire attitudes and impressive physical infrastructure[4] to set up various smuggling, gun-running, human-trafficking, and money-laundering operations.[5] Most significantly, despite Dubai's undoubted usefulness to such groups, the final section of this article will reveal that the UAE has been unable to remain completely in the eye of the storm and has suffered from a number of terrorist attacks on its own soil.

Military Power

The first formal security force tasked with protecting the sheikhdoms of the lower Gulf was set up in the late 1950s. By the late 1960s, the British-officered Trucial Oman Scouts (previously known as Levies) were being funded almost exclusively by Abu Dhabi, as its oil revenues began to accumulate.[6] Britain had anticipated that all regional divisions of the scouts would be amalgamated into one unified force following her withdrawal from the lower Gulf in 1971. However, the newly independent—albeit federated—emirates preferred to set up their own security organisations. By the end of the year, the Dubai Defence Force (DDF) had 500 men and had purchased a number of patrol boats, fighter aircraft, and tanks.[7]

---

[4] For a discussion of Dubai's infrastructural development see Davidson, *Dubai*, pp. 91–99, 106–113. For a discussion of Dubai's early commitment to laissez-faire attitudes see Davidson, *Dubai*, pp. 67–69.

[5] For greater detail on such operations see Christopher M. Davidson, 'Dubai: The Security Dimensions of the Region's Premier Free Port', *Middle East Policy*, 15(2) (2008), pp. 144–152.

[6] Easa Saleh Al-Gurg, *The Wells of Memory* (London: John Murray, 1998), p. 117.

[7] Graeme Wilson, *Rashid's Legacy: The Genesis of the Maktoum Family and the History of Dubai* (Dubai: Media Prima, 2006), p. 307.

Although by the late 1970s the DDF had approximately doubled in size, its commanders accepted that it was impractical to create a full-scale army and thus they preferred to concentrate on buying high quality equipment so that Dubai would have a lightly armed task force capable of rapid deployment in the event of emergency.[8] As such, by the time that the DDF was finally absorbed by Abu Dhabi's much larger Union Defence Force in the mid-1990s, it had become a small but well-trained force with a tightly organised structure (including a specific women's unit[9]) and superior hardware. Problematically, however, given that Dubai had been procuring equipment independently of Abu Dhabi for over 25 years, this meant that the newly reinforced and genuinely federal UAE Armed Forces was made up of largely incompatible hardware and munitions. Perhaps as a symbol of autonomy, for much of the 1980s Dubai had been sourcing its armaments from the USSR, North Korea,[10] and other Warsaw Pact suppliers, whereas Abu Dhabi had been dealing almost exclusively with Western European and North American manufacturers. Even more incongruous was the equipment used by the various other emirate-level defence forces that had followed Dubai's lead and had also agreed to integrate. Most remarkably, the ruling families of Umm al-Qawain and Ajman offered the UAE Armed Forces the services of their predominantly untrained retainers armed with little more than antiquated rifles.[11]

Given the task of phasing out such mismatched weaponry and upgrading Abu Dhabi's existing stocks, the UAE Armed Forces' chiefs of staff since this period have secured military budgets of between $2 and $2.5 billion per annum,[12] have expanded their personnel to over 55,000,[13] and have frequently managed to gain permission from Western governments to purchase the most sophisticated armaments—most of which are normally restricted to NATO allies.[14] In particular, the UAE Armed Forces has procured $3 billion worth of Leclerc main battle tanks from France's Nexter corporation.[15] Interestingly, given that the custom-made UAE versions have additional armour and upgraded guns for desert conditions, they are actually superior to the French Army's Leclercs. In addition, the DDF's old Russian-manufactured BMP-3 armoured personnel carriers have largely been replaced by about 100 Turkish-supplied Savunma Sistemleri carriers. Courtesy of France's Sagem Défense Sécurité, individual soldiers will soon be benefiting from modular infrared units that will allow improved battlefield navigation between men. Moreover, the UAE Armed Forces' artillery capabilities have been greatly enhanced following the purchase of howitzers from South Africa's Denel corporation and from the Royal Netherlands Army. Similarly, the UAE's air force has taken delivery of a large quantity of advanced equipment, including

---

[8] Personal interviews with military advisors, Dubai, January 2007.
[9] Wilson, *Rashid's Legacy*, p. 523. This unit was created at the time of the Kuwaiti crisis.
[10] Hendrik Van Der Meulen, 'The Role of Tribal and Kinship Ties in the Politics of the United Arab Emirates' (PhD thesis, The Fletcher School of Law and Diplomacy, 1997), p. 44.
[11] Personal interviews with military advisors, Dubai, January 2007; Wilson, *Rashid's Legacy*, pp. 343–344.
[12] 'UAE Military Buildup', *Janes Defense Weekly*, 7 February 2007, pp. 1–16
[13] Personal interviews with military advisors, Dubai, January 2007; Van Der Meulen, 'The Role of Tribal', p. 95. Prior to amalgamation, in 1995 the Union Defence Force had about 45,000 personnel.
[14] In contrast, many non-NATO states are not eligible to purchase the most sophisticated equipment unless they receive governmental oversight from the supplier countries. Personal interviews with military advisors, Abu Dhabi, December 2004; Abdulkhaleq Abdulla, 'Political Dependency: The Case of the United Arab Emirates' (PhD thesis, Georgetown University, 1985), p. 208.
[15] Oxford Business Group, 'Emerging Emirates' Report (London: 2000), pp. 58–59.

French-supplied Mirage 2000-9s complete with laser targeting pods and precision-guided missiles, British Aerospace Hawk 128s, Sikorsky Black Hawk helicopters, and about 30 Apache AH64 gunships.[16] Furthermore, given the UAE's recent involvement in several international peacekeeping operations,[17] its air force has needed to improve its long-range capabilities and has duly begun to acquire a number of heavy airlift carriers from the Ukraine. Most notably, the UAE Armed Forces' massive purchase of 80 F16E Desert Falcons in 2004 has made the UAE one of Lockheed Martins' best customers.[18] A few dozen of these have already arrived at Abu Dhabi's Al-Dhafrah airbase, and over the next few years the arrival of the remainder should make the UAE's air force the second most advanced in the Middle East, after Israel.[19]

Unlike most other militaries in the developing world, the UAE Armed Forces has committed itself heavily to purchasing custom-made equipment manufactured by joint ventures between Western arms companies and domestic enterprises. With the reasoning that such products will be better suited to combat conditions in the Middle Eastern theatre, while also promoting the diversification of the economy and generating employment across the federation, the strategy would seem to have found much favour in both government and industry circles. Specifically, in cooperation with a German company, the UAE has begun to manufacture its own military motorcycles and its new Guardian jeeps. Similarly, the air force has commissioned a project to produce the 'Mako' light aircraft to be used for desert reconnaissance, and has consulted with a British company over the development of Al-Hakeem precision guided missiles, and with the European MBDA Corporation over the design of UAE-specific Black Shaheen cruise missiles.[20] Although the UAE's navy has historically been small, with only one marine battalion and one naval squadron, and of less immediate concern than the army or air force, it would appear that the same collaborative strategy is being applied. As part of the UAE Armed Forces' 'Project Baynunah', in conjunction with a French manufacturer and the new Abu Dhabi Shipbuilding Company, a number of new frigates and corvettes in addition to some small amphibious craft and two-person mini submarines are under construction at Abu Dhabi's Mussafah facility, and should be delivered by 2010.[21]

With the UAE Armed Forces' main priority being improved defence, these land, air, and naval procurements will soon be complemented by far more advanced attack warning systems. In particular, a large underground airbase is under construction somewhere in the southern desert of Abu Dhabi. This will have a hardened shelter to allow the air force to survive a direct assault[22] and will be able to link up with an integrated electronic warfare system supplied by Northrop Grumman and a number of newly acquired airborne early warning and control aircrafts (AWACs) provided by Boeing. In addition, underwater surveillance systems are being installed at most of the UAE's naval bases, courtesy of the German Konigsberg corporation, and the UAE Armed Forces will soon benefit

---

[16] Personal interviews with military advisors, Abu Dhabi, March 2007.
[17] Including Somalia in 1992, Bosnia in 1995, and Kosovo in 1999. See Davidson, *Dubai*, p. 172.
[18] Personal interviews with military advisors, Dubai, January 2007; *Counterpunch*, 4 December 2004.
[19] 'UAE Military Buildup', *Janes Defense Weekly*, 7 February 2007.
[20] Personal interviews with academic observers, Dubai, January 2007.
[21] Personal interviews with academic observers, Dubai, June 2006.
[22] 'UAE Military Buildup', *Janes Defense Weekly*, 7 February 2007, pp. 1–16

from strategic data from a new Space Reconnaissance Centre that is located in Abu Dhabi and has access to Russian and North Korean satellite feeds.[23]

The Western Security Umbrella

Despite the absorption of various emirate-level armed forces and several expensive upgrades, the UAE's military strength remains weak. There is considerable concern that the UAE Armed Forces has insufficient personnel with the necessary training to operate such sophisticated hardware. Moreover, there is a fear that given the financially privileged backgrounds of most UAE nationals, most of those employed by the UAE Armed Forces would not actually stand their ground in the event of combat.[24] Indeed, given that military salaries are often much lower than other incomes, especially those derived from family businesses and landlordship, a career in the armed forces is often looked upon as a source of additional status rather than as a source of livelihood. Thus, for lower and middle-ranking servicemen, military misconduct would not lead to complete socio-economic destruction. Perhaps most worryingly, however, as with many other public sector professions in the UAE, including the civil service and the police, there are thought to be a growing number of expatriates employed by the UAE Armed Forces. Certainly, of the 55,000 military personnel, it has been estimated that over 15,000 are foreigners, most of whom are Yemenis and Egyptians.[25] Understandably this has led to much disquiet over the dependency on mercenaries, who cannot be relied upon to the same extent as indigenous professional soldiers.

As such, despite the obvious costs to their legitimacy resources, in particular their commitment to the Palestinian nation and other Arab and Muslim causes,[26] the UAE's ruling families have had little choice but to remain under the security umbrella of Western militaries that are predominantly made up of non-Arab, non-Muslim personnel, and which are directed by governments that are in a *de facto* alliance with Israel. Most notably, France, which has been the UAE Armed Forces' greatest arms supplier since the 1993 Leclerc deal, has agreed to deploy 75,000 troops to the UAE in the event of an emergency, and it is believed that Britain signed a similar defence pact in the late 1990s, albeit without specifying exact troop numbers.[27] Such arrangements have allowed the UAE Armed Forces to assume a more realistic delaying role[28]—should UAE territory be invaded, they can serve to slow down hostile forces until superpower reinforcements arrive.

Since the declaration of the 'war on terror' in September 2001 and the subsequent American invasions of Afghanistan and Iraq, the UAE, or more exactly Dubai with its advanced infrastructure, has been able to provide the Western militaries with an important regional base for their operations. Although never publicly supporting the United States on the same scale as Qatar and Bahrain, which between them house an entire air wing of the US Air Force and the US Navy's Fifth Fleet, in addition to a CIA base and an array of US special forces

---

[23] Personal interviews with military advisors, Dubai, January 2007.
[24] Davidson, *Dubai*, p. 267.
[25] Personal interviews with military advisors, Dubai, January 2007.
[26] See Davidson, *The UAE*, pp. 80–82.
[27] Oxford Business Group, 'Emerging Emirates', pp. 58–59.
[28] Sean Foley, 'The United Arab Emirates: Political Issues and Security Dilemmas', *Middle East Review of International Affairs,* 3(1) (1998), pp. 1–13..

living in compounds,[29] the UAE has nevertheless discreetly made many of its facilities available and will soon host a permanent French military base. Ironically, given the US Congress' hostility to the Dubai Ports World Company's attempted takeover of a number of US ports in early 2006,[30] Dubai's ports have proved indispensable in the war on terror. Notably, in mid-2006 George Bush stated that 'the UAE is a key partner for our navy in a critical region, and outside of our own country Dubai services more of our own ships than any other country in the world'. Similarly, US Rear Admiral Michael Millar commented on the takeover fiasco by declaring that 'in a sense Dubai Ports World has already been responsible for American security because we dock here in Dubai, and from personal experience I can confirm they are wonderfully efficient'.[31] In particular it is thought that Port Jebel Ali is the US Navy's most highly visited liberty port (a port which allows access to friendly foreign navies) with warships such as the USS *John Kennedy* regularly being refuelled or being serviced in Dubai's dry docks,[32] which remains one of only two ship repair yards in the Gulf.[33] It has been estimated that around 4000 US sailors come ashore at Jebel Ali each year, with many revealing in anonymous US Navy surveys that Dubai is their favourite stop-off location due to the availability of alcohol and nightclubs.[34] Moreover, Jebel Ali together with Port Rashid also serve as major transit hubs for US military goods, with most such freight being delivered by three inconspicuous European shipping companies.[35] On a lesser, but still significant scale, Fujairah's deep water port on the UAE's Indian Ocean coastline is also used by the US Navy, with the emirate's major hotels even having a longstanding arrangement to bloc-let many of their rooms to Navy personnel,[36] in much the same way as some of Abu Dhabi's hotels, which have on occasion billeted US soldiers on leave from Iraq.[37]

The use of air infrastructure has also proved to be a key area of cooperation, with Dubai International Airport's Terminal 2 having probably become the busiest airport involved in the war on terror, while the newer Rashid Terminal 1, built in 1998, has been allowed to concentrate on servicing Dubai's more wholesome tourist, business, and transit flights. Significantly, Terminal 2 is one of the few airports in the world that has regular flights to Baghdad and Kabul—offered by African Express, Al-Ishtar, Jupiter, and other somewhat low-key airlines. While some of the passengers are Iraqis or Afghanis hoping to visit their relatives, the bulk of the $400 seats are reserved for US military personnel or for employees of big contractors such as Halliburton. Also lucrative have been Terminal 2's war-related freight facilities, with cargo space on such flights selling for about $2 per kilo, and with many commercial companies shipping US military goods (including armoured vehicles) via the terminal. It has been alleged that US military personnel have been working out of the airport offices of a major multinational courier company so as to bypass Dubai's customs' regulations and

---

[29] Personal interviews with US diplomats, London, July 2006.
[30] Davidson, *Dubai*, p. 108.
[31] 'Dubai Ports Crisis', *Emirates Today*, 26 April 2006, p. 1.
[32] Personal interviews with US diplomats, London, July 2006.
[33] The other dry docks being in Bahrain. See Davidson, *Dubai*, p. 106.
[34] Personal interviews with US diplomats, London, December 2006.
[35] One company being British, one Danish, and the other Norwegian. Personal interviews with military advisors, Dubai, January 2007.
[36] Personal interviews with academic observers, Fujairah, June 2006.
[37] Personal observations, Abu Dhabi, December 2004.

thereby smooth the clearance process for such goods. On a more formal level, Abu Dhabi has made available its airbase in Al-Dhafrah to the US Air Force and to the CIA, with RQ-4 Global Hawk unmanned reconnaissance aircraft being stationed there and with KC-10 tanker aircraft using the base to support operations in Afghanistan. Embarrassingly, in the summer of 2005, it was revealed that U2 aircraft were also being serviced in Al-Dhafrah, following the crash landing of one of the spy planes on its return to Abu Dhabi from a mission in Afghanistan. The incident prompted the US Air Force to confirm that its 380th Air Expeditionary Wing had been based there since 2002.[38] In total, it is thought that there are currently over 100 US military personnel stationed in Al-Dhafrah as of mid-2009.[39]

Iran—A History of Threats

Dubai has historically enjoyed fairly warm relations with Iran, given that many of its immigrant merchants are of Persian origin. Iran has also long been the emirate's principal regional trading partner and Dubai chose to remain neutral in the Iran–Iraq War.[40] Nevertheless, for the federation as whole, the greatest external threat since its inception—and therefore the UAE Armed Forces' greatest fear—has always been an attack from Iran. Spanning over a century and three very different eras of Persian and Iranian administration, a number of islands belonging to Sharjah and Ra's al-Khaimah—the UAE's third and fourth most populous emirates—have been claimed and counter-claimed, and remain a source of great dispute between the UAE and Iran. Worryingly, the largest of these islands is less than 60 miles from downtown Dubai, and is currently occupied by Iranian military personnel. In many ways the UAE's most recent efforts to solidify its Western military umbrella and to improve its war on terror collaboration have exacerbated this risk as the US continues to challenge Tehran over its domestic energy policies.

During the mid-1880s, the Qajari Persian government expanded its influence to the southern coast of Iran and its soldiers occupied the formerly Arab-controlled mainland towns of Lingah, Junj, and Luft, in addition to several Arab-inhabited islands in the lower Gulf, including Qishm and Sirri.[41] Importantly, four smaller but strategically located islands close to the Straits of Hormuz remained in Arab hands following a British warning delivered to Tehran.[42] Even so, by the end of the nineteenth century, Persia had renewed its claims to Henjam, Abu Musa, Tunb al-Kuhbra and Tunb al-Sughra,[43] with Britain finally appearing to acknowledge the Qajari's new sphere of influence.

By the late 1930s, with Persia's name changed to Iran, with nationalist sentiments running high, and with Britain concentrating on developments in Nazi Germany, Reza Shah was encouraged to switch his ambitions to Bahrain—a much greater prize. His son, Muhammad Reza Shah Pahlavi, maintained pressure on Bahrain for many more years following his Anglo-Soviet assisted succession

---

[38] 'US Air Crash', *International Herald Tribune*, 22 June 2005, p. 1.
[39] 'UAE Military Buildup', *Janes Defense Weekly*, 7 February 2007, pp. 1–16; personal interviews with US diplomats, London, July 2006.
[40] Davidson, *Dubai*, p. 227.
[41] *Ibid.*, p. 72.
[42] John B. Kelly, *Britain and the Persian Gulf* (Oxford: Oxford University Press, 1968), pp. 92–93; Al-Gurg, *The Wells of Memory*, p. 5.
[43] Al-Gurg, *The Wells of Memory*, p. 5.

during the Second World War, stating in his own book, *Mission of My Country*, that his divine purpose was to be the saviour of both Iran and the Gulf.[44] By the late 1960s, during the period of federal negotiations preceding British withdrawal, the Iranian Foreign Ministry even claimed that 'Iran has always been opposed to colonialism in all forms, and the so-called federation of the Gulf emirates, by annexing the island of Bahrain to it, is considered a matter which cannot be acceptable to the Iranian government'.[45] However, by the time of Bahrain's declaration of independence in mid-1971 and its concurrent international recognition,[46] Iran had little choice but to return its attention to the lower Gulf, with Abu Musa being regarded as the most attractive consolation prize.[47] Ominously, Tehran informed Britain that it must stop flying over the area, and when Britain uncharacteristically complied[48] there was considerable concern that a secret deal had been struck in which Iran would be allowed to occupy the island when Britain finally left the Gulf.[49] During the months preceding the formation of the UAE in late 1971 such rumours gathered pace, fuelled by news of Britain's completion of the sale of over $200 million worth of Chieftain tanks to Iran, and confirmed by a British envoy's instruction to the rulers that they should negotiate directly with Iran.[50]

Reportedly rejecting an offer of over $30 million,[51] the Qawasim rulers of Sharjah and Ra's al-Khaimah refused Iran's proposed compensations,[52] and Iran duly invaded Abu Musa along with both of the Tunb islands on the eve of Britain's departure. Muhammad Reza Shah claimed this was a necessary action to prevent any 'unfriendly power' from gaining control of the Straits.[53] Following a brief struggle involving some fatalities, the ruler of Sharjah[54] reluctantly agreed to allow Iran to establish permanent bases on certain parts of Abu Musa in exchange for a financial aid package of nine annual payments of about $2 million.[55] Importantly, the more resolute ruler of Ra's al-Khaimah[56] refused to come to an agreement over the Tunb islands, and the UAE duly reported all three islands to the United Nations, requesting international arbitration. Since the formation of the Gulf Cooperation Council in 1981 the liberation of these territories has remained a central component of the six members' foreign policy objectives; however in many ways Iran has managed to extend its control even further.[57] Notably, in 1992, Iran reneged on its 1971 deal with Sharjah, as Revolutionary Guards began to encroach further on Abu Musa's towns, requesting all UAE nationals to obtain

---

[44] Wilson, *Rashid's Legacy*, p. 260.
[45] Ibid., p. 295.
[46] Davidson, *Dubai*, p. 63.
[47] Wilson, *Rashid's Legacy*, pp. 90, 295, 332.
[48] Ibid., pp. 325–326.
[49] Such rumours had begun in Ra's al-Khaimah earlier in the 1960s. See Donald Hawley, *The Emirates: Witness to a Metamorphosis* (Norwich: Michael Russell, 2007), pp. 188–190.
[50] Britain's special envoy was the former British Political Resident in the Gulf, Sir William Luce. It was reported that Luce even brought an Iranian military official with him on his visits to the rulers of Sharjah and Ra's al-Khaimah. Richard A. Mobley, 'The Tunbs and Abu Musa Islands: Britain's Perspective', *Middle East Journal*, 57(4) (2003), pp. 628–644; Wilson, *Rashid's Legacy*, pp. 325–236.
[51] Mobley, 'The Tunbs', pp. 628–644.
[52] Kelly, *Britain and the Persian Gulf*, pp. 92–93.
[53] See Walter Laquer, *The Struggle for the Middle East* (London: Routledge, 1969).
[54] Sheikh Khalid bin Muhammad Al-Qasimi.
[55] Tim Niblock (ed.), *Social and Economic Development in the Arab Gulf* (London: Croom Helm, 1980), pp. 205–215; Van Der Meulen, 'The Role of Tribal', p. 238.
[56] Sheikh Saqr bin Muhammad Al-Qasimi.
[57] Malcolm Peck, *The United Arab Emirates: A Venture in Unity* (Boulder, CO: Westview, 1986), p. 120.

Iranian entry visas.[58] In 1995, Iran forcibly required all residents to exit and then return through the island's Iranian port, and has since then prevented teachers and other UAE public sector employees from re-entering.[59] Ominously, Iran has now also opened an airport, has built a town hall, is constructing a university, and conducts numerous naval exercises in nearby waters.[60]

Today, further instability and skirmishes in the vicinity of the islands remain likely should a beleaguered Iranian presidency need to rebuild national pride. This could hamper both Dubai and Sharjah's oil exports, especially given the close proximity of Sharjah's remaining Mubarak offshore oilfield. Moreover, despite the federal government's attempts to balance the United States and Iran by inviting delegations from both countries to the UAE in the summer of 2007, by declaring to the international media that 'UAE territories will never be used for security, intelligence, or military operations directed against Iran',[61] and by dispatching groups of sympathetic fact-finding clergy to Qom in Iran; any stray anti-ship missiles or Iranian submarine activity in the event of a US–Iran conflict would nonetheless raise tanker insurance rates and thereby greatly harm the UAE's economy.[62] Lastly, it is also important to note that invasion itself, or missile strikes against targets on UAE soil are not an impossibility. Certainly, there exists a certain optimism in the UAE that the United States will eventually reach something of a 'grand bargain' with Iran, as the Americans cannot afford to allow the economies of the Gulf emirates to falter, especially those such as Dubai's that are now so heavily reliant on foreign direct investment, much of which originates from the West. Importantly, this line of thinking grossly underestimates the UAE's ultimate expendability should the United States need to grapple with a state whose weapons may prevent long-term regional stability.

Other Regional Threats

OPEC quota disagreements during the 1980s and the invasion of Kuwait in 1990 led to considerable tension between the UAE and Iraq, with many fearing invasion.[63] However, the Anglo-American enforced regime change in Iraq in 2003 has significantly reduced the UAE's fear of hostilities from Iraq. Over the past three years, the UAE Armed Forces has donated much equipment to the new Iraqi military, including several Bell 206 helicopters, and in a further gesture of friendship has provided training for hundreds of Iraqi policemen and other security officials on UAE soil.[64] Similarly, occasional threats from other Arab Gulf states have now all but disappeared, with the last serious dispute with Oman being resolved in 1989 when the ruler of Dubai[65] stepped in to mediate a disagreement between Muscat and Ra's al-Khaimah over the sovereignty of the Musandam Peninsula that was on the verge of escalating into armed conflict.[66]

---

[58] Van Der Meulen, 'The Role of Tribal', p. 238.
[59] Oxford Business Group, 'Emerging Emirates', pp. 98–99.
[60] Personal interviews with military advisors, Dubai, January 2007.
[61] 'UAE Stands Firm', *Gulf News*, 29 March 2007, p. 2.
[62] Van Der Meulen, 'The Role of Tribal', p. 279.
[63] Davidson, *Dubai*, p. 228.
[64] The training has been provided by German security companies operating in the UAE. 'Germany Trains UAE Police', *Islamic Republic News Agency*, 16 January 2004, p. 1.
[65] Sheikh Rashid bin Said Al-Maktum.
[66] Wilson, *Rashid's Legacy*, pp. 496–497.

Most significantly, the UAE's long history of tension with Saudi Arabia now also appears to have abated. Throughout the nineteenth and early twentieth centuries the rulers of Abu Dhabi and Dubai had resisted the encroachment attempts of the same Wahhabi-inspired Saudis[67] that had managed to gain influence in Ra's al-Khaimah and Sharjah.[68] Crucially, by the early 1950s, the US concession holder for Saudi oil, ARAMCO, was urging its host nation to renew its historical claims to parts of the lower Gulf, especially the towns surrounding the Buraimi oasis, where it had assumed there were large onshore oil deposits. ARAMCO devoted all of its scholarly resources to proving the legitimacy of the Saudi claim, not least by demonstrating that the tribesmen of the area, including those inhabiting the Abu Dhabi-administered town of Al-Ayn, had for centuries paid religious tax to Saudi sheikhs.[69] Following a failed peace conference in Damman in late 1952, a Saudi envoy[70] arrived in Hamasa, another of the Buraimi towns, with an armed force laden with money, food, and presents for the local sheikhs. To reinforce further the Saudi position, it was reported that the envoy even married the daughter of the sheikh of one of the most powerful Buraimi tribes.[71] Although the Trucial Oman Levies were deployed and the Saudis were expelled, with the envoy being shot by a British officer,[72] no real solution was reached between the two parties. Just three years later Saudi Arabia was accused of paying for the assassination of the Abu Dhabi ruler,[73] and in 1959 Saudi Arabia vigorously protested over Abu Dhabi's establishment of a police outpost on the disputed Khor al-Udaid.[74]

Remarkably, when the UAE was formed in 1971 Saudi Arabia refused to acknowledge its existence, and only granted it recognition in 1974 when Abu Dhabi finally agreed to give up Khor al-Udaid in addition to the islands of Khor Duwayham and Huwayat, thereby providing Saudi Arabia with a corridor of land to the lower Gulf between Qatar and Abu Dhabi. Ironically, while oil has never been discovered in the Buraimi region, this conceded territory is now home to the Shaiba and Zarara oilfields, and is therefore one of Saudi Arabia's most resource-rich provinces.[75] Importantly, given that this 1974 treaty was never officially registered, there remains some concern even today that the new generation of Abu Dhabi rulers may attempt to challenge Saudi Arabia over the agreement.[76] Most maps produced in Abu Dhabi today depict the UAE with its pre-1974 Saudi border,[77] perhaps indicating a willingness to re-open the dispute. Nevertheless, since the formation of the GCC and the emergence of greater mutual

---

[67] For example Sheikh Said bin Tahnun Al-Nahyan's assault on the Wahhabis in Buraimi in 1848, and Sheikh Zayed bin Khalifa Al-Nahyan's spirited defence of Buraimi against the Omani-Wahhabi renegade, Said Turki in 1870. Jayanti Maitra and Afra Al-Hajji, *Qasr Al-Hosn: The History and Rulers of Abu Dhabi, 1793-1966* (Abu Dhabi: Centre for Documentation and Research, 2001), pp. 102–103, 177.
[68] Donald Hawley, *The Trucial States* (London: George Allen and Unwin, 1970), p. 101.
[69] *Ibid.*, p. 188.
[70] Turki bin Utaishan.
[71] He married the daughter of an Al-Bu Shamis sheikh. See Hawley, *The Emirates*, p. 160.
[72] *Ibid.*, p. 160.
[73] Sheikh Shakhbut bin Sultan Al-Nahyan.
[74] Hawley, *The Emirates*, p. 104.
[75] Muhammad Fahim, *From Rags to Riches: A Story of Abu Dhabi* (London: Centre for Arab Studies, 1995), p. 159; John Duke Anthony, *Arab States of the Lower Gulf: People, Politics, Petroleum* (Washington DC: Middle East Institute, 1975), pp. 148–149.
[76] Van Der Meulen, 'The Role of Tribal', p. 23.
[77] Oxford Business Group, 'Emerging Emirates', p. 20; Personal interviews with academic observers, Dubai, June 2006.

threats, Saudi Arabia, much like Iraq, has become less likely to threaten the UAE again. Indeed, the greatest threat that Saudi Arabia now poses to the UAE is one of internal regime failure—should Saudi Arabia falter, the military bulwark of the GCC would collapse.

Domestic Vulnerabilities—A History of Terror

Notwithstanding early anti-British movements such as the 'Popular Front for the Liberation of Occupied Arab Gulf' and some sporadic National Front-inspired violence in the 1950s,[78] over the course of the second half of the twentieth century the UAE suffered several spates of serious terrorist attacks and other politically motivated acts of violence on its own soil. While in most cases the UAE has been a victim of cross-fire due to its unfortunate geographic location and its large expatriate population, it is important to note that a number of these incidents were also purposely intended to discredit the establishment and the ruling families, often by highlighting their close relationship with the West.[79]

The first organised attacks that were aimed at destabilising the lower and frightening both the British and the indigenous population were those launched by Omani terrorists in the late 1950s and early 1960s; most of whom were supporting the Imam Ghalib against the government in Muscat,[80] and many of whom would join the more conventional Dhofar Liberation Front later in the decade. Crucially, it would seem that most of the protagonists were based in Dubai, as sympathisers provided them with safe houses and in some cases even British travel documentation, so that they could travel freely without their Omani papers. Land mines were also stored in Dubai, seemingly in cars belonging to associates of both the ruler of Sharjah,[81] and the eldest son of the ruler of Ajman.[82] Shockingly, in 1959 a three-ton lorry transporting Trucial Oman Scouts soldiers was blown up by one of these mines on the road between Dubai and Buraimi,[83] and soon after a Land Rover was blown up in Buraimi itself.[84] As panic spread, all motorists began to place sandbags on the fenders of their cars so as to better absorb such explosions.[85] Throughout 1960 the terror attacks continued, and on one occasion a mine exploded on a private road belonging to the ruler of the informally recognised sheikhdom of Mahadha.[86] Most dramatically, in 1961, the Omani rebels struck at sea and became the perpetrators of one of the greatest acts of terrorism there has ever been in the Middle East. The Dara was the flagship of the British India Steam Navigation Company and was carrying over 800 passengers from Bombay to Basra via Dubai. When she was approaching the coast of Dubai two explosions ripped through her cabins, killing 212 passengers and 24 crew members. Although British salvage vessels managed to tow the ship away, its

---

[78] Davidson, *Dubai*, pp. 41–43.
[79] *Ibid.*, pp. 193–206.
[80] Most of the terrorists were thought to be drawn from the Bani Harth and the Bani Riyam. See Margaret Luce, *From Aden to the Gulf: Personal Diaries, 1956-1966* (Salisbury: Michael Russell, 1987), p. 164; Hawley, *The Emirates*, p. 62.
[81] Sheikh Saqr bin Sultan Al-Qasimi.
[82] Sheikh Ali bin Rashid Al-Nu'aymi, who never became crown prince of Ajman. Personal interviews with academic observers, Dubai, June 2006; Hawley, *The Emirates*, p. 289.
[83] Hawley, *The Emirates*, p. 173.
[84] *Ibid.*, p. 177.
[85] Personal interviews with former British diplomats, Durham, February 2007.
[86] Sheikh Abdulla bin Salim Al-Ka'abi. Hawley, *The Emirates*, p. 220.

burning hull eventually sank two days later off the coast of Umm al-Qawain.[87] Although the exact method of the attack remains unknown, the British agent surmised that timers had been set so that the bombs would explode upon the Dara's arrival in Muscat and that bad weather had caused them to go off early.[88] Indeed, it later transpired that after planting their explosives the terrorists had left the ship when it berthed in Bahrain before eventually being captured in Oman.[89]

Disturbingly, although the Omani threat soon subsided, during the 1970s and 1980s Dubai and the new UAE federation became something of an unwitting proxy battleground for other organised terror groups and freedom fighters that sought international publicity for their causes. In 1973, a Japan Airlines jet en route from Amsterdam to Tokyo was jointly hijacked by members of the Palestinian Liberation Organisation (PLO) and the Japanese Red Army. After the new pirate captain redirected the aircraft to land in Dubai, a youthful Sheikh Muhammad bin Rashid Al-Maktum—the ruler's third son and at that time the commander of the DDF—opened communications with the terrorists from the airport control tower. Having assumed that Muhammad would grant their release given the UAE's international pro-Palestinian stance, the hijackers soon realised their miscalculation and demanded to be refuelled. With little choice, after three days of threat-laden negotiations Muhammad had to grant the aircraft safe passage to Libya where all of the hijackers were allowed to walk free.[90] The following year, a British Airways jet was hijacked by the PLO and also forced to land in Dubai, before being refuelled under similar circumstances.[91] In 1977, the UAE faced an even more difficult year with a Gulf Air flight bound for Muscat being hijacked and landed by an unknown team of terrorists, with explosives being detonated in the offices of the Egyptian Airlines at Sharjah airport.[92] Moreover, a prominent Dubai national and the federal Minister of State for Foreign Affairs[93] were assassinated by gunmen while escorting the Syrian foreign minister to Abu Dhabi airport.[94] Most dramatically, towards the end of 1977, the Baader-Meinhof Gang chose to fly their hijacked Lufthansa jet with 91 passengers on board to Rome and Bahrain, before finally demanding clearance from Dubai. Muhammad was again able to confront the terrorists, delaying their departure for over 48 hours.[95] Crucially, this allowed a German commando team to position themselves around Mogadishu airport where they stormed the jet upon its arrival in Somalia, killing all of the hijackers and releasing all of the hostages. Six years later, tragedy struck once more, when a hijacked Gulf Air flight from Abu Dhabi to Karachi exploded in mid-air somewhere close to Dubai,[96] and in the following year the UAE's ambassador to France[97] was assassinated upon his arrival in Paris by unknown perpetrators. The fear that this killing generated was enough to persuade the ruler of Dubai to finally have plainclothes bodyguards around him during

---

[87] Ram Buxani, *Taking the High Road* (Dubai: Motivate, 2003), pp. 11–12; Wilson, *Rashid's Legacy*, pp. 191–194.
[88] Hawley, *The Emirates*, p. 288.
[89] Personal interviews with former British diplomats, Dubai, June 2006; Luce, *From Aden to the Gulf*, p. 165.
[90] Wilson, *Rashid's Legacy*, pp. 358–360.
[91] *Merchant International Group Strategic Research and Corporate Intelligence*, Report, 25 August 2005.
[92] Ibid.
[93] Saif Said bin Ghubash.
[94] Wilson, *Rashid's Legacy*, p. 431.
[95] Ibid., pp. 429–431.
[96] *Merchant International Group Strategic Research and Corporate Intelligence*, 25 August 2005.
[97] Khalifa bin Ahmad Al-Mubarak.

public appearances.[98] By the mid-1980s, little had improved, with bombs being discovered onboard a Jordanian aircraft in Dubai in 1985, and with bombs exploding at the Syrian Airlines office at Abu Dhabi airport in 1986. More recently, in the 1990s, several foreign intelligence operatives were assassinated in the UAE, including an Iranian intelligence colonel. And, in early 1999, explosives were discovered in one of Dubai's first large-scale shopping malls: Deira City Centre.[99] Infamously, on the Christmas Eve of that year, yet another aircraft was diverted to the emirate when Pakistani hijackers seized an Indian Airlines flight en route from Nepal to Delhi. A hostage was murdered and thrown out of the plane when it reached Dubai, before the hijackers then flew to a warmer welcome in Kandahar. The entire crisis (including the tragedy in Dubai) became the subject of both a National Geographic Channel documentary and a Bollywood action movie.[100]

Since then almost all terror-related incidents in Dubai and the UAE have had at least some connection to Al-Qaeda, or rather organisations purporting to be linked to Al-Qaeda. Certainly, in addition to well-documented money laundering services[101] and the personal involvement of UAE nationals in Al-Qaeda's international attacks, including the Ra's al-Khaimah national Marwan Al-Shehhi, and another of the 11 September hijackers, Fayez Banihammad,[102] there have also been persistent claims that the country has many key sympathisers, and is regularly used as a safe haven and a logistical base by various Al-Qaeda cells and other associated renegades. During the September 11th Commission hearings, the former US Secretary of Defence[103] stated that in 1999 the witness reports of paid agents in Afghanistan had informed the CIA that Osama bin Laden had set up a large hunting camp in the desert of the Helmand province complete with marquees, generators, and refrigerators. Hoping to hit the suspected mastermind of the 1998 African embassy bombings, the Pentagon duly drew up plans for a cruise missile strike, but then had to abort the operation when it was learned that a C130 transport aircraft with UAE markings had landed at the camp's airstrip. According to CIA and Department of Defense officials, US decision-makers were concerned that such an attack might compromise a UAE sheikh or other senior UAE official.[104] Tellingly, the former CIA director later testified that if the strike had gone ahead 'it might have wiped out half of the UAE royal family in the process', while others testified that 'the United Arab Emirates was becoming ... a persistent counterterrorism problem ... as it was one of the Taleban's only travel and financial outlets to the outside world'.[105]

Significantly, although not touching on the widespread rumours that Osama Bin Laden himself had been receiving medical treatment in Dubai during the summer of 2001,[106] the Commission nevertheless also reported that most of the

---

[98] Fahim, *From Rags to Riches*, p. 159; Wilson, *Rashid's Legacy*, p. 355.
[99] *Merchant International Group Strategic Research and Corporate Intelligence*, 25 August 2005.
[100] The 2003 movie *Zameen* starred Abhishek Bachchan.
[101] Davidson, 'Dubai: The Security Dimensions', pp. 149–152.
[102] 'UAE Linked to 9/11', *USA Today*, 2 September 2004. The UAE provided the second largest contingent of 9/11 hijackers after Saudi Arabia.
[103] William Cohen.
[104] Personal correspondence, March 2007.
[105] Iqbal Ismail Hakim, *United Arab Emirates Central Bank and 9/11 Financing* (New York: GAAP, 2005), p. 1; personal correspondence, March 2007.
[106] It was widely rumoured in Dubai that Bin Laden was receiving treatment for his kidney ailments in a Dubai-based hospital during the summer of 2001.

11 September hijackers had flown to the United States via the UAE. It was claimed that 11 Al-Qaeda men of Saudi origin, the presumed 'muscle' for the operation, had travelled in groups of two or three from Dubai International Airport between April and June of that year.[107] In November 2002, journalists learned that the suspected ringleader of the team that had attacked the USS *Cole* off the coast of the Yemen in 2000 had been captured, but were only informed that the arrest had taken place in an undisclosed location in the Gulf. In a good example of carefully timed announcements of sensitive information, it was only revealed a month later that a 'top ten' Al-Qaeda operative had been captured in Dubai. Worryingly, it transpired that the Saudi suspect, Abd Al-Rahim Al-Nashiri, had been apprehended while in the final planning stages of attacks on 'vital economic targets' in the UAE that were aiming to inflict 'the highest possible casualties among nationals and foreigners'.[108] Also in 2002, various international reports were published indicating that hundreds of the Al-Qaeda 'volunteer soldiers' that had been captured in Afghanistan were actually UAE nationals.[109] Moreover, the reports claimed that a number of Dubai and Fujairah-based 'welfare associations' had been sending money to radical groups in Afghanistan and South Asia, and had been encouraging young men to join terrorist groups.[110] In 2004, the perceived links between Dubai and Al-Qaeda were further strengthened by another round of high-profile arrests, leading many to suspect these were merely the tip of the iceberg and that the emirate was still 'playing a key role for Al-Qaeda as a through-point' even three years after the 11 September attacks.[111] Notably, after alleged pressure from the CIA, the Dubai authorities arrested and extradited Qari Saifullah Akhtar, the leader of the Pakistani Al-Qaeda splinter group Haraktul Jihad Islami, who was believed to be responsible for the training of thousands of militants in the Rishkor camp close to Kabul, and for carrying money and personal messages on behalf of Bin Laden. Crucially, he had disappeared from Afghanistan and Pakistan just days before Anglo-American forces arrived in October 2001.[112] Shortly afterwards, the arrest in Pakistan of Al-Qaeda's Ahmad Khalfan Ghailani, a suspect of the 1998 US embassy bombings, provided intelligence concerning two of his South African colleagues and 'several other senior men' who were all either travelling from the UAE to Pakistan or were based in the UAE at that time.[113]

Domestic Vulnerabilities—The Present Threat

As few would dispute, despite the unrestrained development that has taken place in Dubai and elsewhere in the UAE, despite the necessary but often controversial socioeconomic reforms,[114] and despite the close relationship with the West, there exists a certain overconfidence that little can go wrong and that somehow the country will remain aloof from acts of terror on its own doorstep. Along with other Gulf states, there have been accusations that various terrorist organisations have

---

[107] 'UAE Linked to 9/11', *USA Today*, 2 September 2004.
[108] 'Al-Nashri Arrested in the United Arab Emirates', *The Times*, 24 December 2002.
[109] Adam Robinson, *Bin Laden: Behind the Mask of the Terrorist* (New York: Arcade, 2002), pp. 91–93.
[110] John Wilston, 'The Roots of Extremism in Bangladesh', *Terrorism Monitor*, 3(1) (2005), pp. 1–8.
[111] Quotes from Evan F. Kohlmann, a New York-based terrorism researcher.
[112] Personal interviews with military advisors, Dubai, June 2006; 'The Extradition of Akhtar', *Financial Times*, 10 August 2004.
[113] *China Daily*, 9 August 2004.
[114] Davidson, *Dubai*, pp. 114–115.

been 'bought off'.[115] In 2005, the struggling Iraqi president, Jalal Talabani, made dark references to the sources of the funding for his enemies, most conspicuously the insurgent leader Abu Musab Al-Zaraqawi. Disturbingly, he stated that 'they are getting aid from Al-Qaeda and from some financiers among some extremist Muslim organisations abroad ... and from countries that I will not name'. Analysts agreed that these mystery countries were most likely to be the small Gulf states.[116] With specific regard to the UAE, it has similarly been claimed that a number of Islamist organisations, in addition to wealthy individuals, are supporting terror organisations financially.[117] However, regardless of whether these payments are in genuine support of the causes or are simply protection money, it would seem unnecessary for the UAE to have to rely on such measures given that at present most groups continue to benefit from Dubai's openness so long as they can operate in relative freedom and can use the city's infrastructure for their own purposes. Certainly, even if one does subscribe to the belief that there exists some kind of unwritten understanding that the authorities will turn a blind eye to questionable activities, or even if one accepts that Dubai unwittingly permits itself to be used as a logistical terror hub, these steps are unlikely ever to be enough to prevent splinter groups or disaffected individuals from acting unilaterally against an establishment that they undoubtedly perceive to be an ally of the Western powers.

Over the last few years, there have been a large number of threats made to Dubai and the UAE by hitherto unknown groups, many of which refer explicitly to the country's dealings with the United States and its supporting role in the war on terror. Notably, in 2002, a letter signed by the previously unknown 'Al-Qaeda Terrorist Organisation in the United Arab Emirates Government' was intercepted by US intelligence services—it warned UAE officials to stop arresting Al-Qaeda's 'mujahideen sympathisers'. The letter concluded with a boast that 'you are well aware that we have infiltrated your security, censorship, and monetary agencies along with other agencies that should not be mentioned', and demanded that the UAE 'get the idolaters out'.[118] Similarly, in 2003, following the Anglo-American invasion of Iraq, an audio message was recorded by Al-Qaeda's Saleh Al-Aloofi that sought to incite violence in all of the pro-Western Gulf states, including the UAE, by stating 'to the brothers of Qatar, Bahrain, Oman, the Emirates, and to all the lions of jihad in the countries neighbouring Iraq, every one of us has to attack what is available in his country of soldiers, vehicles, and airbases of the crusaders and the oil allocated for them'.[119] Chillingly, since 2005, the frequency and severity of the threats would seem to have increased even further, with underground Islamist websites having publishing warnings that 'Dubai is rapidly changing into a secular state ... with the profound use of non-Islamic ways';[120] with Al-Qaeda representatives having notified the Dubai authorities that they had discovered both the USS *Harry Truman* and the USS *John Kennedy* berthed in Port

---

[115] Senior Qatari officials were recently alleged to have been paying a multi-million dollar annual ransom to Al-Qaeda since 2003 so as to prevent attacks taking place on Qatari territory. 'Terror in the Persian Gulf', *Khaleej Times*, 4 May 2005.
[116] 'Iraq Blames Terror Financiers', *Reuters*, 9 May 2005.
[117] Personal interviews, Beirut, November 2006.
[118] Paraphrased from unclassified document AFGP/2002/603856 located at the Combating Terrorism centre at the US Military Academy at West Point. Also see *Scripps Howard News Service*, 28 February 2006.
[119] Personal correspondence, March 2007.
[120] This statement appeared on the As-Sahwah website in 2005.

Jebel Ali after they had been used to 'bombard the Muslims in Iraq and Afghanistan';[121] with the US Embassy in Abu Dhabi and the US Consulate in Dubai having had to close temporarily due to bomb threats;[122] and with another new group calling itself 'The Al-Qaeda Organisation in the Emirates and Oman' having issued a statement in July 2005 that called for the dismantling of all US military installations in the UAE within ten days, failing which 'the ruling families would endure the fist of the mujahideen in their faces'.[123] As recently as June 2008, the British Foreign and Commonwealth Office raised its terror threat assessment for the UAE from medium to high, following a series of arrests and several weeks of intensified 'chatter' intercepted between UAE-based suspects.[124]

Conclusion

The UAE is now more vulnerable than ever before to uncontrollable external circumstances. This is especially true given that the economic diversification strategies, while superficially successful in reducing the historical dependency on oil exports, have, if anything, intensified the dependency on foreign economies. Notably, in the event of a crisis—whether a terrorist attack, an invasion, or close proximity to regional violence—many of the multinationals with regional branches in Jebel Ali, Dubai Internet City, Dubai Media City, and the various other free zones would most likely withdraw their personnel and close their operations, and would think carefully about returning afterwards. Given the success of Dubai's free zones, other regional cities have set up similar entities,[125] and these are soon likely to position themselves as serious alternatives. Problems in Dubai or elsewhere in the UAE would therefore lead to swift relocations for many companies that wished to maintain a Middle Eastern headquarters. Similarly, international luxury tourists would be unlikely to continue visiting the UAE should its reputation wane as being a safe destination. Many of the European and North American tourists (who now make up nearly 40 per cent of all visitors to Dubai[126]) who choose their holidays from high street travel agency brochures do not really consider Dubai to be part of the Middle East. But if there were to be negative publicity, this misconception would swiftly change. Certainly, in October 2001, most of Dubai's five-star hotels were empty following the US invasion of Afghanistan, with even the iconic Burj Al-Arab having had its power cut off temporarily due to zero occupancy. Tellingly, 2001 was the only year that the total number of visitors to Dubai did not increase, despite the sector's strong performance in the months prior to 11 September.[127] Given the much greater and more diverse population of tourists today, it is likely that demand would be even more elastic should there be a future problem that more directly concerns the UAE, especially as there are many alternative winter sun resorts, most of which offer arguably far superior cultural and historical attractions than those of the

---

[121] This statement was made in March 2005.
[122] These closures took place in late March 2005.
[123] Personal correspondence, March 2007.
[124] 'UAE Terror Threat Raised', *Financial Times*, 16 June 2008.
[125] Jordan's Aqaba free zone was set up in 2000.
[126] In 2006 there were two million European visitors and 0.4 million North American visitors, out of a total of 6.4 million. Data supplied by the Dubai Department of Tourism and Commerce Marketing, 2007.
[127] The Dubai Department of Tourism and Commerce Marketing reported 3.5 million visitors in 2001, compared to 3.4 million in 2000.

lower Gulf. Similarly, should confidence in Dubai's real estate sector be shaken by internal or external threats, a significant proportion of foreign investors would cease further payments and would probably try to sell their deposits, preferring to cut their losses. In much the same way as the emerging competition from new free zones, other developing states are now beginning to adopt elements of Dubai's real estate industry in an attempt to emulate its success.[128] Should the pioneer stumble, these are likely to provide attractive alternative venues for international property investors.

---

[128] In addition to Oman and some of the other Gulf states, prominent examples would include Cape Verde, which has invested heavily in tourist infrastructure (including a new international airport), and has recently launched a real estate sector modelled on similar lines to Dubai's.

Iraq's Gulf Policy and Regime Security from the Monarchy to the post-Ba'athist Era

IBRAHIM AL-MARASHI

ABSTRACT *Domestic regime security has explained Iraq's foreign policy to the Gulf since the birth of the nascent Hashemite kingdom in Baghdad. Saudi Arabia presented one of the first security threats to the Iraqi monarchy, and both King Ghazi and 'Abd al-Karim Qasim sought to invade Kuwait in order to bolster their nationalist credentials at home. Baghdad's policy to Gulf prior to the outbreak of the Iran-Iraq War reflected a perceived threat from the Islamic Revolution in Iran. Thus, ensuring regime security in Baghdad has resulted in tensions with Iraq's Gulf neighbours since the creation of the Iraqi state.*

Introduction

Explaining Iraq's relations to the Gulf as a projection of the state's military power and quest for hegemony ignores the role of regime security and its influence on policy to the region. The rise of the Saudi state presented one of the first security threats from the Gulf to the nascent Hashemite kingdom. King Ghazi and 'Abd al-Karim Qasim both sought to invade Kuwait in order to bolster their nationalist credentials, and secure a naval outlet to the Gulf to strengthen Iraq's military status in the region. Baghdad's Gulf policy leading up to the Iran–Iraq War reflected a perceived threat from the Islamic Revolution in Iran, which threatened to unseat the government of Saddam Hussein as well as the other Gulf monarchies. In this conflict, as well as the ensuing 1991 Gulf War and 2003 Iraq War, regime security was based on support from Saddam Hussein's tribe and fellow clansmen from the Tikrit region, who predominated in the upper echelons of the military and security apparatus. A final shift in Gulf policy occurred following 2003 when a fledgling Iraqi government sought to develop its crumbling infrastructure and lure investment from the Gulf.

The Hashemite Monarchy and the Gulf: 1921–1958

One of the first security threats from the Gulf to the nascent Hashemite kingdom emerged from within Saudi Arabia. An expanding Saudi state threatened King

Faysal's regime, as the House of Sa'ud was hostile to the Hashemite monarchy and would later incorporate the domains of his father in the Hijaz. At this juncture Iraq's borders with Iran were contested, and the newly formed Republic of Turkey claimed the city of Kirkuk. In the south of Iraq marauding Saudi Ikhwan tribesmen violated Iraq's borders and undermined Faysal's ability to guarantee the security of the newly formed state. In March 1922, the Ikhwan leader Faysal Al-Dawish of the Mutayr tribe attacked elements of the Iraqi Muntafiq tribe in the south, and since the Iraqi military did not have the numbers nor the training to patrol the porous borders of the south, the raid was ultimately repelled by the British Royal Air Force in Iraq.[1] In the month following the attack, a conference was convened in Karbala by Shaykh Mahdi al-Khalisi, a Shi'i cleric, along with 200 Shi'a religious leaders and tribesmen, calling upon the King to provide protection from the Ikhwan raids.[2]

Ikhwan raids continued into the south of Iraq through 1929 despite deployments of Iraqi military forces. A friendship treaty was signed in 1931 between Saudi Arabia and Iraq, but the failure of Iraq's military to prevent the Ikhwan attacks, in addition to the growing strength of the Turkish and Iranian militaries were among numerous reasons that King Faysal demanded a stronger army to be levied through conscription.

The state of Iraq's military touched off a battle between the King and London, with the former keen to develop an indigenous Iraqi army, crucial to Faysal's state-building policy and his efforts to build alliances with elites to prop up his regime. The elites with whom Faysal sought to build alliances consisted primarily of ex-Sharifian officers who had served as the King's Damascus entourage, and who moved with him upon assuming the Iraqi throne. These officers included Ja'far Al-'Askari, the first Minister of Defence, and Nuri Al-Sa'id, who held a variety of executive posts and initially served as Deputy Commander-in-Chief of the Army.[3] Other ex-Sharifians included the soldier-politician Yasin Al-Hashimi, who forged ties with the military through his brother Taha, who would become Chief of the General Staff.[4] These officers formed the core of Faysal's regime, and all of them shared a desire for the formation of a conscripted Iraqi Army to serve as a means of cementing the loyalty of the nation's disparate ethnic and sectarian groups. Iraq's inability to fend off marauding tribes, along with the rise of Iran and Turkey, provided the conscription lobby within Faysal's government a powerful argument against London, which sought to maintain a small Iraqi military that was easier to control.

The security dilemmas faced by King Faysal upon assuming the Iraqi throne included forging alliances and maintaining the loyalty of the differing factions of the Sharifian elite that accompanied him from Damascus to Baghdad. Regime security was defined during Faysal's period as maintaining cohesion of the Sharifian elite and instilling some sense of Iraqi citizenship that included loyalty to the Hashemite throne. Conscription emerged as the solution to deal with Faysal's security dilemmas. A conscripted army would bring all Iraqi citizens into the

---

[1] Stephen Hemsley Longrigg, *Iraq, 1900 to 1950: A Political, Social, and Economic History* (Oxford and London: Oxford University Press, 1953), p. 160.
[2] *Ibid.*, p. 141.
[3] Hanna Batatu, *The Old Social Classes and the Revolutionary Movements of Iraq* (Princeton, NJ: Princeton University Press, 1979), p. 333.
[4] Public Record Office, Foreign Office (FO) 371/20015, 30 November 1936.

national project, as well as create a force that could match Turkey and Iran, in addition to protecting the Kingdom from Wahhabi incursions. In this context, Iraq's relationship to the Gulf was characterized by the threat from Saudi Arabia, in that the Ikhwan raids demonstrated Baghdad's inability to guard its borders or protect its citizens. Unlike his successors, Faysal was not in a position to pursue external aggression, or anti-imperialism as an official policy as a means to make his own regime more secure. Iraq did not have an indigenous military to pursue such policies, and anti-imperialism targeting the UK would have been counter-productive as his throne depended on British support. Furthermore the Sharifian elites did not exhibit the anti-British attitude of younger military elites that would seize power during Ghazi's reign. Thus, the only policy option available to Faysal was to request of the House of Sa'ud to control the Ikhwan tribesman, which Riyadh agreed to albeit with difficulties.

In 1933 King Faysal died and his son Ghazi assumed the throne. Ghazi proved unable to stabilize the fractious political elites in the domestic political arena. The military and government during Ghazi's reign were divided between pan-Arab nationalists (*qawmiyyun*) versus the 'Iraq-firsters' (*wataniyyun*), who realized that Iraq was part of the Arab world but were more concerned with domestic affairs rather than entangling Iraq with events in other Arab states. As early as 1929, a cell of young pan-Arabist officers began to coalesce around Salah Al-Din Al-Sabbagh, who hailed from a mercantile family in Mosul. He formed a working partnership with three other like-minded colonels, Fahmi Sa'id, Mahmud Salman and Kamil Shabib, known as the 'Four Colonels' or the 'Golden Square'. These young officers shared a common background, coming from middle class Sunni Arab families from the northern provinces in the vicinity of Mosul, a region that suffered economically after the creation of the Syrian border, which limited trade.[5] Al-Sabbagh was cultivated by the Arab nationalist Yasin Al-Hashimi, one of the ex-Sharifian officers who became prime minister in 1935, and both gathered the ideological support of the pan-Arabist Muthanna Club.[6]

Al-Sabbagh's aspirations for the Iraqi military are documented in his memoirs, where he criticizes British interference in the expansion of a nationalist Iraqi army that could serve the cause of Arab unity. An autonomous Iraqi military did not exist at that juncture, and was primarily operated, funded, and trained by the British. In his opinion, this army possessed the symbolic potential of an institution that could foster solidarity between soldiers and the Iraqi masses under 'the flag of Arabism'.[7] He envisioned the Iraqi military growing into the largest army in the region to reunite the disparate Arab states through force.

Arab nationalism had not only taken root in Iraq, but also in its small neighbour to the south—Kuwait. An Arab nationalist movement emerged in the sheikhdom, petitioning Sheikh Ahmad Al-Jabir Al-Sabah for greater reforms in April 1938. Ghazi, along with the pan-Arabist officers in the regime, gave refuge to these Kuwaiti nationalists, just as they had given refuge to the Mufti of Jerusalem, Hajj Amin al-Husayni. The Iraqi regime supported their movement within Kuwait by orchestrating a propaganda campaign against the Sheikh. The Kuwaiti Arab

---

[5] Eric Davis, *Memories of State: Politics, History and Collective Identity in Modern Iraq* (Berkeley: University of California Press, 2005), p. 147.
[6] FO 317/23217/ E 5661/72/93, 10 August 1939.
[7] Salah Al-Din Al-Sabbagh, *Fursan al-'Urubah: Mudhakkirat al-Shahid Salah al-Din al-Sabbagh* [The Knights of Arabism: The Memoirs of the Martyr Salah Al-Din Al-Sabbagh] (Rabat: Tanit li Nashr, 1994), p. 43.

nationalists supported by Iraq coalesced into The National Bloc (*Al-Kutla al-Wataniyya*), demanding in July 1938 a consultative government and an elected assembly. While the Bloc depended on Iraqi support, it did not officially declare a desire for the merger between Kuwait and Iraq. The timing of the dissent within Kuwait was fortuitous, given that in September 1938, Iraq indicated its desire to develop a port on Kuwaiti territory to enhance Baghdad's position in the Gulf, facilitate the export of oil, and counter Iran's rising influence in the vicinity.[8] Britain was strongly opposed to Iraq trying to assert its influence in Kuwait, fearing that Baghdad might threaten its own interest in the Sheikhdom.[9] Subsequent Iraqi attempts to establish a port facility on the islands of Warba and Bubiyan were rejected by the British.[10] The attempts to develop a port and navy, accrue rents from oil, and check Iran's growth were all key elements of strengthening Iraq's military status in the region. However, for its security strategy, the regime could have used its policy to Kuwait in order to bolster its nationalist credentials.

In March 1939, Ghazi addressed the Kuwaitis: 'We are Iraqis by flesh and blood. Our history supports the annexation of Kuwait to Iraq. We live and die under the Hashimite flag.'[11] According to the Iraqi scholar Ahmad Shikara, 'since Kuwait was under British aegis, attacks on it had a favourable impact on the Arab nationalists, who regarded such criticism as heroic acts directed against the powerful British'.[12] Ghazi's annexation scheme was part of a larger campaign that called for the liberation of Arabs, particularly in Palestine from British and French colonial interference, as well as union between not only Iraq and Kuwait, but Iraq and a Greater Syria. Britain grew alarmed when Ghazi declared that Iraqi–Kuwaiti unity would be achieved through military means.[13] A violent pro-Iraqi uprising occurred in Kuwait on 10 March to overthrow the Sheikh, arousing suspicions among the British that the German delegation in Baghdad was behind the disturbances in order to justify Ghazi's military intervention.[14] At this juncture British military intelligence assessed that Iraq had already devised a military plan for an invasion of Kuwait.[15] This assessment appeared to materialize as Ghazi mobilized the Iraqi Army at Zubair, near the Kuwaiti border.[16] However, the King never deployed Iraqi forces into Kuwait, and the attempts to annex its southern neighbour faltered when Ghazi was killed in a car accident on 4 April 1939 leaving his infant son Faysal II to assume the throne.[17]

Analyses of this episode in Iraqi policy to the Gulf tend to focus on the role of King Ghazi and his personal ambitions for pan-Arab leadership and his attempts to exert Iraqi influence to the Gulf. The British suspected that Fritz Grobba, the Nazi envoy at the German Legation in Baghdad, had orchestrated the Iraqi propaganda campaign against the Sheikh: 'To the British authorities, German influence was clearly apparent in the promotion of Kuwait as the southern province of Iraq

[8] FO 371/21860/E 5477, 7 September 1938.
[9] FO 371/21860/297/N38, 23 June 1938.
[10] FO 371/21860/E4994, 26 August 1938.
[11] FO 371/23181/05050, 7 March 1939.
[12] Ahmad Abdul Razzaq Shikara, *Iraqi Politics 1921-41* (London: LAAM, 1987), p. 153.
[13] *Ibid.*, p. 154.
[14] *Ibid.*, p. 155.
[15] FO 371/23181, 23 May 1939.
[16] FO 371/23/80, 24 March 1939.
[17] FO 371/23181/E 3016/178, 20 April 1939.

(i.e., the Sudetenland of Iraq). Indeed, the Iraqi press called the southern provinces (Basrah and Kuwait) "Sudeten Territories".[18] However, focusing on Ghazi as the primary actor during the Kuwait crisis, or the Germans or the Kuwaiti nationalists as influencing the King, fails to address the role of the Four Colonels in the Iraqi regime power structure at the time. Ghazi's policy was also contested from within the regime, when the prime minister at the time, Nuri Al-Said, complained to the British Ambassador of the King's policy declaring, 'a few discontented young Kuwaitis had gained access to His Majesty and had cajoled him into "taking up their cause"'.[19]

Since their coup in 1937, the Four Colonels under Al-Sabbagh's leadership had influenced King's behaviour through their 'veto', the implicit or overt threat of a coup. The Colonels constituted a 'moderator regime', exercising power behind the scenes, without overthrowing the monarchy or taking direct control over the government. The Colonels had on seven occasions replaced one civilian government with another that was friendlier, thus maintaining a cabinet that served their pan-Arab interests, as well as that of the armed forces. Just a few months before the escalation of the Kuwait crisis, on 24 December 1938 the Colonels deployed a military detachment outside of Baghdad, demonstrating the forces at their disposal. One of the officers met with King Ghazi and asked him to dissolve cabinet of a rival, the ex-Sharifian Jamil Al-Midfa'i, to which the King promptly acquiesced.[20] Thus the Colonels acted as the de facto regime, with Ghazi agreeing with their foreign policy desires.

The dilemma facing King Ghazi involved his reliance on the Four Colonels. However, both shared a common Arab Sunni background ruling over a nation where they were a minority. Ghazi's Kuwait venture occurred at a time when rival Iraqi national and supranational pan-Arab visions conflicted, with the latter adopted by the Four Colonels and Ghazi. Pan-Arabism served the interests of Ghazi and the Colonels, who came from an Arab Sunni regime ruling over a population of Arab Shi'as, Kurds, and other minorities. The banner of pan-Arabism held the prospect of subsuming the Arab Shi'a into a regional project that could legitimize their minority rule. As Sunni Arabs, these officers sought to enhance their minority status in Iraq by linking their nation's identity with that of the greater Sunni Arab world. The Colonels sought to use their power to assume their dream of creating an Arab Prussia to expel imperialist influences in the region, unite the various Arab countries, and come to the rescue of Palestine, which seemed to be on the road to partition. The Colonels' and Ghazi's legitimacy rested on an anti-British and pan-Arabist platform, during a time when Palestine and Syria were under respective British and French control. In their positions of power, they had the coercive measures to ensure the government did not stray from this path. Ghazi's policy for uniting with a Greater Syria, expelling the British from the region, and his Kuwait policy fell under the officers' greater vision of Iraq's role in the Arab world.

Just as the Colonels had seized power in a military coup, they were ever vigilant that another faction in the military could overthrow them if their activist pan-Arab foreign policy failed to produce results. When factions within Kuwait began agitating against the Sabah royal family, this provided a further opportunity to

---

[18] Shikara, *Iraqi Politics*, pp. 154–155.
[19] *Ibid.*
[20] Ibrahim Al-Marashi and Sammy Salama, *Iraq's Armed Forces* (London: Routledge, 2008), p. 57.

enhance the pan-Arabist and anti-imperialist credentials of the regime of Ghazi and the Colonels, and secure a foothold in the Gulf through a friendlier Kuwaiti government that would allow Iraq to develop naval facilities on the Bubiyan and Warba islands.

Pan-Arabism emerged as an ideological tool to bolster the regime during the tenure of Ghazi and the Four Colonels, and thus influenced Ghazi's interventionist policy over Kuwait. While securing naval facilities for Iraq as well as facilitating oil exports were equally important variables, these issues emerged during the activist pan-Arab regime of the Colonels, who were Arab Sunnis, rather than the Sidqi-Sulayman regime, (who were of mixed Kurdish and Turkish origins) who actively pursued an Iraq first policy, which resulted in a foreign policy behaviour seeking alliances with Iran and Turkey. The anti-British posture among the Colonels was affected by London's policy towards Palestine, as well as its role in the division of the Arab homeland, sentiments clearly expressed in al-Sabbagh's memoirs.

The Colonels' strategy proved successful until a British invasion unseated them and their ally, Prime Minister Rashid Ali al-Gaylani in 1941. Indeed, Nuri Al-Sa'id, the premier who seized power in the aftermath of the British war and ruled while Faysal the II was growing up, failed to adopt a successful strategy of regime security. Failing to address the agenda of pan-Arabism, and relying on the British for his regime's survival, would not protect the monarchy from Iraqi nationalist and pan-Arabist officers during their coup in 1958.

The Early Republican Era and the Aborted Kuwait Invasion: 1958–1968

The officers from 1936 to 1941 emerged as a 'moderator regime', moderating factions within the government, preventing the accession of politicians that could threaten their regime interest. By contrast, the post-revolutionary regime of General 'Abd Al-Karim Qasim represented a regime in which Qasim dominated political, economic, and social life, as well as driving Iraq's Gulf policy.

Challenges to Qasim's regime came from a divided core of officers who presided over a divided army and an Iraqi populace rife with political divisions, such as communism, Ba'athism, and Nasirism. Qasim's Gulf policy needs to be seen within the framework of attempts to develop and maintain a regime comprised of officer networks within the military. Qasim tried to enhance his own patronage network among the officers, appeasing the military establishment by allocating it 40 per cent of the national budget, increasing the number of promotions and the pay of the officers, and providing them with housing compounds with their own schools, cinemas, swimming pools and health facilities in the Officers' City (*Madinat al-Dhubbat*).[21] However, while Qasim struggled to build up a sustainable patronage network in the officer corps, he failed to create a cohesive regime based on ideological, tribal, clan, or regional belonging.

Qasim, like King Ghazi before him, reoriented Iraq's policy toward the Gulf. In 1961, Baghdad was the first government to designate the 'Persian Gulf' as 'the Arabian Gulf', and Iraq encouraged students from Arab Gulf countries to attend

---

[21] Issam Al-Khafaji, 'War as a Vehicle for the Rise and Demise of a State-Controlled Society: The Case of Ba'thist Iraq', in Steven Heydemann (ed.), *War, Institutions and Social Change in the Middle East* (Berkeley: University of California Press, 2000), p. 265.

Iraqi universities, while Iraqi scholars began to conduct research about the Gulf.[22] However, despite this interest in the Gulf, Qasim did not seek to create a Gulf identity for Iraq. According to Dawisha: 'The long-standing patronizing attitude—even contempt—felt by Iraqis toward the inhabitants of the Gulf precluded the possibility of utilizing a "Gulf" identity to mobilize domestic and regional support for the leaders' policy.'[23] Even when Qasim laid claim to Kuwait in 1961, he did not invoke a Gulf identity, as doing so would do little to bolster the legitimacy of his regime.

When Britain recognized Kuwait's independence, Qasim sent ambiguous messages to the Shiekhdom failing to acknowledge its new status. On 25 July 1961, Qasim declared that Kuwait was a part of Iraq, basing his claim on an argument that would be used exactly 30 years later during the 1990 Gulf crisis; Qasim argued that Kuwait had once been a district of the Basra *vilayet* under the Ottomans.[24] Whatever military units were not pegged down in the north to suppress a revolt launched by the Kurds under Mullah Mustafa Barazani were mobilized near the Kuwaiti border, but were hardly enough to launch an invasion. Nevertheless, British forces deployed to the Sheikhdom and the Arab League rallied behind its newest member, Kuwait.

Due to conflict in the north, Iraq did not have the forces in 1961 to invade and seize Kuwait. Perhaps Qasim sought to coerce concessions from a weak Kuwait, such as being allowed to develop a naval facility on the two Kuwaiti islands. To bolster his legitimacy, Qasim pursued an anti-British and anti-imperialist agenda, while criticizing Jamal 'Abd al-Nasir's regime in Egypt (who was angered by Iraq's refusal to join his United Arab Republic). Indeed, the insecurity of Qasim's regime was demonstrated by a Nasirist uprising and coup attempt in Mosul in 1959 and an attempt against his life launched by the Ba'thists. While Qasim tried to develop an in-group of pro-communist military officers to protect his regime from pro-Nasirist and Ba'athist officers in the military, he also sought to ensure that the Iraqi Communist Party did not become powerful enough to challenge his rule. Even though the communists supported Qasim's regime, a 'communist' identity could not be imposed on all Iraqi officers, and thus he had to deal with pan-Arab aspirations within the military elite.

The withdrawal of British forces from Kuwait provided Qasim an opportunity to formulate a foreign policy with nationalist and pan-Arab overtones to appeal to the anti-imperialist and anti-British communist officers within his regime and build alliances among the Nasirists and Ba'athists. An external conflict with Kuwait increased internal cohesion among his in-groups, in addition to his allies in the Communist Party. Qasim's regime had already witnessed the dangers of conflicts of sub-national groups in Iraq, such as the Kurdish–Turkmen infighting in Kirkuk a few years earlier, and the re-emergence of the Barazani rebellion. Furthermore, the rise of communism among the Arab Shi'a alienated the Shi'a clerical establishment from Qasim.

Qasim's claims to Kuwait placated the pan-Arab Nasirists and Ba'athist officers. But his failure alienated his enemies within the military, as Qasim stepped down in the face of 'imperialism' when Britain deployed to protect Kuwait.

---

[22] Phebe Marr, *The Modern History of Iraq* (Boulder, CO: Westview, 1985), p. 180.
[23] Adeed Dawisha, 'Footprints in the Sand', in Shibley Telhami and Michael Barnett (eds), *Identity and Foreign Policy in the Middle East* (Ithaca, NY: Cornell University Press, 2002), p. 127.
[24] Marr, *The Modern History*, p. 181.

According to Charles Tripp, the Kuwait crisis greatly undermined Qasim: 'The revival of this ever powerful theme in Iraqi politics opened old wounds and shook the confidence even of some of Qasim's supporters.'[25] After this event, Qasim's only allies were a Communist Party, which he had intentionally weakened, and a few loyal army officers who were growing disenchanted with the war against the Kurds. The failure to even attempt to stand up to the British in Kuwait (or decisively deal with the Kurdish rebellion) demonstrated Qasim's inability to deliver on the rhetoric he used to bolster his own regime. Two years after the Kuwait venture, Qasim was overthrown and executed by Arab nationalist and Ba'athist officers under 'Abd al-Salaam 'Arif in February 1963.

Ba'athist Iraq and the Gulf: 1968–1990

The Ba'ath Party failed to consolidate power after the 1963 coup, but was successful after another military coup in 1968. Civilians, like Saddam Hussein, were promoted to sensitive security positions, and a disproportionate number came from his hometown of Tikrit. Hussein's Al-Bu Nasir tribe had some 20,000 people at that time of the 1968 coup and served as loyal network that sought to benefit from the favours that could be accrued from their fellow tribesmen's rise to power.[26] Thus, a new base of regime support coalesced within Iraq's power structure. While this group's proximity to the security forces meant that they buttressed the regime, they also posed a challenge to it at the same time as they could unseat Saddam Hussein if he failed to guarantee their interests or survival.

Iraq's policy to the Arab Gulf became more pragmatic in the 1970s. Rather than perceiving the Gulf states as 'imperial stooges', Baghdad pursued a moderate policy to the region, and followed Saudi Arabia's lead on oil pricing. It even extended financial loans to the British-allied Sultan Qabus of Oman to fight the leftist Dhofari rebellion.[27] One of the valuable documents dating from this time is a report issued by Iraqi military intelligence entitled, 'The American Threats to Occupy the Oil Resources in the Arab Gulf: 1979'. The report examines the possible scenarios of a US military action in the region during the energy crisis. The introduction of the report reads:

> The genesis of the possibility of American military intrusion in the Middle East and the Arab Gulf particularly, started in 1974 when then Secretary of State Henry Kissinger declared during a visit to the region that the United States will interfere in the case of oil stoppage because it threatens America's national interest. In recent years various studies and thoughts concerning American occupation of the oil reserves were published. Initially it started as an introduction into the energy crisis in the Gulf and its impact on international relations. Then it was followed by official statements and declarations by American officials that stressed that uninterrupted oil import from the Gulf is an American national interest. These statements came as one of the tools of imperialism.[28]

The document invokes the themes of 'Western imperialism' encroaching on the Gulf, similar to the frames employed by King Ghazi and Qasim, and that would re-emerge during the 1991 Gulf Crisis. While the document was produced in 1979, it reveals fears among the Iraqi regime in 1974, at a time when Hussein was

---

[25] Charles Tripp, *A History of Iraq* (Cambridge: Cambridge University Press, 2000), p. 166.
[26] *Ibid.*, p. 199.
[27] Dawisha, 'Footprints in the Sand', p. 140
[28] Kuwait Data Set (KDS) Folder CD 10 File 108-10-005, p. 2.

consolidating power and trying to assert control over the military. Furthermore, the notion of an American threat to the Gulf's oil could be seen at that time as a threat to the regime's main source of revenue.

In the early 1970s, the emergence of an American allied Iran as a regional power clashed with the Iraq's attempt to enhance its position in the Gulf. The expansion of military power in both countries was facilitated by the increase in Iraqi revenues after the oil crisis following the 1973 war, which allowed for surplus funds to be devoted to a significant increase in the hardware needed to project Iraq's military power. Tensions with Iran over Abu Musa and the Tunbs Islands were also related to portraying Iran as a threat to the 'Arab Gulf' and thus legitimized a massive arms build-up of the Iraqi military. The expansion of the military in the 1970s served as a means to buttress Saddam Hussein's leadership, projecting the image of the Arab power in the Gulf, an alternative to Iran. On the domestic level, Hussein demonstrated the development and technological strength of the armed forces to the Iraqi public. According to Chubin and Tripp, the massive modernization and expansion of the military also presented Hussein with another threat: creating such a force was of little use to the Iraqi leader unless he could employ it in a decisive demonstration of his power.[29] The perceived threat to Hussein's regime emanating from Khomeini's Islamic Revolution in 1979 ultimately provided Baghdad with the opportunity to use this expanded military in such a demonstration of power and assert his regional dominance in the Gulf, if not the entire Arab world.

The Iran–Iraq war changed the dynamics of Gulf politics for the following eight years. During this time, Saddam Hussein's most important supporters were the elite group of insiders whose loyalty he cultivated. This in-group was made up primarily of civilian Ba'athists, including members of his own clan that he promoted to key security positions once he was in power. Other regime supporters formed clusters around this inside group, including the higher echelons of his security services, tribal leaders who declared their loyalty to the president, a new class of economic entrepreneurs who benefited from Hussein's patronage, and the officers who represented the interests of the military. During the Iran–Iraq war, Hussein never allowed himself to be threatened by any of these collective interests, particularly those of the military at a time when Iraq was facing setbacks on the battlefront. Rather than becoming dependent on any one cluster during the war, he played one off against the other. At the same time he played off his loyal core of insiders against the military, convincing the former of their common plight of losing their status and privilege if the career officers of the armed forces were to launch a coup in response to their failing fortunes on the battlefield with Iran.

Iraq's decision to invade Iran in September 1980 was a result of regime insecurity, as the Revolution had the potential to incite its Shi'a to agitate against a minority Sunni Arab and secular Ba'athist government. Regime security provided Baghdad with a motive to cooperate with the Gulf, as Iraq's overriding priority remained the defeat of Iran, or after 1982 bringing Teheran to a stalemate. Common ethnic and sectarian affinities with the Arab Sunni regimes of the Gulf ensured a shared threat perception in the face of a Shi'a Persian enemy.

[29] Shahram Chubin and Charles Tripp, *Iran and Iraq at War* (Boulder, CO: Westview, 1988), p. 243.

Iraq and Kuwait during the Gulf Crisis: 1990–2003

At the end of the Iran–Iraq War, and prior to the invasion of Kuwait, the Iraqi leadership perceived a threat from an American conspiracy, with the aid of Israel and Kuwait. The invasion of Kuwait was not an offensive operation but rather a pre-emptive manoeuvre to prevent this American scheme from succeeding. The perception of the US in the early nineties was based on the notion that the Americans intended to assume the role that the British played in the Middle East after the collapse of the Ottoman Empire. The US was maintaining the colonial legacy of Great Britain, and given that the Soviet Union was collapsing, the Iraqis maintained that there was no power to check American designs for the Middle East. Such rhetoric was designed for consumption in the Arab world, as such tactics sought to rally Arab opinion, particularly in states that were supporting a growing coalition based in Saudi Arabia that had the potential to not only fight for Kuwait, but to undermine Saddam Hussein's regime by invading Baghdad. Such a threat emanating from the Gulf would provide a compelling narrative to maintain internal cohesion among Hussein's inner core prior and during the Gulf Crisis.

Several speeches delivered by Saddam Hussein reveal how the Iraqi leadership justified its policy to the Gulf. In a speech on 8 August 1990, in which he announced Iraq's annexation of Kuwait, Saddam Hussein stated that, 'The pen of colonialism and the scissors of the evil ones have drawn the maps and divided the nations to make sure that all the independent states will become weak and ineffectual, unable to participate in an Arab renaissance and Arab unity'.[30] This speech justified the absorption of Kuwait to a mass Arab audience, depicting the US as preventing Iraq's historic mission of uniting the Arab nation.

Saudi Arabia posed a potent threat to Iraq as it served as a base for the coalition forces. Regime security in Baghdad dictated that the otherwise secular Ba'ath regime adopt Islamic rhetoric to undermine the religious credentials of the House of Sa'ud, who had let 'infidels' occupy Islam's holiest cities of Mecca and Madina. On 10 August 1990, Hussein delivered what has been euphemistically referred to as the 'jihad speech':

> Arabs, Muslims, believers in God ... this is your day to rise and spread quickly in order to defend Mecca, which is captive to the spears of Americans and Zionists ... Burn the soil under their feet. Burn the soil under the feet of the aggressors and invaders who want to harm for your families in Iraq. Until the voice of the right rise up in the Arab world, hit their interests wherever they are and rescue holy Mecca and the grave of the Prophet Mohammed in Medina.[31]

Such an appeal sought to communicate to Riyadh that Iraq had the capability to inspire audiences in Saudi Arabia and the entire Muslim world. This Islamist appeal served as a rhetorical tool to undermine the base of a coalition that had the potential to unseat him militarily.

A transcript of a session with Hussein's most valuable domestic in-group reveals another dynamic in Iraqi policy to the Gulf that has rarely been examined. On 3 October 1990, Hussein convened a meeting of the heads of his security services. He used the occasion to repeat his conviction that most Iraqis believed that Kuwait was an integral part of Iraq, separated from it by 'British imperialism'.

---

[30] KDS Folder 1215-1429 File 565-2-3, pp. 76–78.
[31] Jerry M. Long, *Saddam's War of Words: Politics, Religion, and the Iraqi Invasion of Kuwait* (Austin: University of Texas Press, 2004), p. 95.

Hussein's tirade against the Kuwaiti rulers and the British demonstrated this belief: 'The detachment of Kuwait is a British trap, and I was convinced that the Al-Sabah have conspired with the British.'[32] Hussein highlighted this view: 'They (the Kuwaitis) will compensate us for the losses due to the British conspiracy, because Kuwait is Iraqi, and I know the detachment is a loss for Iraq.'[33] These verbal attacks in the presences of the security apparatus had a specific motive according to Tripp:

> In this connection Saddam Hussein made frequent use of ridicule and contempt in references to the al-Sabah, the al-Sa'ud, and other Gulf dynasties. Metaphorically, if in no other way, the Iraqi leader was seeking to include all Iraqis—and perhaps many other Arabs—in the collective identity closest to his heart: that of membership in a once disadvantaged rural clan despised by people with more impressive pedigrees and greater wealth.[34]

The Iraqi leader's rhetoric, embellished with themes of class hostility, exemplified the discourse directed to his regime insiders, or what Tripp described as an Iraqi 'resentment of the arrogance and pretensions of the al-Sabah and other Gulf dynasties'.[35] This 'resentment' is amply apparent when Hussein directly insulted the origins of the royal family in this speech: 'The Al-Sabah were originally bastards. They used to sell bubble gum and sweets to women; they have been kicked out of more than one place. They came to Iraq and conspired with the English to detach a part for them that will prevent Iraq from having a sea shore.'[36] Afterwards, he resorted to insulting the morality of the family itself: 'They wanted to make the Iraqi women naked,' and said, 'The house of corruption cannot coexist with the house of honour and the corrupt cannot coexist with the good-hearted.'[37] Hussein argued that the Iraqis had to invade due to the personal insults hurled at them from the Kuwaitis: 'After we placed our troops on the borders, they made fun of us.'[38] On top of that, the Kuwaitis and Jabir al-Sabah, the Amir of Kuwait had the 'audacity' to take Hussein's warnings lightly: 'In spite of that, I have suggested to Jabir to settle the borders, but his answer was to leave this issue to the group and he procrastinated on the subject. I said that these were the principles we have discussed.'[39] Such comments were particularly insulting from the Kuwaiti side, as in the aftermath of the Iran–Iraq war, Iraq developed a myth that due to its sacrifices in 'protecting the Gulf' during its conflict with Persian Iran, it emerged as the rightful defender of the Arab states as well the most powerfully armed nation in the region.

The discourse he employed differed from his usually flowery comments of rectifying past colonial injustices, delivered to the Iraqi and Arab masses. Given that this was a closed session meeting, his candid statements justifying the invasion are revealing. Tripp's work characterizes the relationship between Saddam Hussein and his ruling apparatus as cemented through the ties of

---

[32] KDS Folder CD 10 File 111-9-005, pp. 4–6.
[33] *Ibid.*
[34] Charles Tripp, 'Symbol and Strategy: Iraq and the War for Kuwait', in Wolfgang F. Danspeckgruber and Charles Tripp (eds), *The Iraqi Aggression Against Kuwait: Strategic Lessons and Implications for Europe* (Boulder, CO: Westview, 1996), p. 27.
[35] *Ibid.*, p. 23.
[36] KDS Folder CD 10 File 111-9-005, pp. 4–6.
[37] *Ibid.*
[38] *Ibid.*
[39] *Ibid.*

patronage, where familial and sectarian commonalities between the regime insiders guaranteed their loyalty to the president as long as he could provide them with powerful positions and privileged access to the largesse of the state. The rhetoric in the 3 October 1990 meeting illustrates the dynamics of the language of patronage.

Saddam Hussein needed to generate some kind of victory over Kuwait to maintain the security of his regime, proving to insiders that the invasion produced tangible results. Unlike Ghazi or Qasim, Hussein was constrained by his own words, so that when he had the option of withdrawing from Kuwait before the 15 January 1991 deadline or engaging the coalition in a battle he was sure he could not win militarily, he chose the latter. Failure to do so would mean he would have failed to live up to his promises of reunifying Kuwait. Such an admission would demonstrate the leader's weakness to the Iraqi public, the military, and most importantly his Tikriti inner core, leading to a possible coup.

Iraq's regime insecurity after the Iran–Iraq war was related to international phenomena, such as the collapse of the USSR, American unipolarity in the Middle East, and regionally, the Kuwaiti refusal to forgive Iraq's debts and the allegation that Kuwait was serving as the base for an American–Israeli conspiracy to unseat the Saddam Hussein government. All these perceived threats created internal cohesion among the Iraqi ruling apparatus, at a time when Iraq's economy was shattered after the eight-year war, and Iran could no longer provide a convenient scapegoat, as Saddam had declared his victory over Teheran. By 1990, Saddam Hussein redefined the threats to the regime from the Persian foe to a Gulf-American-Zionist tripartite threat. Creating such an enemy provided Hussein with a dilemma, since he was forced to stand up to this threat coalescing in the Gulf rather than retreating from Kuwait with his military forces intact on the eve of the 1991 war. His initial justification for invading Kuwait to reunify the Iraqi nation and pre-empt these international and regional threats to the regime would prove to be Hussein's undoing, as it initiated the 1991 Gulf war, more than a decade of sanctions and culminated in the 2003 Iraq war which ultimately unseated him, ushering in a new era in Iraq–Gulf relations.

Iraq's Post-Ba'athist Gulf Policy

Since 2003, the Iraqi government's policy to the Gulf has been primarily defined by abandoning its policy of hostility toward the south. Iraq did not have the military forces to even consider this option, and its priorities remained the reconstruction of its infrastructure. The new regime faced difficulties in governing and could not deliver basic services to its citizens. Iraq's priorities included asking the Gulf states to write off its debts and aid in its reconstruction. For example, in July 2006, Iraqi Prime Minister Nuri Al-Maliki asked Kuwaiti investors to invest in Iraq during a meeting of the Kuwait Chamber of Commerce and Industry.[40] On the same day, Al-Maliki declared that, 'The Saddam symphony that Kuwait is part of Iraq has vanished. For me this issue is a rubbish matter.'[41]

[40] 'Iraqi PM Calls Upon Kuwait Businessmen to Invest in His Country', Kuwait News Agency (KUNA), OSC GMP20060705649005, 5 July 2006.
[41] 'Trial of Saddam Wouldn't Take Long, His Execution Is Coming Soon—Maliki', KUNA, OSC GMP20060705649004, 5 July 2006.

Nevertheless, the tensions that have marked Iraq–Kuwaiti relations have not disappeared, despite aforementioned statements by the Iraqi prime minister. On 2 August 2005, exactly 14 years after Iraqi troops rolled into Kuwait, Jawad Al-Maliki, chairman of the Iraqi Parliament's Security and Defense Committee, accused Kuwait of erecting a fence that reached a kilometre deep into Iraqi territory. He declared that such an act constituted a 'transgression against Iraq's borders, sovereignty, and vital resources by laying their hands on deep waters [of the shores of Umm Qasr], which are considered a vital resource in the Iraqi maritime and trade industries'. He also said: 'They left us some shallow waters that are no more than six meters deep'.[42] The perceived insecurity of Iraq failing to develop a deep-water port continued to exist in Iraq despite the ouster of the Ba'athist government.

Conclusion

This study has sought to portray Iraq's Gulf policy as an outcome of regime security in Iraq. The history of Iraqi–Gulf relations can be characterized by several dynamics. In order to bolster regime security, the Iraqi state attempted to occupy Kuwait on three occasions within the twentieth century to gain a naval outlet on the Gulf as well as preempting threats to the stability of the ruling apparatus in Baghdad. Gulf policy was developed by insular regimes, whether it was the Four Colonels' and Ghazi's policy to Kuwait, or Saddam Hussein's policy to the same state used to appeal to and protect himself from his Tikriti inner core. The failure to demonstrate strength to the in-groups of the regime had drastic consequences. Qasim's indecisiveness during the Kuwait crisis of 1961 could be considered as one of the factors that led to his overthrow and execution in 1963.

The overriding factor in Iraq's Gulf policy was determined by the Kuwait issue, an issue that factored in Iraq's policy since its creation. The use of nationalist symbols and images in the rhetoric of the state regarding Kuwait demonstrated that the leadership had the ability to choose themes that could resonate among constituents in the regime. While Iraq's forces failed to take action in 1938, 1961 or were overwhelmed in 1991, the leadership had diligently endeavoured to inspire regime insiders with a notion of 'reunified homeland'.

Ensuring regime security in Baghdad has resulted in tensions with Iraq's Gulf neighbours since the creation of the Iraqi state. The survival of the Iraqi government in the aftermath of the 2003 Iraq War will depend on a legitimacy derived from providing basic services to its citizens. The security situation in Iraq improved in 2007, and thus the administration in Baghdad had the means to concentrate on restoring Iraq's infrastructure. In this context, the Gulf will be crucial in terms of investing and rebuilding Iraq, and at least in the near future, the twenty-first century may well be marked by greater cooperation between Iraq and the members of the Gulf Cooperation Council.

---

[42] 'Iraq: Assembly Member Accuses Kuwait of "Encroaching on" Iraqi Territories', Al-Sharqiyya Television, OSC GMP20050802547001, 2 August 2005.

Islamic Utopian Romanticism and the Foreign Policy Culture of Iran

ARSHIN ADIB-MOGHADDAM
St. Edmund Hall and Department of Politics and International Relations, University of Oxford

The disappearance of utopia brings about a static state of affairs in which man himself becomes no more than a thing.... Thus, after a long tortuous, but heroic development, just at the highest stage of awareness, when history is ceasing to be blind fate, and is becoming more and more man's own creation, with the relinquishment of utopias, man would lose his will to shape history and therewith his ability to understand it.[1]

On account of his dualistic and contradictory nature, man, this dialectical phenomenon, is compelled to be always in motion.... How disgraceful, then, are all fixed standards. Who can ever fix a standard? Man is a 'choice,' a struggle, a constant becoming. He is an infinite migration, a migration within himself, from clay to God; he is a migrant within his own soul.[2]

During the winter of 1978–79, Michel Foucault cogitated about the Iranian Revolution in a series of reports for *Corriere della sera* describing the protests as a revolt against the 'planetary system,' inspired by a 'religion of combat and sacrifice,' a counter-hegemonic mass movement that could bring about the 'transfiguration' of the world. Witnessing the departure of Iran's last shah, few analysts doubted that the demise of the Pahlavi dynasty was one of the central events of post-Second World War history.[3] Like Iranians themselves,

---

The author would like to thank Charles Jones and Zaheer Kazmi for their insightful comments on earlier drafts of this paper. The article also benefited from presentations and seminars at the University of Cambridge, the University of Hamburg, the School of International Relations in Tehran and from numerous conversations with Iranian foreign ministry officials.

[1] Karl Mannheim, *Ideology and Utopia: An Introduction to the Sociology of Knowledge* (London: Routledge, 1991), p. 236.
[2] Ali Shari'ati, *On the Sociology of Islam: Lectures by Ali Shari'ati*, Hamid Algar (Trans.) (Berkeley: Mizan Press, 1979), pp. 92–93.
[3] On Foucault and Iran in English, see among others Didier Eribon, *Michel Foucault*, Betsy Wing (Trans.) (London: Faber and Faber, 1991), p. 281ff.; James Miller, *The Passion of Michel Foucault* (London: HarperCollins, 1993), p. 306ff; Janet Afary and Kevin B. Anderson (2005), *Foucault, Gender, and One Iranian Revolution: The Seductions of Islamism* (Chicago: University of Chicago Press). See also Foucault's essays 'Open letter to Mehdi Bazargan' and 'Useless to revolt?,' in: Michel Foucault, *Power: Essential Works of Foucault, 1954–1984*, vol. 3, Robert Hurley et al. (Trans.) (London: Penguin, 1997).

Foucault perhaps underestimated the authoritarian moment of Iran's Islamic enterprise, whilst overestimating its potencies, but his reports adequately captured the universal claim and 'libidinous' idealism intrinsic to the revolutionary process. Like the French, Russians, Chinese, and Cubans before them, Iranians believed in the imminence of change, brought about by an Islamic international that would shatter the prevalent status quo. Their political and spiritual guide, Ayatollah Rouhollah Khomeini, who made unmistakably clear that the Islamic Revolution did not belong exclusively to Iran, nurtured this idealism, declaring that 'Islam [was] revealed for mankind and the Muslims. ... An Islamic movement, therefore, cannot limit itself to any particular country, not even to the Islamic countries; it is the continuation of the revolution by the prophets.'[4]

This article explores how the revolutionary reality of late 1970s Iran transmuted into a new identity for the Iranian state and how core principles of the revolution—radical cultural and political independence, economic autarky, diplomatic and ideological mobilization against Zionism and resistance against US interference in regional and domestic affairs—continue to guide the country's foreign policy elites. My argument is that Iran continues to challenge the international system in general and the US state as its most dominant power in particular, because of a 'utopian-romantic' meta-narrative that constitutes the Iranian foreign policy culture. The way the phrase is used here, 'foreign policy culture' does not refer merely to cognitive filters through which impulses from the international system are processed.[5] Reverting to ideas developed by critical theorists and historical sociologists, I contend that one can attribute analytic autonomy to foreign policy culture as a structured system constituted by intersubjective knowledge, e.g., ideologies, norms, identities, institutions, and other cultural artifacts. Foreign policy culture thus is conceived of as a systemic phenomenon that transcends the concrete minds of its agent— the cultural manifestation of the dominant *Weltanschauungen* carried by elites and which gives meaning to power and content to interest. To deconstruct this culture and to establish how it informed the grand foreign policy preferences of the Islamic Republic is what this narrative tries to demonstrate. To that end, the article is divided into two parts: one, theoretical-abstract, the other, empirical-descriptive.

The first section of this article presents a 'four-dimensional dialectic' of culture and foreign policy preferences. I am aware that some readers will find this part of the argument too abstract, too 'theoretical.' But I found it necessary to sketch the *Herkunft* of culture to its 'base'—human inventions—in order to avoid the perils of cultural reductionism that have sometimes infested 'orientalist' discourse on our subject matter. I found such an interpretative approach toward culture helpful to show that cognitive beliefs about the world are neither predetermined ontologically nor are eternally valid. As it is pursued here, analysis of culture is 'not an experimental science in search of law but an interpretative one in search of meaning.'[6]

Moreover, a dialectical approach toward culture focuses as much as possible on the manufacturing, reification, theorization and institutionalization of culture. How is culture produced, reproduced, legitimated, ideologized, contested and changed? How is

---

[4] Sermon delivered on 2 November 1979 and quoted in Farhang Rajaee, *Islamic Values and World View: Khomeyni on Man, the State and International Politics*, vol. XIII (London: University Press of America, 1983), p. 82.
[5] Most foreign policy theorists rate ideas as secondary to material factors; see further Judith Goldstein & Robert Keohane (Eds) *Ideas and Foreign Policy* (Ithaca: Cornell University Press, 1993).
[6] Clifford Geertz, *The Interpretation of Cultures* (Basic Books: New York, 1993), p. 5.

the meaning of culture fixed or stabilized historically via theory and political practice? How does culture affect strategic preferences? Framing the empirical analysis with a four-dimensional dialectic is helpful to trace historically the emergence and constitution of cultural constructs and their corresponding effects upon collective action. My method is essentially to sketch—and it certainly does not claim to be more than a sketch—the 'functioning' of culture in relation to strategic preferences of the post-revolutionary Iranian state. What I contend about Iran's foreign policy culture is that it is not only a set of ideas but also a mentality, a *Geist*, a systemic phenomenon that is strong enough to penetrate the strategic thinking of Iran's foreign policy elites to its core. Thus, it is claimed, culture has both an internal consistency and a highly articulated set of relationships to its agents. My analyses consequently try to show the ideational shape of culture as pertinent to Iran's grand strategic preferences which requires some discussion about the emergence, perseverance, and transformation of culture.

The second part of this article focuses on the emergence of Iran's grand foreign policy preferences. Primarily, it is addressed to those readers who wonder why Iran is repeatedly challenging central tenets of international society. It demonstrates how utopian-romantic ideals formulated during the revolutionary years, and institutionalized as central narratives of the Islamic Republic, constitute the contemporary grand strategic preferences of the Iranian state. By arguing that the Islamic Republic has not discarded certain core principles formulated during the revolutionary period, I question interpretations of Iranian foreign policies as thoroughly status-quo oriented, 'pragmatist' or 'realist.'[7] It is not at all obvious that challenging the international status quo and the United States as its dominant guardian is considered irrational from the perspective of the Iranian state. Nor is it clear that Iran has discarded the export of the Islamic republican model. Like other revolutionary entities—China, Cuba, France—the Iranian state and Iranians themselves have a nostalgic self-perception about the role of their country in world affairs. While the means to advocate Iran's international agenda may have changed, the motivational drives toward challenging international realities continue to be strong.

Culture and Foreign Policy: Toward a Four-dimensional Dialectic

If we aspire to look over the shoulders of decision makers, as Hans Morgenthau so famously advocated, we have to strengthen our empathetic understanding of the 'mindset' of decision makers, and this in turn requires going through the pains of exploring the cultural fabric producing that mindset.[8] In contrast to political realists, who tend to take existing social structures for granted, cultural and sociological theorists agree that the essential factor of the social world that humans create is socially constructed meaning.[9] Depending on how they order their environment, humans infuse their own meanings or interpretations into reality. The surrounding social order hence is not preordained

---

[7] See, for example, Anoushiravan Ehteshami, *After Khomeini: The Iranian Second Republic* (London: Routledge, 1995); and Adam Tarock, *Iran's Foreign Policy since 1990: Pragmatism Supersedes Islamic Ideology* (Commack: Nova Science Press, 1999).

[8] See further Hans Morgenthau, *Politics among Nations* (New York: Alfred Knopf, 1948).

[9] For a comprehensive critique of (neo)realist methodologies and ontologies, see R. B. J. Walker, *Inside/Outside: International Relations as Political Theory* (Cambridge: Cambridge University Press, 1993), esp. chap. 5.

or biologically given. It is an 'ongoing human production. It is produced by man in the course of his ongoing externalisation.'[10]

Both Marx and Hegel argued that human externalization, that is the ongoing outpouring of human activity in society, is an act of anthropological necessity. In order to be an acting being, man requires reference to the social world. A comparable dialectic may be established between the nation-state and international society. In order to give meaning to the external, international world, nation-states constitute themselves *in relation to* international society, and more specifically in relation to other members of that society. They interact with other countries (economically, politically, diplomatically) in the course of their ongoing externalization. Like man who is not merely *Homo socius* but also *Homo faber/Homo pictor*, the nation-state is both world and culture maker. In this sense international relations exist only as a human product and—by extension—as a product of the nation-state (itself a product of individual action).

In a second dialectic between man and society, sociological theory suggests that socially constructed meaning attains the status of objective reality. 'Human expressivity,' Berger and Luckmann, observe 'is capable of objectivation, that is, it manifests itself in products of human activity that are available both to their producers and to other men as elements of a common world.'[11] The most obvious signs and symbols of the objectivated world surrounding us are norms, values, traditions or institutions and other cultural artifacts. Ultimately, they tell us what is good and bad and sometimes even who we are. They are *there*, external to us, invented by history, but nonetheless claiming objective validity, commanding a persistence that is beyond our control. This goes to the heart of what Marx meant when he observed that 'Men make their own history ... not under circumstances they themselves have chosen but under the given and inherited circumstances with which they are directly confronted.'[12] It also points toward a comparable dialectic in our international world. Both the nation-state and its product, international society, are objectivated human activity. The nation-state, the producer, and international society, the product, exist *only* as human objectivity. Their meaning, importance, legitimacy, indeed their very existence, is mediated to us via their cultures—norms, institutions, traditions, values, etc. These cultural artifacts define subjectively plausible representations of reality, morally sanctioned codes of collective behavior, rules of social discourse and a general plot for the conduct of the day-to-day affairs of the state. Culture in this sense functions as shared, 'factualized' ideational patterns that permit the nation-state to interpret its relationship with the external environment (alter, or international society) and to order the internal self (ego, or self-identity).

The Social Construction of Cultural Systems

It has been suggested that, through the process of externalization, a structured cultural system is constructed that is experienced as an intersubjectively shared object of reality in common with others. To understand culture as externalized, objectivated systems of

---

[10] Peter L. Berger & Thomas Luckmann, *The Social Construction of Reality: A Treatise in the Sociology of Knowledge* (Harmondsworth: Penguin, 1979), pp. 69–70.
[11] Ibid., p. 49.
[12] Karl Marx, 'The Eighteenth Brumaire of Louis Bonaparte,' in: Karl Marx, *Survey from Exile*, David Fernbach (Ed.) (Harmondsworth, Penguin, 1973), p. 146.

knowledge is close to Wilhelm Dilthey's observations regarding the relationship between cultural system and the individual. According to Dilthey:

> The individual slant which colours the personal knowledge of life is corrected and enlarged by the common experience. By this I mean the shared beliefs emerging in any coherent circle of people. These are assertions about the passage of life, judgements of value, rules of conduct, definition of goals and of what is good. It is characteristic of them that they are the products of the common life. They apply as much to the life of individuals as to that of communities. As custom, tradition and public opinion they influence individuals and their experience; because the community has the weight of numbers behind it and outlasts the individual, this power usually proves superior to his will.[13]

The last sentence is crucial and introduces the third moment of the dialectic between culture and individual. Dilthey discerns that culture emerges as aggregations of meaning constituted by human experience. Once externalized, objectivated as custom, tradition and values, the cultural structure reacts back on the individual, exercising a power that 'proves superior to his will.' If we attribute structural qualities to interaction, the cultural system under focus develops *emergent* properties that may have causal impacts on its constituent agents. To say that a cultural system has emergent properties refers to a paradox in the dialectic between culture and individual. The cultural system, having emerged as an externalized, objectivated human product, is experienced by man as something other than his own invention. Once externalized through human action and objectivated through reification and institutionalization, culture appears as an externalized product, which implies it has acquired a measure of distinctiveness from the elites who produced it (it has acquired systemic qualities).[14] As an external cultural system, it exercises a certain degree of hegemony over the culture bearer, which at times is overwhelming, at times reformed through consistent resistance, and at times overthrown *in toto* by revolutionary force. Culture conceived of in this sense is objectified as a facticity external to its creators, and hence is experienced as an outer objective reality in common with others.[15] Sociologist Margaret Archer argues in a comparable vein:

> As an emergent entity the Cultural System has an objective existence and autonomous relations amongst its components. ... At any moment the CS [Cultural System] is the product of historical Socio-Cultural interaction, but having emerged (emergence being a continuous process) then *qua* product, it has properties of its

---

[13] Wilhelm Dilthey, *Selected Writings* (Cambridge: Cambridge University Press, 1976), p. 179.

[14] Most contemporary sociological and constructivist analyses, in international relations and other disciplines, subscribe to that viewpoint. See further Mlada Bukovansky, *Legitimacy and Power Politics: The American and French Revolutions in International Political Culture* (Princeton: Princeton University Press, 2002); Alexander Wendt, *Social Theory of International Politics* (Cambridge: Cambridge University Press, 1999), esp. chap. 4; Margaret S. Archer, *Culture and Agency: The Place of Culture in Social Theory*, rev. ed. (Cambridge: Cambridge University Press, 1996); and Nicholas Onuf, *The Republican Legacy in International Thought* (Cambridge: Cambridge University Press, 1998), chap. 8.

[15] I have drawn on sociological theory here; see further Peter Berger & Stanley Pullberg, 'Reification and the sociological critique of consciousness,' *History and Theory*, 4(2) (1965), pp. 196–211; Peter Berger, *The Sacred Canopy* (Garden City: Doubleday, 1966); and Berger & Luckmann, *Social Construction*, n. 8.

own. Like structure, culture is man-made but escapes its makers to act back upon them.[16]

Archer speaks of an objectively existing cultural system that is the product of interaction and acts upon its constituent parts. This idea not only corresponds to my argument about the relative autonomy of the cultural system as an external, objectified reality transcending its makers but also with my second proposal regarding the social construction of culture. If the cultural system is produced, reproduced, and reified in interaction with others, as Archer argues, the formation of culture is an intrinsically social process. Individuals and nation-states do not retain integrity as they engage in interaction; they do not 'function' in encapsulated habitats. They have myriad relationships with the international world, with other nation-states, and with other actors in international society. This 'sociality' suggests two central characteristics of cultural systems: it is through externalization of socially produced knowledge that culture is a product of individuals; and it is through objectification that culture becomes a reality *sui generis*. What needs to be provided in a third step is the link between that cultural system and the emergence of preferences and interests.

Foreign Policy Culture and Grand Strategic Preference Setting

If externalization constitutes a cultural system and objectification makes it appear as reality, it should follow that this objectivated world is reabsorbed by agents who are the addressees of the reflexive reality. This process is termed 'internalization' in sociological theory. Sociologists argue that agents internalize culture through the process of socialization—a dialectic, continuous process whereby the contents and meanings of culture are mediated, and the agent is habituated to accept the ideational attributes of the structure of that cultural system (e.g., identities, roles, norms, institutions). Relating our argument back to the findings in the previous section, this would mean that the third dimension of the production and workings of culture has 'reactive' qualities: (1) it is through externalization that culture is a human product; (2) it is through objectification that culture becomes a reality *sui generis*; and (3) it is through internalization that agents are products of culture. The behavioral component—intrinsic to all three moments of this cultural dialectic—manifests itself most forcefully in the dimension of internalization through socialization in culture, because it is during this moment where external structures affect the subjective structures of the consciousness of the agent itself, not only transcending the external-internal divide but also transposing the outer cultural system into the inner self. It is this moment of the cultural process that transforms agents from culture *maker* to culture *taker*.

If cultural systems react to shape their makers, we may talk about a process of 'introjection,' in a manner that the 'radical' Frankfurt School theorist Herbert Marcuse employed the term. In a provocative form, this quality of culture reveals that socialization in cultural systems has not only mediating or causal impacts but also *constitutive* effects. According to Marcuse:

> The efficiency of the system blunts the individuals' recognition that it contains no facts which do not communicate the repressive power of the whole. If the individuals find themselves in the things which shape their life, they do so, not by

---

[16] Archer, *Culture and Agency*, p. 107, n. 14.

giving, but by accepting the law of things—not the law of physics but the law of their society.[17]

Reinterpreted, Marcuse's dramatic argument about the deterministic impact of society on man may be transferred to our cultural milieu. By its very constitution, both as an intersubjectively shared objectified reality and formally institutionalized and codified fact, culture not only penetrates agents but also 'introjects' them with objectivated meanings (fundamentally through language).[18] The invented artifacts of the culture—norms, identities, institutions, etc.—are maintained not simply by their coercive ability but by implicit and sometimes formally explicit claims to legitimacy.[19] They possess a degree of historically legitimated moral authority which signals that conforming to the dominant culture is morally right and dissent is morally wrong. Socialized in such an authoritative yet invented cultural milieu, agents are penetrated ideationally 'all the way down,' shaped to take on the roles and attitudes communicated by the dominant cultural system.[20]

Following the symbolic-interactionist school of social psychology in the tradition of George Herbert Mead, one further may assert that social roles have particular identities (or an identity set) attached to them.[21] These *role identities* are socially constructed representations of the Self (ego), which by implication require representation of an alter Other: 'By taking a particular role identity Ego is at the same time "casting" Alter in a corresponding counter-role that makes Ego's identity meaningful. One cannot be a trader without someone to trade with, a proselytiser without a convert, or a conqueror without a conquest.'[22] Culture in this sense functions as a source for identity, it differentiates 'us' from 'them.' Boundaries of identity expressed by abstract 'typologies' that differentiate the 'in-group' from the 'out-group' would not make sense without reference to shared knowledge or culture. The self-depicted identities would not be recognizable if individuals or states would not constantly act out, reproduce, and legitimate them. Once cognitively internalized and formally institutionalized, the cultural system constitutes the preferred self-identification or identity of the agent in relation to the Other, guiding him in relation to both *goal-oriented preferences* (interest) and *strategy* (means). Reconstituted for our understanding of foreign policy culture, a four dimensional dialectic emerges: (1) it is through externalization that culture is a human product; (2) it is through objectification that culture becomes a reality *sui generis*; (3) it is through internalization that agents are products of culture; and (4) it is through introjection that culture constitutes the identities, interests and preferences of agents. These are, of course, ideal-typical categorizations that are not meant to define separable positions in a causal transmission belt. Here and elsewhere there is no suggestion that there are benchmarks which would define the transformation of one dialectic into another. What has been presented here is a preliminary four-dimensional dialectic of culture that may offer mnemonic (yet ephemeral) value for the relationship between agents (individuals, nation-states) and cultural systems

---

[17] Herbert Marcuse, *One-dimensional Man: Studies in the Ideology of Advanced Industrial Society* (London: Routledge, 1964), p. 11.

[18] The centrality of language is accentuated by the 'semiotic' approach to culture; see, among others, Ferdinand Saussure, *Course in General Linguistics* (New York: McGraw Hill, 1964).

[19] For the social construction of legitimacy, see Bukovansky, *Legitimacy*, esp. pp. 2–3, n. 14.

[20] See Wendt, *Social Theory*, chap. 3, p. 92ff., n. 14.

[21] See George H. Mead, *Mind, Self, and Society* (Chicago: University of Chicago Press, 1934).

[22] Wendt, *Social Theory*, p. 329, n. 14.

(society, the international system). Culture conceived of in this sense is 'not a power, something to which social events, behaviors, institutions, or processes can be causally attributed causally; it is a context, something within which they can be intelligibly—that is, thickly—described.'[23]

Framing Iran's Foreign Policy Culture

The suggested cultural dialectic offers a general framework to trace the relationship between cultural system, identity construction and the definition of goal-oriented preferences. In this case, we are dealing with a specific manifestation of culture, attempting to address the relationship of one specific agent (Iran) with its external environment (international society). To that end, it makes sense to commence by exploring the emergence of ideas, institutions, and norms as pertinent to the contemporary grand strategic preferences of Iran. But how do we specify the location of them? Where do we 'look' for the production and reproduction of shared knowledge? I suggest two interdependent sources of Iran's foreign policy culture: 'cognitive-introjective,' referring to the intellectual production and processing of categories of the Self and the Other; and 'institutional-introjective,' denoting the formal institutionalization of cultural artifacts as authoritative narratives of the state. Both moments of cultural production and reproduction claim the quality of objectiveness, resisting attempts to be altered. Both are interdependent, i.e., they 'inhabit' the same foreign policy culture. Both are legitimated by authoritative narratives of discourse, wielding mechanisms of social control to enforce their reality. However, both also are under permanent pressure from competing and oppositional ideas, which may succeed in transforming the prevalent culture altogether.

Cognitive-introjective Sources of the Iranian Foreign Policy Culture

The ideational introjection of masses by intellectuals has figured prominently in discourse about the workings of culture. According to Max Weber, intellectuals are a group of people 'who by virtue of their peculiarity have special access to certain achievements considered to be "culture values" [*Kulturwerte*] and who therefore usurp the leadership of a "culture community" [*Kulturgemeinschaft*].'[24] It was Antonio Gramsci, of course, who highlighted the hegemonic fulcrum of culture, observing that intellectually produced and legitimated ideologies are particularly deterministic and functional in perpetuating and reproducing the dominant social system. 'The intellectuals,' Gramsci observed, 'are the dominant group's "deputies" exercising the subaltern functions of social hegemony and political government.'[25] The hegemony of the dominant ideas articulated by intellectuals is not, however, unalterable. With the formation of a revolutionary cadre of 'organic' intellectuals, Gramsci argued, a counter-hegemonic movement may succeed in spreading ideas that organize the masses against the exploitation of the ruling groups. From

---

[23] Geertz, *The Interpretation of Cultures*, p. 14, n. 6.

[24] Max Weber, *From Max Weber: Essays in Sociology* (London: Routledge, 1998), p. 176.

[25] Antonio Gramsci, *Selections from Prison Notebooks* (London: Lawrence & Wishart, 1971), p. 12. Writing in the Marxist tradition, Gramsci distinguished between 'organic' intellectuals and 'traditional' intellectuals. Whereas the former are created by dominant social classes to give them homogeneity and awareness of their function, the latter category refers to intellectuals (most notably the clergy, but also administrators, scholars, philosophers, scientists and theorists) who are already in existence and seem to represent historical continuity.

Gramsci's perspective, then, intellectuals are manufacturers, re-manufacturers *and* inventors of culture.

Whereas followers of Gramsci perhaps would accentuate the function of intellectually sanctioned culture primarily as a servant of power, I focus on the formative and inventive moment of the intellectual manufacturing of ideational systems. In the pre-revolutionary Iranian context it was the 'inventive manufacturer' of intellectual ideas who was instrumental in producing a counter-hegemonic political culture that ushered in the revolution in 1979.[26] Whereas the Pahlavi state adhered to the representation of the monarchy and Iran as the heir of pre-Islamic Persian empires at the gates of reconstituting a 'great civilization' (*tamadon-e bozorg*), the opposition to the metaphysics propagated by the Pahlavi state reverted to Shi'i-Islamic anti-imperialist imageries as the dominant narrative of the Iranian self. The actual existing and ongoing order of the Pahlavi state ('topia') was counteracted with 'wish-images' suitable to function as a counter-hegemonic, revolutionary rallying call for the opposition (utopias).[27] Romanticizing, yet frugal in their exaltations of the millenarian cause, erudite, yet bellicose in their manifestos for political emancipation, opprobrious, yet sanctimonious in their language of protest, and passionate, yet myopic in their promises about a better future, pre-revolutionary Iranian intellectuals managed to organize the Iranian population around powerful ideas, advocating not only revolutionary domestic change but also the transformation of the identity of the Iranian state from a monarchic-nationalistic status quo power to a revolutionary-universalistic people's movement perceived to be in the vanguard of the fight for a new, equitable world order. This utopian-romantic, perhaps even hubristic, self-perception constituted the nucleus of the foreign policy culture of post-revolutionary Iran. Employing the outlined theoretical framework, the following paragraphs investigate the cognitive-introjective production and reification of this foreign policy culture, followed by an exploration of its institutional-introjective manifestations.

Protesting Identity: Intellectual Foundations of Iran's Foreign Policy Culture

Carried by a cadre of revolutionary visionaries equipped with a range of counter-hegemonic utopias (Marxist, Communist, Maoist, Islamist, etc.), the political culture of Iran experienced a radical change during the 1960 s. While the domestic aspect of this cultural shift that led to the revolution in 1979 is well documented, the consequences for Iran's grand strategic foreign policy preferences have not been studied rigorously.[28] Nevertheless, the protests against the Pahlavi state did not reflect dissatisfaction only with domestic issues. The historical claim accentuated by the Iranian movement, which was inherent in the revolutionary internationalist ethos, transcended the nation-state, creating the dynamism that propelled the movement to spiral out of the Iranian context.

---

[26] For an examination of this political culture, see Mehrzad Boroujerdi, *Iranian Intellectuals and the West: The Tormented Triumph of Nativism* (Syracuse: Syracuse University Press, 1996).

[27] I have employed the terminology of Karl Mannheim here; see his *Ideology and Utopia*, p. 174, n. 1. Here, utopianism is *not* synonymous with ideology as E. H. Carr claimed; rather, utopianism refers to rationalization of political change (termed realism by Carr). See Edward Hallett Carr, *The Twenty Years' Crisis, 1919–1939: An Introduction to the Study of International Relations* (London: Macmillan, 1961). For an examination of the differing uses of terms common to Carr and Mannheim, see Charles Jones, *E. H. Carr and International Relations: A Duty to Lie* (Cambridge: Cambridge University Press, 1998).

[28] For a perceptive analysis of Iran's domestic political culture, see especially Boroujerdi, *Iranian Intellectuals*, n. 26; and Samih K. Farsoun & Mehrdad Mashayekhi, *Iran: Political Culture in the Islamic Republic* (London: Routledge, 1992).

Oppositional Iranian activists and intellectuals not only protested against the institution of monarchy but also demanded the redefinition of the country's identity and the redirection of relations with the whole world. As Morteza Mottahari argues:

> If it is decided that [the] basis in determining the limits of the Iranian nation is the Aryan factor, the ultimate end of that is proclivity toward the Western world. But this proclivity in our national and political mission involves submissions and consequences, the most serious being a severance with neighbouring Islamic nations that are not Aryan and an attachment to Europe and the West. ... [I]f we [would choose as] the foundation of our nation our intellectual, behavioural and social heritage over the past fourteen centuries, [however,] we would have a different mission and other costs. ... Therein, Arab, Turk, Indian, Indonesian and [Chinese] would become our friends, even kinsmen.[29]

In order to legitimate the monarchy, the Pahlavi state emphasized the ancient, pre-Islamic Persian heritage of Iran's identity. Moreover, both Mohammad Reza Shah (r. 1941–79) and his father, Reza Shah Pahlavi (r. 1925–41) nurtured the idea of 'Iranianism,' embedding the Iranian self in the romantic discourse about a superior 'Aryan' nation (*mellat-e aryan*), married to Indo-European heritage because of common linguistic roots and hence different from the 'Arab-Semitic other.'[30] Demonstrating affinity with orientalist views about the supremacy of the Indo-European peoples and the mediocrity of the 'Semitic race' characteristic of the writings of Ernest Renan and others,[31] late nineteenth-century figures of Iranian nationalism such as Mirza Fath Ali Akhonzadeh or Mirza Aqa Khan Kermani were the forerunners of the 'metaphysical mendacity' of racially coded Iranian supremacy adopted by the Pahlavi state and secular intellectuals.[32] Iranian nationalist discourse idealized the status of pre-Islamic Persian empires, while negating the 'Islamicization' of Iran by Muslim forces. The Shah's celebration of 2500 years of Iranian empire in Persepolis in 1971 and his decision to abandon the Islamic solar *hegra* calendar in favor of an imperial one exemplify his adherence to the 'Iranianist' topia. Nurtured by the dream of reviving ancient Persian grandeur and establishing the ultimate 'great civilization' (*tamadon-e bozorg*), externalizing the Muslim identity of Iran from the Persian-Aryan self was meant to rationalize the Pahlavi claim to 'natural' affinity with the 'Western' world.[33] In her examination of the image of Arabs in modern Persian literature, Joya Blondel Saad reaches a similar conclusion:

---

[29] Morteza Mottahari, *Islam and Iran* (Beirut: Dar al-Ta'aruf, n.d.), p. 22, quoted in Wajih Kawtharani, 'Mutual awareness between Arabs and Iranians,' in: Khair el-Din Haseeb (Ed.) *Arab–Iranian Relations* (Beirut: Centre for Arab Unity Studies, 1998), p. 74.

[30] Indeed, one of the many titles of Mohammad Reza Shah included *Aryamehr*, which means 'light of Aryans' in Persian. His father, Reza Khan, who established the Pahlavi dynasty, promoted the name 'Iran' (Land of Aryans) instead of Persia and supported the elimination of Arabic terms from the Persian language.

[31] For a critical deconstruction of Ernest Renan's study of 'semitic' and 'orientalist' discourse, see Edward W. Said, *Orientalism* (London: Penguin, 1995), esp. pp. 140–150.

[32] See Firoozeh Kashani-Sabet, 'Cultures of Iranianness: the evolving polemic of Iranian nationalism,' in: Nikki R. Keddie & Rudi Matthee (Eds) *Iran and the Surrounding World: Interactions in Culture and Cultural Politics* (Seattle: University of Washington Press, 2002), pp. 162–181.

[33] For a comparison of the representation of 'Self' and 'Other' in textbooks before and after the revolution see Golnar Mehran, 'The presentation of the "Self" and the "Other" in postrevolutionary Iranian school textbooks,' in ibid., pp. 232–253.

For some Iranian nationalists, the Other has been not so much the West, but the Arabs and Islam. Identifying Iran with the West, as fellow 'Aryan' nations, allowed for the acceptance of Western modernisation and the importation of Western culture. ... The myth of the common origin of Iranians, 'proved' by categories of race ('Aryan') and language (Indo-European), and the myth of the pre-Islamic Golden Age, allowed Iran to fit the Western national model.[34]

If the Pahlavi state attempted to externalize the Arab-Semitic other from the Iranian-Aryan self in order to position Iran more firmly in the 'Western' camp, oppositional intellectuals constructed the narrative of *gharbzadegi* to protest Iran's state-sanctioned 'Westernization.' Jalal Al-e Ahmad's publication of *Gharbzadegi* in the fall of 1962 put forward one of the most influential anti-dependency theories in Iran, disseminated beyond the pre-revolutionary intellectual context in the country. Al-e Ahmad equated penetration by and dependency on the 'West' with a state of cultural and economic mediocrity he termed *gharbzadegi* (westtoxification, occidentosis or westitis), defined as

> a complex of circumstances which comes about in the life, culture, civilization, and way of thinking of a people in one spot on the globe without any kind of supporting cultural context or historical continuity, or any evolving method of integration, coming about only as a result of the charity of machines.[35]

Employing a medical analogy, Al-e Ahmad deprecated the decadent, mediocre and inauthentic status of Pahlavi Iran. If left untreated, he argued, the spread of the disease-like status would lead to the demise of the country's cultural, political and economic independence, because society was made susceptible to 'Western' penetration. Moving beyond the Iranian context, Al-e Ahmad saw the struggle against *Gharbzadegi* in terms of a conflict between the 'Occidental West' and the 'Oriental East.' Employing the metaphor of 'the machine,' he argued that while the 'West' had learned to master the 'technology of modernity,' the mediocre 'East' was kept in a state of political and economic dependency. The definition of this milieu of subjugation and power was dramatized as a means to alert the 'Eastern mind' about the creeping intrusion of 'west-toxification' and its corrupting symptoms on societies programmed to be subservient to their imperialist masters:

> Our sense of competition has been lost and a sense of powerlessness has taken its place, a sense of subservience. ... One would think that all of our own standards are extinct. It has reached such a state that we are even proud to be their vermiform appendix. Today the fate of those two old rivals is, as you see, this: one has become a lowly groundskeeper and the other the owner of the ballpark. And what a ball game it is! Nine innings of genitals and thighs, charges of stupidity, mutual flattery, and bluster.[36]

---

[34] Joya Blondel Saad, *The Image of Arabs in Modern Persian Literature* (Lanham: University Press of America, 1996), p. 134.
[35] Jalal Al-e Ahmad, *Plagued by the West (Gharbzadegi)* (New York: Caravan, 1982), p. 10.
[36] Ibid., p. 19.

The second dominant narrative that had a determining impact on Iran's shifting self-perception and its relationship to the 'Western other' emerged from the writings of Ali Shariati. Echoing the views of Al-e Ahmad, Shariati developed a comparably critical position toward imperialism and cultural, political and socio-economic dependency on the 'West.' During his education at the Sorbonne in Paris, Shariati was in contact with figures of the French left whose political outlook and intellectual paradigms were influential in his later writings. Those included Catholic Islamologist Louis Massignon to whom he was a research assistant between 1960 and 1962, the Jewish-Russian émigré George Gurvitch who was his professor in sociology, Islamologist Jacques Berque whose class on the 'Sociology of Islam' Shariati audited in 1963–64, Frantz Fanon whose seminal *The Wretched of the Earth* he translated (in collaboration with others) into Persian, and Jean-Paul Sartre whose attempt to reconcile existentialism with Marxism and humanism had an important influence on Shariati's own attempt to synthesize social scientific concepts with Shia-Islamic political thought.[37] Ironically, he employed aspects of these ('foreign') ideas in one of his main publications entitled *Bazgasht beh-khish* (Return to oneself), which appeared as serialized articles in the Iranian daily *Kayhan* between 22 April and 22 June 1976. Shariati argued that discovering the 'true identity' of Iran as a nation requires rejecting 'Western' cultural influences and foreign ideologies and reverting instead to the 'authentic' Iranian-Islamic self. Pointing toward the corrupting influences of 'Western' culture, he demurred the subordination of indigenous ideas, values, and morals of the people in favor of an uncritical imitation of alien worldviews.[38] Comparable to the views of Al-e Ahmad, then, Shariati developed his ideas in close relation to the 'imperialist' other which made the invention of the necessary journey back to the 'Iranian-Islamic self' possible in the first place.

The romantic dimension of Shariati's worldview can be attributed to his interest in Sufism (Islamic mysticism) and the role he attributed to it in the political arena. While the trajectory of his intellectual thought makes it difficult to discern a genuine Sufi tendency, nonetheless one might argue that he presented elements of Sufism as a revolutionary and libertarian program, suitable to challenge the status quo in Pahlavi Iran. As Ali Rahnema argues in his perceptive political biography of Shariati:

> In a way Shari'ati argued that an individual's gnostic experience was an educational process which paved the way for the meaningful dedication of one's life to the cause of the people. By the time the Sufi wayfarer is free of all worldly chains including his love for life and ready to be accepted by Him, he has acquired all the attributes of a true warrior for the cause of God. ... Thus Shari'ati replaces the Sufi concept of self-annihilation and subsequent assimilation or living in God with self-annihilation and subsequent assimilation of living in 'the people.' This is certainly a novel interpretation. According to it, Che Guevara becomes an armed and socially responsible reincarnation of Hallaj and 'Ayn al-Quzat Hamadani [two Persian Sufis executed on charges of heresy]. They are both selfless martyrs of love.[39]

---

[37] See Ali Rahnema, *An Islamic Utopian: A Political Biography of Ali Shariati* (London: I. B. Tauris, 2000), pp. 119–128.

[38] Ibid., p. 345. In an interesting insight into the identity politics of Pahlavi Iran, Rahnema notes that Shariati's articles were printed next to another serialized article entitled 'Reza Shah the Great, saviour and reconstructor of Iran.'

[39] Ibid., p. 159.

The romantic imageries intrinsic to the narratives of *Bazgasht beh-khish* and *Gharbzadegi* constituted the apotheosis of the socialist, third-worldist and revolutionary Islamic *Zeitgeist* dominating Iranian society during the 1970s. The agents of that political culture engineered situationally transcendent ideas that promised to succeed de facto in the realization of their projected contents. 'Only those orientations transcending reality,' Karl Mannheim argues 'will be referred to ... as utopian which, when they pass over into conduct, tend to shatter, either partially or wholly, the order of things prevailing at the time.'[40] According to Mannheim, such 'chiliastic' utopias are expressions of the ideal that is realizable in the here and now. 'For the real Chiliast,' he elaborates, 'the present becomes the breach through which what was previously inward bursts out suddenly, takes hold of the outer world and transforms it.'[41] Paul Ricoeur argues in a similar vein, elaborating that Chiliasm 'has the idea of a millennial kingdom coming from heaven ... [it] assumes a transcendent point of departure for a social revolution based on religious motives.'[42] The concept of chiliastic utopianism appears to be immediately relevant to the events in Iran. Once the religiously framed, anti-imperialist discourse was codified as a revolutionary narrative it developed a dynamism of its own, 'shattering the order of things' not only in Iran but also beyond. As lay religious intellectuals whose ideas appealed to the disillusioned middle-class urban youth in 1970s Iran, Shariati and Al-e Ahmad introduced Islamic-revolutionary ideas to a wide audience outside the religious seminaries, giving impetus to the emergence of a systematic, Islamic culture of revolt. Translated by the organized political movements into revolutionary action, the force of this systemic movement transcended the powers of both its makers and its agents—it engendered its own dynamism, its own 'utopian reality' rendered transcendent by its intoxicating claim. Introjected with such a powerful, authoritative discourse, Iranians were driven by the belief that the revolution *was* a revolt against the *mostakbaran* (oppressors), that the shah *was* the incarnation of Yazid, that Iran *was* the battlefield where the party of God (*hezb'allah*) was struggling against the Greater and Lesser Satan, that Imam Khomeini *was* the messianic chaperone guiding the slave revolt in its mission to smash the idols (*bot*) of the imperial masters. This revolutionary reality penetrated Iranian thinking to its core (even Foucault could not escape its force). After the success of the revolution, the Islamic Republic institutionalized the revolutionary utopias as central ideological precepts of the Iranian state—a process that established Iran as a revisionist power in international affairs.

Institutional-introjective Structure of Iran's Foreign Policy Culture

What gave Iran's revolutionary narrative its force was its religious passion. The revolutionary reality transmuted the paradigms of *gharbzadegi* and *bazgasht beh-khish* into a radical counter-culture that succeeded in destroying one of the most powerful states in the Persian Gulf. Glorifying the symbols of Iranian and Shia romanticism—the aesthetics of *shahadat* (martyrdom), the sufferings of Imam Hussein, the just age of the Imam Mahdi—they

---

[40] Mannheim, *Ideology and Utopia*, p. 173, n. 1.
[41] Ibid., p. 193.
[42] Paul Ricoeur, *Lectures on Ideology and Utopia*, George H. Taylor (Ed.) (New York: Columbia University Press, 1986), p. 276.

extracted, channeled, and dispersed the emotional energy onto the receptive revolutionary masses.[43] Once internalized, this emergent culture appeared as an objectified reality to its agents. This aestheticized political reality had its own structure, meaning, symbols and imagery. Hence, the *Shuhada* (martyrs) were not merely freedom fighters giving their lives for the revolutionary cause. The revolutionary reality represented them as the 'candles of society [who] burn themselves out and illuminate society.'[44] Martyrdom was not a loss, it was a choice 'whereby the warrior sacrifices himself on the threshold of the temple of freedom and the altar of love and is victorious.'[45] Likewise, Imam Hussein—the exalted, almost eponymous hero of the revolutionary play—was not merely a religious-political personality among others. 'He was that individual who negated himself with absolute sincerity, with the utmost magnificence within human power.'[46] This 'ideal man,' Shariati contended

> holds the sword of Caesar in his hand and he has the heart of Jesus in his breast. He thinks with the brain of Socrates and loves God with the heart of Hallaj. ... Like the Buddha, he is delivered from the dungeon of pleasure-seeking and egoism; Like Lao Tse, he reflects on the profundity of his primordial nature; ... [l]ike Spartacus, he is a rebel against slave owners ... and like Moses, he is the messenger of jihad and deliverance.[47]

After the triumph of the revolution, the newly created Islamic Republic under the leadership of Ayatollah Khomeini fused the revolutionary energies and channeled them into politics, transforming the self-attribution of Iran from a systematically legitimated status quo power to an internationalist Islamic movement, equipped with the transnational mandate for the export of the revolution (*sudur-e enghelab*). How was this abstract self-identification institutionalized and how did it shape Iran's grand strategic preferences?

Due to the dominance of the persona of Ayatollah Khomeini, the philosophical-theoretical context of the self-bestowed universal mandate, which emerged as the foundation of the foreign policy culture of the Islamic Republic, was shaped by Shi'i political theory and its interpretation by the charismatic leader.[48] Speaking authoritatively both because of his institutionalized position as the leader of the revolution (*rahbar-e enghelab*) and supreme jurisprudent (*vali-e faqih*) and his broad support among the elites and the populace,[49] Khomeini frequently employed the imagery of the millenarian struggle between the 'oppressed' and the 'oppressors' in order to rally the Iranian

---

[43] One of the main tenets of Iran's *Ja'afari* or Twelver Shia school is that the Twelfth Imam went into hiding (*gheiba*) and will return to establish the just rule of God on earth.

[44] Mortada [Morteza] Mutahhari, 'Shahid,' in: M. Abedi & G. Leggenhausen (Eds) *Jihad and Shahadat: Struggle and Martyrdom in Islam* (Houston: Institute for Research and Islamic Studies, 1986), p. 126.

[45] Ali Shari'ati (n.d.), 'Arise and bear witness,' available at < htttp://www.shariati.com > (accessed 24 March 2003).

[46] Idem, 'A discussion of Shahid,' in: Abedi and Leggenhausen (Eds), *Jihad*, p. 233, n. 44.

[47] Ali Shari'ati, *On the Sociology of Islam*, p. 122.

[48] See Roy P. Mottahedeh, 'Shi'ite political thought and the destiny of the Iranian Revolution,' in: Jamal S. al-Suwaidi (Ed.) *Iran and the Gulf: A Search for Stability* (Abu Dhabi: The Emirates Center for Strategic Studies and Research, 1996), pp. 70–80; and esp. Juan R. I. Cole & Nikki R. Keddie (Eds), *Shi'ism and Social Protest* (New Haven: Yale University Press, 1986).

[49] The doctrine of *velayat-e faqih* was put forward by Ayatollah Khomeini in *Hokumat-e Islami* in the early 1970s. For an English translations of Khomeini's main arguments, see Ayatollah Rouhollah Khomeini, *Islam and Revolution: Writings and Declarations of Imam Khomeini*, Hamid Algar (Trans.) (Berkeley: Mizan Press, 1981).

population behind the revolutionary cause. That Manichean *mostazafan-mostakbaran* dichotomy was central to the *Weltanschauung* of Khomeini, representing a modification of the traditional Islamic differentiation of world affairs in *dar al-Islam* (the abode of Islam or the place of peace) and *dar al-harb* (the abode of war, or the place of non-believers).[50] Borrowing from anti-imperialistic terminology of the Iranian left and touching upon the country's Third World populist and socialist *Zeitgeist* during the 1970s, Khomeini referred to a wider struggle not only between Muslims and non-Muslims but also between justice and injustice.[51] According to that ideological dualism, the ongoing clash between the 'oppressed,' who have been deprived of their political, cultural, natural and economic resources, and the 'oppressors,' who have subjugated the 'disinherited,' is zero-sum in nature. Elevating the position of Islamic Iran to the highest 'moral high-ground,' the aspiration to effect a total change of that 'unjust' system was rendered explicit. Confirming that goal, the preamble of the Constitution of the Islamic Republic declared that the revolution aims to bring about the triumph of the *mostazafan* against the *mostakbaran*. Moreover, it is stated that the Constitution 'provides the necessary basis for ensuring the continuation of the Revolution at home and abroad.' Illustrated in accordance with the Quranic verse 'This, your nation, is a single nation, and I am your Lord, so worship Me (21:92),' it is further declared that the Constitution 'will strive, in concert with other Islamic and popular movements, to prepare the way for the formation of a single world community.'[52]

Iran's Foreign Policy Culture and the Challenge to International Society

Despite contradictory sections in the Constitution where abstention from 'aggressive intervention in the internal affairs of other nations' is accentuated (see, for example, Article 154) and the overall anti-militaristic tenor during the early days of the Islamic Republic, the Iranian revolutionaries did as much as any revolutionary movement to propagate their message abroad.[53] Khomeini explicitly endorsed the export of the revolutionary idea, but he also cautioned: 'This does not mean that we intend to export it by the bayonet. We want to call [*dawat*] everyone to Islam [and to] send our calling everywhere.'[54] Although covert support to 'liberation movements' in Afghanistan, Iraq, Lebanon, and Palestine was sometimes justified openly, exporting the *idea* of the Islamic Republic without military aggrandizement was rather more central.[55] Reliance on *dawat* (calling) and *tabligh* (propagation, advertisement, dissemination) hence substituted for the militaristic coercion periodically characteristic of the shah's reign. In accordance with that disposition, the Islamic Republic cancelled the shah's multi-billion dollars defense contracts with the United States and Western Europe and abandoned Iranian military installations in Oman. Conscious of the appeal of the Islamic republican model to the Muslim world and caught in a momentum of revolutionary intoxication, Iran relied on its ideological power transmitted by the charisma of Ayatollah Khomeini and transplanted by

---

[50] For Khomeini's perception of international affairs, see Rajaee, *Islamic Values and World View*, n. 4.
[51] See Ervand Abrahamian, *Khomeinism: Essays on the Islamic Republic* (London: I. B. Tauris, 1993).
[52] Hamid Algar (Trans.), *Constitution of the Islamic Republic of Iran* (Berkeley: Mizan Press, 1980), p. 19.
[53] For a comparative analysis, see Fred Halliday, *Revolution and World Politics: The Rise and Fall of the Sixth Great Power* (Durham, NC: Duke University Press, 1999).
[54] Ayatollah Rouhollah Khomeini, *Sahifey-e nur*, vol. 18 (Tehran: Vezarat-e Ershad, 1364/1985), p. 129.
[55] See, among others, Rajaee, *Islamic Values and World View*, pp. 83–84, n. 4; and R. K. Ramazani, *Revolutionary Iran: Challenge and Response in the Middle-East* (Baltimore: Johns Hopkins University Press, 1986), pp. 26ff.

sympathizing movements in the region and beyond.[56] It was this self-confidence about the justness of the revolutionary cause and the spiritual superiority of religious values that motivated Khomeini to write a letter to Soviet leader Mikhail Gorbachev in January 1989, attempting to persuade him to consider religion in general and Islam in particular as an alternative to the materialism of capitalist societies. He argued in a similar vein in his response to a letter from Pope John-Paul II (in the midst of the hostage crisis) in May 1980:

> I ask His Honor to warn the U.S. government of the consequences of its oppressions, cruelties and plunders, and advise Mr. Carter, who is doomed to defeat, to treat nations desiring absolute independence of global powers on the basis of humanitarian principles. He should be advised to observe the guidelines of Jesus Christ and not to expose himself and the U.S. Administration to defamation.[57]

The occupation of the US embassy by the *daneshjuan-e musalmanan-e piramun-e khatt-e imam* (Muslim Students following the line of the Imam) in November 1979 was perhaps the most explicit rejection of the pillars of international society and here specifically the institutions of international law. Denying diplomatic immunity to more than 50 US American embassy personnel was intended to symbolize the revolution's protest against imperialism, and specifically what was perceived to be an unjust and oppressively hierarchical world order. The 'hitherto prevailing conventions of diplomatic immunity and representation' were considered 'worthy of attack,' because of the legitimating force of revolution.[58] In other words, here and elsewhere, the long-term image and ideological symbolism of the revolution superseded crude, short-term cost-benefit calculations. Rejection of central tenets of international political culture was deemed conducive to appeal to other revolutionary movements, representing '[t]he Islamic Revolution of Iran [as] a new achievement in the ongoing struggle between the peoples and the oppressive superpowers.'[59] Ayatollah Khomeini condoned the occupation, because it reiterated Iran's revolutionary aspirations and symbolized the combatant-Islamic state identity he favored. Moreover, the hostage crisis was taken as an opportunity by the *khatt-e imam* (the Imam's line) revolutionary wing of the Iranian factions to encourage a process of internal radicalization and subdue their liberal-left competitors organized around Prime Minister Mehdi Bazargan.[60] The preferred state identity espoused by that faction was to be offensive, revolutionary, and idealistic, rather than conservative, accommodating, and status quo oriented. As the closest manifestation of the omnipotence of the United States, whose government was deemed to be the prime agent of anti-Iranian conspiracies,[61] occupying the 'den of spies' (*laneh-e jasusan*), as the US embassy was called, was meant to reiterate the revolutionary, anti-imperialistic character of the Iranian movement, symbolizing the 'total' victory of the Islamic revolution, kindling 'flames

---

[56] For further analysis see Farhang Rajaee, 'Iranian ideology and worldview: the cultural export of revolution,' in: John L. Esposito (Ed.) *The Iranian Revolution: Its Global Impact* (Miami: Florida International University Press, 1990), pp. 63–80.

[57] Letter from Ayatollah Ruhollah Khomeini to Pope John-Paul II,' in: Massoumeh Ebtekar, *Takeover in Tehran: The Inside Story of the 1979 U.S. Embassy Capture* (Vancouver: Talonbooks, 2000), p. 246.

[58] Halliday, *Revolution and World Politics*, p. 96, n. 53.

[59] First Communiqué of the Muslim Students Following the Line of Imam,' in Ebtekar, *Takeover in Tehran*, p. 70, n. 57.

[60] See Fred Halliday, 'Iranian foreign policy since 1979: internationalism and nationalism in the Islamic Revolution,' in: Cole & Keddie (Eds) *Shi'ism*, p. 96, n. 48.

[61] The occupation occurred about two weeks after the shah was allowed to come to the United States for medical treatment.

of hope in the hearts of the enchained nations' and creating 'a legend of self-reliance and ideological steadfastness for a nation contending with imperialism.'[62]

A comparable rationale propelled Ayatollah Khomeini to pursue a second controversial challenge to the central tenets of international political culture. By issuing a religious verdict (*fatwa*) against Salman Rushdie and the publishers of *The Satanic Verses*, Khomeini negated the very basis of the international nation-state system, whereby the citizens of a sovereign state are subject only to the jurisdiction of territorial state law and, where applicable, to secular international law. From Ayatollah Khomeini's perspective, the extension of *sharia* law to someone who used to be part of the *umma* had become an apostate member of the Islamic community, and who had insulted the Quran and the Prophet Mohammad was not only legitimate but also an obligation.[63] Mandated by his religious status as *marjay-e taqlid* (source of emulation, highest Shi'i religious rank) and legitimated by a popular revolution in the name of Islam and on behalf of the 'wretched of the earth' (to employ Frantz Fanon's famous phrase), Khomeini positioned divine law above secular international law during periods when safeguarding the *maslahat* (interest) of the Islamic state and—by extension—the Muslim *umma* demanded political expediency. In both cases—hostage taking and the *fatwa* against Rushdie—Ayatollah Khomeini found it conducive to assert the Iranian state identity as the anti-imperialist, revolutionary-Islamic power house, because in both cases asserting that identity was helpful to fend off domestic dissent and claim the leadership of the Muslim *umma* externally. Seeking acknowledgement and support for the primacy of the revolution's spiritual and political power, calculations were made on the basis of the *absolute* ideological appeal of the revolutionary idea rather than the *relative* costs of confrontation. Ironically, the more international society turned against Iran, the more this reaction confirmed the self-perception of the Iranian state as the leader of an 'oppressed' nation, facing the overwhelming force of the 'arrogant powers'—a deeply internalized perception that was reiterated by the Iraqi invasion and the international silence about Saddam Hussein's repeated employment of chemical weapons. The revolutionary state closely related this imagery to the sufferings of Shi'is at the hands of unjust rulers and the martyrdom (*shahadat*) of the Shi'i Imam Hussein during the Battle of Karbala against the Umayyad monarch Yazid in 680 CE:

> Imam Husayn was not to be killed again. Thus, he defeated Yazid [i.e., the shah] in Iran last year. Imam Husayn, who now is leading a battle against a greater Yazid [i.e., imperialism], also will triumph, God willing. The revolutionary Imam Husayn in Iran, who is fighting imperialism, is not alone now. In addition to some 35,000,000 Iranians who bravely and devotedly rally around him, there are billions of Muslims and non-Muslims everywhere in Syria, Libya, Algeria, Lebanon, Palestine, Pakistan, Africa, the Omani liberation front, Eritrea, the Chilean resistance, the Chadian liberation movement, the Canary Islands' liberation movement, the Futami liberation movement, Spain, Korea and many other places as well as the entire Islamic world, and the oppressed all over the world, who all support Iran, the revolution and Imam Husayn, represented in leader Imam Ayatollah Khomeini.[64]

---

[62] See n. 59.
[63] See David George, 'Pax Islamica: an alternative new world order,' in: Abdel Salam Sidahmed & Anoushiravan Ehteshami (Eds) *Islamic Fundamentalism* (Boulder: Westview, 1996), pp. 80ff.
[64] *BBC Survey of World Broadcasts*, Part IV (A), The Middle East, 24 November 1979, ME/6280/A/8.

The anti-imperialist norm advocated by Al-e Ahmad and Shariati and adopted by the revolutionary state, central as it was to the language and symbols of the Islamic Republic during the first decade of its existence, became a dominant institution in revolutionary Iran.[65] Inextricably linked to the identity of the Islamic state, the rhetoric about the struggle of the 'oppressed' against the 'arrogant powers' soon broke the boundaries between political idiom and political action, explaining the Iranian belligerence toward the prevalent rules and institutions of international society. Consistent with Islamic leftist concepts and the prominent intellectual discourse about *Gharbzadegi*, encroachment on the Islamic world by 'corrupting' 'Western' concepts was deemed poisonous for the evolution of a just society and the emergence of the ultimate *Homo Islamicus*. In theory, regaining authenticity—in Shariati's terminology returning to the self (*bazgasht beh-khish*)—and retaining independence required detachment from the bipolar international system that was perceived as 'dangerous for humanity.'[66] Alluding to the intellectual production of that mindset, Mehrzad Boroujerdi has suggested a causal link between the anti-imperialist disposition of Iranian intellectuals and the challenges of revolutionary Iran to the international system:

> [Iranian thinkers] believe in the telos of living a moral, sensible, passionate and authentic life. Authenticity is tantamount to taking hold of one's existence and traditions in a manner that is genuine, trustworthy, and sincere. To be 'authentic' is to embrace one's time and culture critically, and, yet to keep an eye on the overriding sense of loyalty and belonging. For the prototypical Iranian intellectual this has translated into a rejection of the apish imitation of the West on the grounds that mimicry and submission are fraudulent and counterfeit states of being. This explains why anti-Westernisation and anti-imperialism have become two of the fixed hallmarks of the modern Iranian intelligentsia's identity discourse. The formidable ideological permeation of the West and its (neo)colonial exploits lead many Iranian intellectuals as well as the common people of Iran, in search of indigenisation, authenticity, and freedom, to turn toward nativism and Islamicism. In their desire not to be a prolegomenon to Western philosophical texts or a nodal point in the Western imperialist maps, some of these intellectuals and social movements, alas, succumb to cultural xenophobia toward the West and adopt essentialist world-views. As a result, precarious policies (i.e., hostage taking, export of revolution, the death sentence against Salman Rushdie) should not come as a surprise.[67]

Boroujerdi suggests that anti-imperialism, cultural authenticity, and independence constituted the central parameters of Iran's identity discourse after the revolution because the revolutionary elites had deeply internalized the three norms and were hence an immediate factor of Iran's delineation between itself and the 'Other.' In turn, this would suggest that it was due to this ideational mindset that the foreign policy norm of *na sharghi*

---

[65] See Abrahamian, *Khomeinism*, n. 49.
[66] Ayatollah Rouhollah Khomeini, Sermon delivered on 5 November, in *Kayhan* (Tehran), 6 November 1982, and quoted in Rajaee, *Islamic Values and World View*, p. 75, n. 2.
[67] Mehrzad Boroujerdi, 'Iranian Islam and the Faustian bargain of Western modernity,' *Journal of Peace Research*, 34(1) (1997), p. 4.

na gharbi, jomhuri-ye islami (neither Eastern nor Western, only the Islamic Republic) entered the revolutionary program, pitting the Islamic Republic against the established (bipolar) order of the international nation-state system. R.K. Ramazani agrees:

> The policies of the state of the faqih, aiming as they do at the eventual creation of ... an Islamic world order, will inevitably entail confrontation between that state and the superpowers. Such a conflict is inevitable because the superpowers have arrogated all power (*qudrat*) to themselves.... It is in the context of these basic ideas that the Iranian slogan 'neither East, nor West, only the Islamic republic' ... should be understood, not the irrelevant notions of equidistance or non-alignment.... These ideas in effect accept the Western notion of power politics, whereas Khomeini's religious, millenarian, and idealistic view rejects the global role of both superpowers; they are both considered to be illegitimate players in the international system they dominate.[68]

Hence, given that anti-imperialism emerged as a central institution of Iran's foreign policy culture, it should not come as a surprise that the Iranian state acted upon that disposition by ending the country's membership of Cold War institutions such as the Central Treaty Organization (CENTO), challenging established norms of appropriate behavior in the conduct of international affairs, turning into a passionate advocate of the Non Aligned Movement (NAM), supporting the Palestinian quest for self-determination, and transforming its alliance with the United States into a relationship of enduring antagonism. The costs of these policies were accepted, even if that meant that the country would be isolated, and labeled as a 'rogue' or 'outlaw' state by international society.

Islamic Utopian Romanticism and Iran's Contemporary Political Order

It has been argued that Iran's contemporary foreign policy culture is rooted in the revolutionary paradigms formulated in the 1970s and that this cultural system informed the country's grand strategic preferences. Institutionalized as central narratives of the state, the Islamic Republic followed the revolutionary utopias not only at the level of behavior but also of interest. In other words, the radical wing that took over the post-revolutionary Iranian state did not see a contradiction between the revolutionary ideals and 'the' national interest of the state. On the contrary, from their perspective, realizing those ideals *was* in the national interest of the Islamic Republic and—by implication—the Muslim *umma*. Iranian foreign policy elites were aware that the appeal of the revolution in the Muslim world (and in some parts of the Third World) would be enhanced greatly if the counter-hegemonic rhetoric were to be backed up by action. If the United States was the 'Great Satan,' conquering the moral high ground in international affairs required confrontation. If the Islamic Republic wanted to propagate its revolutionary claim, it needed to confront real and perceived imperialism both at home and abroad. If the revolution was to act as a model for other Third World countries, it had to assert its legitimacy, if necessary, through violent action. In the Iranian case, then, as elsewhere, utopia offered both 'a vantage point from which to perceive the given, the already constituted' and, more importantly, 'new possibilities above and beyond the given.'[69]

---

[68] R. K. Ramazani, 'Shi'ism in the Persian Gulf,' in: Cole & Keddie (Eds) *Shi'ism*, p. 33, n. 48.
[69] 'Editor's Introduction,' in: Ricoeur, *Lectures*, pp. xxviii–xxix, n. 42.

The composition of Iran's contemporary foreign policy culture shows both residual elements of the revolutionary utopias and signs of an emergent counter-culture that signals loyalty to the country's commitment to a rather more equitable world order, yet less 'raucous' methods to achieve that goal.[70] In the Iranian context, as elsewhere, culture does not appear as a monolithic system resistant to changes from below. 'The reality of any hegemony,' Raymond Williams argues 'is that, while by definition it is always dominant, it is never either total or exclusive. At any time, forms of alternative or directly oppositional politics and culture exist as significant elements in the society.'[71] One needs only to consider the speeches of women activists such as Noble Peace Prize Laureate Shirin Ebadi and intellectual paradigms developed by oppositional figures such as Mohsen Kadivar, Akbar Ganji or Abdolkarim Soroush (or even watch the movies of directors Abbas Kiarostami, Mohsen Makhmalbaf and his daughter Samira or Majid Majidi) to conclude that Iran's post-revolutionary cultural order (yesterday's utopia turned today's topia) is undergoing rapid transformations.[72] Undeniably, this emergent counter-culture—which has manifested itself in a multi-dimensional movement for democracy—has already had an impact on the country's foreign policies (e.g., cooperation with regional states, détente with the European Union, and at some stages even with the United States under Mohammad Khatami's 'dialogue among civilizations' policy). It would be reductionist, however, to attribute these policies to power struggles between pragmatic 'reformers' organized around Khatami and pan-Islamic 'conservatives' supported by Leader Ali Khamenehi. This dichotomous notion, too often presented in mono-causal terms (i.e., reformism equals pragmatism and pro-Western policies while conservatism equals pan-Islamicism and anti-Western agitation), is inadequate to address why Iranian foreign policy elites have remained committed to certain core strategic principles of the state. Does the Islamic Republic not continue to represent itself as a 'moral superpower,' as a force for change in international affairs? Does it not challenge US foreign policies repeatedly, in the Persian Gulf, in Iraq, in Central Asia? Does it not continue to support the Palestinian cause, with conferences, ideological propaganda, organized diplomatic initiatives? Does the episode with the eight British servicemen in June 2004 and the continued standoff with the International Atomic Energy Agency (IAEA) over the country's nuclear program not indicate Iran's obstinate adherence to the independence norm?[73] Does the country not continue to advocate the case for the Islamic republican alternative both at home and abroad? Like other states, it appears, the Iranian republic adheres to certain grand strategic preferences that transcend the faultlines of day-to-day politics.

Moreover, from the perspective of contemporary Iranian decision makers there appears to be no contradiction between the utopian-romantic *Leitmotif* of the revolution and multilateral engagement and détente—two institutions that are central to

---

[70] For a conceptualization of 'residual,' 'dominant,' and 'emergent' culture see Raymond Williams, *Marxism and Literature* (Oxford: Oxford University Press, 1977), esp. pp. 121–127.

[71] Ibid., p. 113.

[72] See further Arshin Adib-Moghaddam, 'The contemporary political landscape of Iran: the eclectics of post-revolutionary politics,' Part I, 8 November 2004, *The Tharwa Project*, available at < http://www.tharwaproject.com/English/Main-Sec/Features/Feat_ 11_29_04/index.php?option = com_keywords&task = view&id = 817&Itemid = 0; and idem, Part II, 29 November 2004, available at < http://www.tharwaproject.com/English/Main-Sec/Features/Feat_11_29_04/index.php?option = com_keywords&task = view&id = 814&Itemid = 0 > .

[73] See further *BBC News*, 'Iran releases British servicemen,' 24 June 2004, available at < http://www.news.bbc.co.uk/2hi/middle-east/3835313.stm > (accessed 24 August 2004); and International Crisis Group, 'Iran: where next on the nuclear standoff?,' 24 November 2004, available at < http://crisisgroup.org/home/index.cfm?id = 3118&1 = 1 > (accessed 13 May 2005).

the 'dialogue among civilizations' initiative put forward by the Khatami administration. Although the Islamic Republic has distanced itself from some of the confrontational polices characteristic of the first decade of the revolution, *tabligh* and *dawat* continue to provide the strategic means to realize the grand foreign policy preferences of the state:

> Fulfilling the utopian vision of the revolution's devotees inside and outside of Iran is a pressing necessity to ensure our survival. To assert our identity it is necessary to be present in all world forums and to defend Islam and Iran effectively in all international tribunals and conventions. But we cannot ultimately flourish and make our weight felt in the international scene—whose rules are set by our opponents—unless we maintain our unique idealism.[74]

To open a parenthesis here, I am not claiming that there is a consensus among the different factions of Iranian politics on every foreign policy decision. That would oversimplify the differences between the spectrum of political parties and institutions in Iran. After all, there are at least six institutions involved in Iran's foreign policy process: the office of the Leader, the Foreign Ministry, the office of the President, the Head of the Expediency Council, the Supreme National Security Council, and the Parliament (primarily through its National Security and Foreign Policy commissions). There is no doubt that these institutions follow different agendas. But there appears to be a culturally constituted consensus about the country's role in international affairs that is strong enough to transcend the factions of—and fractions in—Iranian politics. This foreign policy culture refers to a higher level of abstraction than the day-to-day affairs of the state. It functions as the guardian of identity, represents a web of shared ideals, images, norms, institutions, and provides for the foreign policy elites a coherent, if systematically abstract, overall orientation in the conduct of international affairs. Pro-Palestinian sentiments, anti-Zionism and anti-imperialism, Islamic communitarianism, 'third-worldism' (recently reinvigorated by Iran's close relationship with Cuba and Venezuela), and cultural and political independence have functioned as the ideational points of fixation reconstituting the Iranian self during the revolutionary process of the 1960s and 1970s and are not easy to discard. They have acquired the status of cognitively objectified and formally codified social institutions reabsorbed by Iran's contemporary elite, one that is introjected with the penetrating ideational force of this cultural reality. Despite the current power struggles in Iran, the shared interests of reformers and conservatives meet where their competition ends: at the junction of Iran's foreign policy culture and—by implication—the grand strategic preferences of the state.[75]

It is not at all obvious, then, that Iran's current strategic preferences represent a break from the ideals of the revolution. Nor is it clear that they result from 'socialization' in international structures, although the war against Saddam Hussein's Iraq played its part in confronting Iran with the brute realities of international life. A utopia is always in the process of being realized because it is as much legitimization of what is, as it is an aspiration of what could be

---

[74] Mohammad Khatami, *Islam, Dialogue and Civil Society* (Canberra: Centre for Arab and Islamic Studies, 2000), p. 62; see also Javad Zarif, 'Indispensable power: hegemonic tendencies in a globalized world,' *Harvard International Review*, 24(4) (2003), available at < http://www.ceip.org/files/Publications/2003-04-01-brumberg-HIR.asp?from = pubdate > (accessed 13 November 2003). Zarif is Ambassador and Permanent Representative of the Islamic Republic of Iran to the United Nations.

[75] Arshin Adib-Moghaddam, 'But what about Iran's grand strategic preferences?,' *The Daily Star*, 26 August 2004.

(this is the essential difference to ideology, which does not hold the prospect for change, but legitimates the status quo). Iranian-Islamic utopianism is alive and well because it is still in the process of realizing its dual aim: democratization at home and positioning Iran as a central international player abroad. The current reform movement pursues an eclectic reinterpretation of these goals and does not represent a revolt against the system.[76] Its vehicle is a reconstituted counter-utopia, a 'liberal-humanitarian' utopia that is directed against the 'chiliastic' moment of Iran's revolution. The crucial difference between the chiliastic and liberal-humanitarian utopia, Karl Mannheim argues, manifests itself in the sense of time.[77] While the latter avow the instantaneity of their promise—the transcendent moment is here and now, the immediateness of the transcendent overcomes the distance between the utopia and reality—liberal-humanitarian utopias emphasize evolutionary change. 'There is a sense of unilinear progress,' Ricoeur elaborates, 'and this philosophy of progress is directed exactly against the time sense of the chiliastic utopia.... The idea is *post tenebras lux* (after darkness, light); in the end, light wins.'[78] It could be said, then, that the Iranian utopia of *imminent change* has transmuted into the utopia of *generic growth*. This appears to be the philosophical faultline of Iran's contemporary political culture: it manifests itself in the fight between an intellectual and scientific (enlightened?) worldview and a theocratic or clerical (orthodox?) worldview. The influential ideas of the contemporary Iranian philosopher Abdolkarim Soroush are emblematic of the former:

> If science develops, it would modernize and develop our politics, it would give meaning to justice and freedom ... and [it] would determine the rights of people. We should not forget that in the New World politics is scientific politics and management is scientific management. The new science modernizes even philosophy. Islamic philosophy is dear, but ... [w]e should not think that the answer to all questions could be found in this philosophy. Even on the scene of philosophy we should seek progress and renewal.[79]

The paradigmatic turn advocated by Soroush and others has engendered the critical deconstruction of Iran's pre-revolutionary identity discourse. According to the 'Kian school of Iranian philosophy,' neither the 'return to the self' nor the idea of 'west-toxification' have sufficiently addressed Iran's conflict with itself. Instead of essentializing Iran's Islamic heritage and castigating the 'West,' Soroush argues, Iranian thinkers need to evaluate critically the country's national (Persian), religious-Islamic (Shia) *and* Western heritage.[80] 'The difficulty arises,' Soroush asserts,

> when some people unreflectively assume a fixed and eternal cultural identity and distinguish friend and foe accordingly. Such people never realize that the self must be created, that it does not come prefabricated and maintenance-free. ... The bid to 'return to oneself' will remain an empty slogan at best (and a slayer of culture and

---

[76] For a perceptive, anthropological analysis of Iranian modernity, see Fariba Adelkhah, *Being Modern in Iran*, Jonathan Derrick (Trans.) (London: Hurst, 1999).

[77] See Mannheim, *Ideology and Utopia*, esp. chap. IV, n. 1.

[78] Ricoeur, *Lectures*, p. 278, n. 42.

[79] Abdolkarim Soroush, 'Scientific development, political development,' *Kian Monthly Review*, 10(54) (2000), available at < http://www.drsoroush.com/English/By_drsoroush/E-CMB-19990500-Seminar_on_Tradition_and_Modernism_held_in_Beheshti_University.html > (accessed 12 June 2004).

[80] Abdolkarim Soroush, *Reason, Freedom & Democracy in Islam: Essential Writings of 'Abdolkarim Soroush*, Mahmoud Sadri & Ahmad Sadri (Trans. and Eds) (Oxford: Oxford University Press, 2000), p. 156.

a source of stagnation at worst) if the boundaries of the self remain unspecified, if flexibility is denied. We cannot countenance a 'return to the self' that is counterposed to the reconstruction of the self.[81]

The contemporary foreign policy preferences of the Iranian state oscillate between the emerging, liberal-humanitarian utopia articulated by an increasingly vocal civil society and the chiliastic meta-structure woven into the institutional and intellectual fabric of the country during the revolutionary process. A critical, discursive, reconfiguring continuation rather than a break with the ideals of the revolution, this emergent culture has guided the Khatami administration toward advocating reform at home and abroad, while prioritizing an essentially conservative purpose: the preservation of the revolutionary-Islamic character of the Iranian system and the projection of Iranian power both regionally and globally. Managing the intrinsic dichotomies of this 'utopian-romantic realism' will depend on the ability of the Iranian state to accommodate the calls for internal reform and its diplomatic resources to engage an international society struggling to accommodate the desires of a demanding Leviathan shaken by the events on 11 September 2001.[82]

Mnemonics of Iran's Foreign Policy Culture

We began our journey with the assertion that utopian-romantic ideals constituted the preference setting and goal orientation of the post-revolutionary Iranian state. What had emerged as a counter-hegemonic political culture during the 1960s and 1970s, it was argued, was codified as a revolutionary narrative and appeared as a transcendent, de facto reality, reacting on its agents. The introjection of the utopia of the just state, mantled in the romantic imagery of the millenarian Shi'i struggle for emancipation, constituted the pool of shared knowledge that determined the foreign policy culture of the Iranian state after the Islamic Revolution in 1979. Once this aestheticized political reality was internalized cognitively and legitimated institutionally, the self-identification of the Iranian state as the vanguard of an international movement for emancipation guided the country toward challenging the international status quo that was perceived as inherently unjust and overbearingly hierarchical. Thus, for the sake of abstraction, we may assume that the morphology of Iran's foreign policy culture may be attributed to a four-dimensional, dialectical process: (1) the elite-driven invention of utopian-romantic Islamic theories in the 1960s and 1970s engendered a total redefinition of Iran's relationship with the world based on a new, Muslim-revolutionary identity for the Iranian state; (2) through the process of mass internalization of the revolutionary ideals and institutionalization in the post-revolutionary period, the utopias generated a powerful dynamism of their own (they attained systemic qualities); (3) socialized in this omnipresent, ideological system, Iranian foreign policy elites were habitualized to accept Iran's new role as legitimate and a reflection of the revolutionary ideals as formulated by Ayatollah Khomeini and others; (4) that process of institutionalization and habitualization constituted Iran's contemporary role identity par excellence—it introjected foreign policy

---

[81] Ibid., p. 165. *Kian* is the journal founded by Soroush in 1992.
[82] The emerging 'post-Islamicist' moment in Iran's foreign relations led in January 2004 to the renaming of a Tehran street after Khaled Islambouli, the assassin of Egyptian President Anwar Sadat (1981), thus opening up the current rapprochement with Egypt. Irish Republicans in January 2001 launched an Internet campaign urging the Iranian government not to rename a street in Tehran that was named after the IRA hunger striker Bobby Sands after his death in 1981.

elites with the idea that Iran's self-attributed moral high ground legitimates the country's special place in international affairs, which, by necessity, motivated (and motivates) them to challenge the prevalent status quo.

Let me conclude with a necessary autocritic. First, the way I framed my dialectical argument may suggest that the change from one dialectic to another occurs in a temporal sequence: elites externalize culture, culture is objectified, internalized, etc. I may have left room for the critique that I am suggesting a causal transmission belt from one cultural dialectic to another. Such a conclusion would be erroneous. It is important to remember that this paper has sketched a *continuous* dialectical process composed of four moments. Because they occur simultaneously, analysis of foreign policy culture needs to explore the full cycle of the four-dimensional dialectic. In other words, there is no real beginning or end to the dialectical process. Our search for analytical signposts and significance is essentially a modest (perhaps even 'primitive') one. It is limited to finding constitutive events that informed the grand strategic preferences of the country in question and to establishing how they were formed, transformed and maintained to fit the central preferences of the state. Every political entity experienced such constitutive periods. How, for instance, can we divorce the idea of *la grande nation* from France's role in international affairs, the concept of *Handelsstaat* from Germany's international conduct or Wilsonian idealism from the international role of the United States? Few analysts would contend that these self-perceptions did not condition how successive governments in those countries perceived their mission in international affairs. Fewer still would doubt that formative periods such as the American Revolution, the French Revolution and the 'Third Reich' influenced the way future generations of decision makers in those countries interacted with other nations. To give meaning to the outside world, the bearer of culture needs to revert to the pool of knowledge accumulated from previous experiences. Inventions of the past *have* an impact on the present. The practice of foreign policy depends on the existence (and introjection?) of intersubjective 'precedents and shared symbolic materials—in order to impose interpretations upon events, silence alternative interpretations, structure practices, and orchestrate the collective making of history.'[83] Appeals to the past explain why the US state is typically represented as an idealistic force committed to international justice, the German state as an anti-militaristic economic powerhouse, and the French state as a European superpower.[84] None of these abstract typologies would make sense without reference to culture and none of them would be effective if the states in question would not act out, reproduce and legitimate their self-depicted identities. I think it is a central purpose of dialectical analysis to identify and to unravel critically those cultural reification processes.

Second, it may be charged that my argument does not address sufficiently the degree of cultural pressures on foreign policy interests. How deterministic is culture in setting grand strategic preferences? The method pursued in this paper suggests that it is difficult to discern a priori if and when foreign policy culture has an impact on interests and preferences, and the impact needs to be investigated in conjunction with the empirical analysis. In other words, to explore the causal and constitutive effects of culture is a matter

---

[83] Richard K. Ashley, 'Foreign policy as political performances,' *International Studies Notes* (1998), p. 53.

[84] For the German case, see Thomas U. Berger, *Cultures of Antimilitarism: National Security in Germany and Japan* (London: Johns Hopkins University Press, 1998); and John S. Duffield, 'Political culture and state behavior: why Germany confounds neorealism,' *International Organization*, 53(4) (1999), pp. 765–803. For the impact of norms and ideas on French military doctrine, see Elizabeth Kier, 'Culture and military doctrine: France between the wars,' *International Security*, 19(4) (1995), pp. 65–93.

of the dialectical analysis, and is by no means predetermined in advance by theoretical signposts. It is important to remember that cultural inventions, however monolithic and deterministic they may appear, are essentially human fabrications. Their objective status does not divorce them from human action. The relationship between the individual, the producer, and the cultural world, the product, is and remains a dialectical one. Both are in constant interaction with each other. These aspects receive their proper recognition once cultural systems are understood in terms of an ongoing dialectical process composed of the four moments of externalization, objectification, internalization, and introjection. I regret that the unsolved puzzles within these dialectic moments could not have been explored more fully; had we moved further down our path, we might have come to understand the inner dynamics and structure of our ideal types.

Finally, by entering the well-maintained garden of 'Middle Eastern' studies with the heavy boots of critical cultural theory, some empirically spirited readers may ask: why bother with theory? My initial response to such valid criticism would be that theories are at the heart of what individuals and governments think and say about the determinants of international politics; they also become the method that governments use to define their identity and their differences to others. The main issues in international relations are about war and peace, of course. But when it comes to who had the right to attack the other country, who had the right to dominate and exploit it, who was a legitimate resistance movement and who a terrorist, and who was 'our' enemy in the first place—these issues are debated, contested and sometimes decided within theory. Indeed, the seminal study of Eric Hobsbawm and Terence Ranger on the invention of tradition and Hobsbawm's ideas on the construction of nationalist ideologies provide enough incentive to think of nation-states themselves as theoretical constructs.[85] The power of theory, or to block alternative theories from emerging, is very important to the legitimation of culture and national and international policies. Indeed, our case might have demonstrated that the 'libidinous' energies of theory mobilized millions of people in Iran to rise up and oust the omnipresent shah; a comparable force motivated the Russians, Chinese, Cubans and other movements with the principal aim to subvert established hierarchies of master and servant, top and bottom, have and have-nots. Is opposition to theory hence not too often 'really directed against the transformative activity associated with critical thinking'?[86] Does critical thought not emancipate and open up room for intellectual exchange that partakes neither of orthodoxy nor of the partisan affirmation about the supremacy of one worldview?[87] These questions refer to issues left embarrassingly incomplete in this study. An important task for future research would be to synthesize the vast critical theory literature with the international politics of the 'Third World,' to ask how one can study the political cultures of non-Western societies from a critical, or a non-deterministic and non-manipulative, perspective. Projects like these may engender rather

---

[85] See Eric Hobsbawm & Terence Ranger (Eds), *The Invention of Tradition* (Cambridge: Cambridge University Press, 2004); and Eric Hobsbawm, *Nations and Nationalism since 1780: Programme, Myth, Reality*, 2nd ed. (Cambridge: Cambridge University Press, 2004).

[86] Max Horkheimer, 'Traditional and critical theory,' in: *Critical Theory: Selected Essays* (New York: Seabury Press, 1972), p. 232.

[87] In international relations, the return to critical theory has constituted a serious challenge to mainstream portrayals of international relations. For overviews see, among others, Andrew Linklater (Ed.) *International Relations: Critical Concepts in Political Science* (London: Routledge, 2000), esp. vols. IV and V; and Richard Wyn Jones (Ed.), Critical Theory and World Politics (London: Lynne Rienner, 2001).

more multicultural discourse among the growing international studies community, strengthening the case of those among us who advocate the benefits of inter-cultural dialogue.

References

Abrahamian, E. (1993) *Khomeinism: Essays on the Islamic Republic* (London: I.B. Tauris).
Adelkhah, F. (1999) *Being Modern in Iran* J. Derrick (Trans.) (London: Hurst).
Adib-Moghaddam, A. (2002) Global intifadah: September 11th and the struggle within Islam, *Cambridge Review of International Affairs*, 15(2), pp. 203–216.
Adib-Moghaddam, A. (2004) But what about Iran's grand strategic preferences?, *The Daily Star* (Beirut), 26 August, available at <http://www.dailystar.com.lb/article.asp?edition_id=10&categ_id=5&article_id=7698>.
Adib-Moghaddam, A. (2004) The contemporary political landscape of Iran: the eclectics of post-revolutionary politics (Part I), *The Tharwa Project*, 8 November, available at <http://www.tharwaproject.com/English/Main-Sec/Features/Feat_11_29_04/index.php?option=com_keywords&task=view&id=817&Itemid=0>.
Adib-Moghaddam, A. (2004) The contemporary political landscape of Iran: the eclectics of post-revolutionary politics (Part II), *The Tharwa Project*, 29 November, available at <http://www.tharwaproject.com/English/Main-Sec/Features/Feat_11_29_04/index.php?option=com_keywords&task=view&id=814&Itemid=0>.
Adib-Moghaddam, A. (forthcoming) *The International Politics of the Persian Gulf: A Cultural Genealogy* (London: Routledge).
Afary, J. & Anderson, K.B. (2005) *Foucault, Gender, and the Iranian Revolution: The Seductions of Islamism* (Chicago: University of Chicago Press).
Al-e Ahmad, J. (1982) *Plagued by the West (Gharbzadegi)* (New York: Caravan).
Algar, H. (Trans.) (1980) *Constitution of the Islamic Republic of Iran* (Berkeley: Mizan Press).
Archer, M. S. (1996) *Culture and Agency: The Place of Culture in Social Theory*, rev. ed. (Cambridge: Cambridge University Press).
Ashley, R. K. (1988) Foreign policy as political performances, *International Studies Notes*.
BBC News (2004) Iran releases British servicemen, 24 June, available at <http://www.news.bbc.co.uk/2/hi/middle-east/3835313.stm> (accessed 24 August 2004).
BBC Survey of World Broadcasts (2004) Part IV (A), The Middle East, ME/6280/A/8, 24 November.
Berger, P. L. (1966) *The Sacred Canopy* (Garden City: Doubleday).
Berger, P. L. & Luckmann, T. (1979) *The Social Construction of Reality: A Treatise in the Sociology of Knowledge* (Harmondsworth: Penguin).
Berger, P. L. & Pullberg, S. (1965) Reification and the sociological critique of consciousness, *History and Theory*, 4(2), pp. 196–211.
Berger, T. U. (1998) *Cultures of Antimilitarism: National Security in Germany and Japan* (London: Johns Hopkins University Press).
Boroujerdi, M. (1996) *Iranian Intellectuals and the West: The Tormented Triumph of Nativism* (Syracuse: Syracuse University Press).
Boroujerdi, M. (1997) Iranian Islam and the Faustian bargain of Western modernity, *Journal of Peace Research*, 34(1), pp. 1–5.
Bukovansky, M. (2002) *Legitimacy and Power Politics: The American and French Revolutions in International Political Culture* (Princeton: Princeton University Press).
Carr, E. H. (1961) *The Twenty Years' Crisis, 1919–1939: An Introduction to the Study of International Relations* (London: Macmillan).
Cole, J. R. I. & Keddie, N. R. (Eds) (1986) *Shi'ism and Social Protest* (New Haven: Yale University Press).
Dilthey, W. (1976) *Selected Writings* (Cambridge: Cambridge University Press).
Duffield, J. S. (1999) Political culture and state behavior: why Germany confounds neorealism, *International Organization*, 53(4), pp. 765–803.
Ebtekar, M. (2000) *Takeover in Tehran: The Inside Story of the 1979 U.S. Embassy Capture* (Vancouver: Talonbooks).
Ehteshami, A. (1995) *After Khomeini: The Iranian Second Republic* (London: Routledge).
Eribon, D. (1991) *Michel Foucault*, B. Wing (Trans.) (London: Faber and Faber).
Farsoun, S. K. & Mashayekhi, M. (1992) *Iran: Political Culture in the Islamic Republic* (London: Routledge).

SECURITY IN THE GULF: HISTORICAL LEGACIES AND FUTURE PROSPECTS

Foucault, M. (1997) *Power: Essential Works of Foucault, 1954–1984*, vol. 3, in: R. Hurley et al. (Trans.) (London: Penguin).
Geertz, C. (1973) *The Interpretation of Cultures* (New York: Basic Books).
George, D. (1996) Pax Islamica: an alternative new world order, in: A. S. Sidahmed & A. Ehteshami (Eds) *Islamic Fundamentalism*, pp. 71–90 (Boulder: Westview).
Goldstein, J. & Keohane, R. (Eds) (1993) *Ideas and Foreign Policy* (Ithaca: Cornell University Press).
Gramsci, A. (1971) *Selections from Prison Notebooks* (London: Lawrence & Wishart).
Halliday, F. (1986) Iranian foreign policy since 1979: internationalism and nationalism in the Islamic Revolution, in: J. R. I. Cole & N. R. Keddie (Eds) *Shi'ism and Social Protest*, pp. 88–107 (New Haven: Yale University Press).
Halliday, F. (1999) *Revolution and World Politics: The Rise and Fall of the Sixth Great Power* (Durham, NC: Duke University Press).
Hobsbawm, E. (2004) *Nations and Nationalism since 1780: Programme, Myth, Reality*, 2nd ed (Cambridge: Cambridge University Press).
Hobsbawm, E. & Ranger, T. (Eds) (2003) *The Invention of Tradition* (Cambridge: Cambridge University Press).
Horkheimer, M. (1972) Traditional and critical theory, in: M. Horkheimer (Ed.) *Critical Theory: Selected Essays*, pp. 183–243 (New York: Seabury Press).
International Crisis Group (24 November 2004), Iran: where next on the nuclear standoff?, available at <http:www.crisisgroup.org/home/index.cfm?id=3118&1=1 > (accessed 13 May 2005).
Jones, C. (1998) *E. H. Carr and International Relations: A Duty to Lie* (Cambridge: Cambridge University Press).
Kashani-Sabet, F. (2002) Cultures of Iranianness: the evolving polemic of Iranian nationalism, in: N. Keddie & R. Matthee (Eds) *Iran and the Surrounding World: Interactions in Culture and Cultural Politics*, pp. 162–181 (Seattle: University of Washington Press).
Kawtharani, W. (1998) Mutual awareness between Arabs and Iranians, in: Khair el-Din Haseeb (Ed.) *Arab-Iranian Relations* (Beirut: Centre for Arab Unity Studies).
Khatami, M. (2000) *Islam, Dialogue and Civil Society* (Canberra: Centre for Arab and Islamic Studies).
Khomeini, R. (1981) *Islam and Revolution: Writings and Declarations of Imam Khomeini*, Hamid Algar (Trans.) (Berkeley: Mizan Press).
Khomeini, R. (1985) *Sahifey-e Nur*, vol. 18 (Tehran: Vezarat-e Ershad).
Kier, E. (1995) Culture and military doctrine: France between the wars, *International Security*, 19(4), pp. 65–93.
Linklater, A. (Ed.) (2000) *International Relations: Critical Concepts in Political Science* (London: Routledge).
Mannheim, K. (1991) *Ideology and Utopia: An Introduction to the Sociology of Knowledge* (London: Routledge).
Marcuse, H. (1964) *One-dimensional Man: Studies in the Ideology of Advanced Industrial Society* (London: Routledge).
Marx, K. (1973) *Survey from Exile*, David Fernbach (Ed.) (Harmondsworth: Penguin).
Mead, G. H. (1934) *Mind, Self, and Society* (Chicago: University of Chicago Press).
Miller, J. (1993) *The Passion of Michel Foucault* (London: HarperCollins).
Morgenthau, H. J (1948) *Politics among Nations* (New York: Alfred Knopf).
Mottahari, M. (n.d.) *Islam and Iran* (Beirut: Dar al-Ta'aruf).
Mottahedeh, R. P. (1996) Shi'ite political thought and the destiny of the Iranian Revolution, in: J. S. al-Suwaidi (Ed.) *Iran and the Gulf: A Search for Stability*, pp. 70–80 (Abu Dhabi: The Emirates Center for Strategic Studies and Research).
Mutahhari, M. (1986) Shahid, in: M. Abedi & G. Leggenhausen (Eds) *Jihad and Shahadat: Struggle and Martyrdom in Islam* (Houston: Institute for Research and Islamic Studies).
Onuf, N. (1998) *The Republican Legacy in International Thought* (Cambridge: Cambridge University Press).
Rahnema, A. (2000) *An Islamic Utopian: A Political Biography of Ali Shariati* (London: I.B. Tauris).
Rajaee, F. (1983) *Islamic Values and World View: Khomeyni on Man, the State and International Politics*, vol. XIII (London: University Press of America).
Rajaee, F. (1990) Iranian ideology and worldview: the cultural export of revolution, in: J. L. Esposito (Ed.) *The Iranian Revolution: Its Global Impact*, pp. 63–80 (Miami: Florida International University Press).
Ramazani, R. K. (1986) *Revolutionary Iran: Challenge and Response in the Middle-East* (Baltimore: Johns Hopkins University Press).
Ricoeur, P. (1986) in: G. H. Taylor (Ed.) *Lectures on Ideology and Utopia* (New York: Columbia University Press).
Saad, J. B. (1996) *The Image of Arabs in Modern Persian Literature* (Lanham: University Press of America).
Said, E. W. (1995) *Orientalism* (London: Penguin).
Saussure, F. (1964) *Course in General Linguistics* (New York: McGraw Hill).

Shariati, A. (1979) *On the Sociology of Islam: Lectures by Ali Shari'ati* Hamid Algar (Trans.) (Berkeley: Mizan Press).
Shariati, A. (accessed 24 March 2003) Arise and bear witness, available at <htttp://www.shariati.com>.
Soroush, A. (2000) Scientific development, political development, *Kian Monthly Review*, 10(5), available at <http://www.drsoroush.com/English/By_drsoroush/E-CMB-19990500-Seminar_on_Tradition_and_Modernism_held_in_Beheshti_University.html> (accessed 12 June 2004).
Soroush, A. (2000) in: M. Sadri & A. Sadri (Trans. and Eds) *Reason, Freedom & Democracy in Islam: Essential Writings of 'Abdolkarim Soroush* (Oxford: Oxford University Press).
Tarock, A. (1999) *Iran's Foreign Policy since 1990: Pragmatism Supersedes Islamic Ideology* (Commack: Nova Science Press).
Walker, R. B. J. (1993) *Inside/Outside: International Relations as Political Theory* (Cambridge: Cambridge University Press).
Weber, M. (1998) *From Max Weber: Essays in Sociology* (London: Routledge).
Wendt, A. (1999) *Social Theory of International Politics* (Cambridge: Cambridge University Press).
Williams, R. (1977) *Marxism and Literature* (Oxford: Oxford University Press).
Wyn Jones, R. (Ed.) (2001) *Critical Theory and World Politics* (London: Lynne Rienner).
Zarif, J. (2003) Indispensable power: hegemonic tendencies in a globalized world, *Harvard International Review*, 24(4), available at <http://www.ceip.org/files/Publications/2003-04-01-brumberg-HIR.asp?from=pubdate> (accessed 13 November 2003).

Index

Page numbers in *Italics* represent tables.

Abdullah, Crown Prince: peace initiative (2002) 88–91
Abdullah, King 92, 93, 94
Abu Dhabi 97
Abu Musa (island) 104; invasion by Iran 104; Iranian construction on and control of 105
Adelman, M.A. 47
Adib-Moghaddam, Arshin 7, 8, 21, 129–56
Afghanistan: Soviet Union's invasion (1979) 32
Afrasiabi, K.L. 6
Ahmadinejad, President Mahmud 92
Akhtar, Qari Saifullah 110
Al-Bu Nasir tribe: Iraq 122
Al-e Ahmad, Jalal 7; *Gharbzadegi* 139
The Al-Qaeda Organisation in the Emirates and Oman 112
Al-Qaeda Terrorist Organisation in the United Arab Emirates Government 111
al-Qaida 109
al-Qaida on the Arabian Peninsula (QAP) 68; motives 71–2; *The Prophet's Guidance on Targeting Emergency Forces* 71, see also QAP campaign
Algerian insurgents: Eisenhower administration support 46
Al-Alkim, Hassan Hamdan 4, 5
Al-Aloofi, Saleh 111
American intentions: Saudi suspicion or ambivalence 35
American threat: Gulf's oil 123
Anthony, John Duke 18
anti-Soviet coalition: Arab states with Israel 88
Arab Gulf sheikhs 17
Arab League: Riyadh inter-Arab summit 94
Arab League Conference: Fez, Morocco (1982) 86
Arab nationalism 117

Arab nationalism (1950s) 32
Arab Peace Initiative (2002) 88, 92–3
Arab solidarity 84
Arab summit: Fez, Morocco 85
Arab-Israeli conflict 85
Arab-Israeli war (1973) 42
Aramco 106
'Aramco advantage' 48
Aramco workers: strike and Army intervention 63
Archer, Margaret: cultural system 133–4
Asia and Africa: agricultural operation investment 56
Assiri, Abdul-Reda 8
authoritarian rule: as a social preference 36
autonomy: and sovereignty 44–5
AWACS airplanes 85, 100

Baader-Meinhof Gang: Lufthansa hijacking (1977) 108
Ba'athist Iraq and the Gulf 122–3
Bazargan, Prime Minister Mehdi 144
Beirut Plan 91
Beirut Summit (2002) 90
Berger, P.L.: and Luckmann, T. 132
bin Laden, Osama 53, 67, 109
bin Nayef, Prince Muhammad 70
Boroujerdi, Mehrzad 146
British Airways: hijacking PLO (1974) 108
Buraimi oasis 106
Buraimi region 106
Bush, President George H.W. 53
Bush, President George W.: Middle East peace policy 91

Calabrese, John 4, 5, 7
The Camp David Accords (1979) 84, 86, 87
Central Treaty Organization (CENTO) 147
Chiliasm 141
Cho, David 57
Chubin, Shahram 19; and Tripp, Charles 14
Clinton, President Bill: 'dual containment' policy 54

INDEX

Cold War 31, 45
Commodity Futures Trading Commission (CFTC) 57
Conge, Patrick: and Okruhlik, Gwenn 25–40
Cordesman, Anthony: *The Gulf and the Search for Strategic Stability* 11
counter-hegemonic utopias 137
cultural formation 22; Iran and Iraq 21
cultural systems: Archer on 133–4; social construction 132–4
cultural systems and the individual: Dilthey on 133
currency fluctuations 57

Damascus Declaration 16
Davidson, Christopher M. 97–113
Al-Dawish, Faysal 116
Dawisha, A. 8
Dawisha, Adeed 121
Deira City Centre: bomb plot (1999) 109
Denel corporation: military equipment sales UAE 99
Dhofar Liberation Front 107
Dilthey, Wilhelm: cultural systems and the individual 133
dissimilarity and exceptionality 27–38
domestic infrastructure: public-private partnerships 59
domestic power generation: alternative energy sources 59
Dubai: Iran relations 103
Dubai Defence Force (DDF) 98–9
Dubai International Airport's Terminal-2 102
Dubai Ports World Company 102; US ports attempted take over 102
Dubai and the United Arab Emirates: domestic vulnerabilities history 107–10; domestic vulnerabilities present threat 110–12; Iran a history of threats 103–5; military power 98–101; other regional threats 105–7; security threats 97–113
Dubai's dry dock service: USS *John Kennedy* 102

Egypt: violent state repression 73
Eisenhower administration: Algerian insurgents support 46
energy security: aims 41–3; before OPEC 43–6; domestic insurgencies threat 41–2; and *la longue durée* 41–59; OPEC heyday 46–9; and Russia 57–8
English-language literature: international relations 4
exceptionality and dissimilarity 27–38

Fahd, Crown Prince 84, 85, 87
family elites 16

Fatah 95
Faysal, King 116; security dilemmas 116
Fez, Morocco: Arab League Conference (1982) 86; Arab summit 85
food insecurity 56
foreign military presence: Saudi Arabia 67
foreign policy culture: and grand strategic preference setting 134–6
foreign policy studies 4–11
Foucault, Michel: Iranian Revolution 129–30
Fuller, Graham 8

Gates, Secretary of Defense Robert 26
Gause, Gregory 19
gharbzadegi 141, 146; definition 139
Gharbzadegi (Al-e Ahmad) 139
Ghazi, King 117
global economy: fundamental changes 55
globalization: oil market 49–50, 55–7
Golan Heights: Israeli withdrawal 89
gold standard: and US inflation 48
Gramsci, Antonio 136–7
Grobba, Fritz (Nazi envoy) 118
Guazzone, Laura 9
Gulf: Arab side of 18; US foreign policy 45
Gulf Air: hijacking (1977) 108
Gulf Cooperation Council (GCC) 4, 8, 92, 104; institutional alternative identity 17; members strategic incompatibilities 12
The Gulf and the Search for Strategic Stability (Cordesman) 11
Gulf states: foreign policies 6; oil price collapse (1986) 51
Gulf War first (1980–1988) 50–1
Gulf War second (1990–1991) 34, 53, 67; postwar reconstruction projects 16; UN-mandated sanctions 42
Gulf War third (2003–2010) 54; oil reserve benefits 54
Gulf wars and security 50–5
Gulf's oil: American threat 123

Hamas 95
Haraktul Jihad Islami 110
'Haramain Brigades' 71
Hegel, Georg W. 132
Hegghammer, Thomas 61–82
History of the Peloponnesian War (Thucydides) 30
Hizbollah of the Hijaz 64
Hizbullah 91
Hobsbawm, Eric: and Ranger, Terence 153
Hollis, Rosemary 16
Homo socius 132
al-Hudhayf, Abdallah 67
Hussein, Imam Shi'i: martyrdom 145

INDEX

Hussein, Saddam 122; fall of 98; Gulf dynasties and al-Sabah royal family rhetoric 125; Gulf policy speeches 124; 'jihad speech' 124, 125; Kuwait victory as prop to his regime 126; military expansion 123

Hussein's Iraq 123, 149

hydrocarbon industry 43; Arab Gulf 45

Ikhwan revolt 65

Imam Ghalib 107

Indian Airlines: hijacking (1999) 109

Indyk, Martin 94

inflation: global 48; USA and gold standard 48

inter-state interaction 18–22

International Atomic Energy Agency (IAEA): Iranian defiance 148

International Energy Agency (IEA) 48

international oil companies (IOCs) 43–4; US-based tax provision 46–7

international relations: English-language literature 4; scholarship 3–23

Iran: culture and foreign policy preferences 130; disputed island territories with UAE 103; domestic instability 10; ethno-sectarian dispute 10; foreign policy preferences 131; Iraqi invasion 15; Islamic utopian romanticism 129–56; oil pipeline 58; US embassy occupation (1979) 144, *see also* Islamic Republic

Iran foreign policy culture 129–56; anti-imperialism 147; challenge to international society 143–7; framing 136–51; mnemonics 151–4

Iran-Iraq war 123

Iranian ascendancy 91–5

Iranian philosophy: Kian school 150

Iranian Revolution 32, 151; Foucault on 129–30; oil spot price spikes 49; religious passion 141

Iranian security 5

Iranian-Aryan self 139

Iranian-Islamic utopianism 150

Iranians: myth of the common origin 139

Iraq: Al-Bu Nasir tribe 122; Ba'athist Iraq and the Gulf 122–3; British invasion (1941) 120; conscripted army 1930s 117; domestic regime security 115; early republican era 120–2; financial heavy debt 52; 'Four Colonels' or the 'Golden Square' 117, 119; Gulf policy and regime security 115–27; Hashemite Monarchy 115–20; Ikhwan raids 117; Kuwait part of declaration (1961) 121; Kuwaiti investors 126; military actions Iran (1980) 15; military growth 1930s 116; Officers' City (*Madinat al-Dhubbat*) 120; oil boycott 53; oil production post second Gulf War 54; post-Ba'athist Gulf policy 126–7; regime insecurity post Iran-Iraq war 126; relations to the Gulf 115; threat from Khomeini's Islamic Revolution 123; UN sanctions 53

Iraq and Kuwait: Gulf crisis (1990–2003) 124–6

Iraq-Kuwaiti relations 127

Iraqi Communist Party 121

Iraqi invasion: Iran 15

Iraqi military intelligence: possible US military action 1970s 122

Iraqi oil 54

irredentist violence 66

isba (moral policing) 67

'Islamic army' (*'Fatah al-Islam'*) 93

Islamic Republic 10, 131, 142; confrontational policies 149; expansionism 9; language and symbols 146, *see also* Iran

Islamic revisionism 21

Islamic Revolution *see* Iranian Revolution

Islamic utopian romanticism: Iran 129–56

Islamist violence: Egypt and Algeria 62; Saudi Arabia 61–82; Saudi Arabia, lack of grievances 73–4; Saudi Arabia, patterns 73

Israel: Arab states territorial claims 89

Japan Airlines: hijacking PLO and Japanese Red Army (1973) 108

Joffé, George 17

Kantian 'zone of peace' 22

Kechichian, Joseph 8

Khalid, King 84, 86

Khatami, Mohammad: 'dialogue among civilizations' 148

Khomeini, Ayatollah Ruhollah 32, 130, 142; *fatwa* against Rushdie 145; letter to Gorbachev 144; letter to Pope John-Paul II 144; *Weltanschauung* 143

Khomeini regime 9

Kian school: Iranian philosophy 150

Kissinger, Henry 48

Kostiner, Joseph 12, 83–95

Kuwait: Arab League support again Iraq (1961) 121; border fence infringement 127; British aegis 118; British forces withdrawal 121; Iraqi invasion (1990) 53, 124; *majlis* movement 58

Kuwait and Iraq: Gulf crisis (1990–2003) 124–6

Kuwaiti emir 44; assassination attempt 52

Lawson, Fred H. 3–23

Lockheed Martins: sales to UAE Armed Forces 100

INDEX

Long, David 8, 18
la longue durée: and energy security 41–59
Luckmann, T.: and Berger, P.L. 132
Lufthansa hijacking (1977): Baader-Meinhof Gang 108

Mahdi Army 91
Al-Maliki, Jawad: Kuwait border fence infringement 127
al-Maliki, Prime Minister Nuri 91, 126
al-Mani, Saleh 13
Mannheim, Karl 141, 150
Al-Marashi, Ibrahim 115–27
Marcuse, Herbert 134–5
Marshall Plan 45
martyrs (*Shuhada*) 142
Marx, Karl 132; 'Men make their own history...' 132
Mead, George Herbert 135
military equipment (for UAE): Denel corporation 99; join ventures 100; Royal Netherlands Army 99
military power: UAE and Dubai 98–101
Møller, Bjørn 20
Morgenthau, Hans 131
Mossadeq government: oil nationalization (Iran) 45
Mottahari, Morteza 138
Musandam Peninsula 105
mutual identification: societal level 17

narrative (power of): Saudi Arabia and USA 25–40
Abd Al-Nashiri, Al-Rahim 110
[sq]Abd al-Nasir, President Gamal 83
National Action Charter: Bahrain 22
The National Bloc (*Al-Kutla al-Wataniyya*) 118
National Security Council (NSC) 29, 37; memo (1954) 34
nationalism: and socialism 32; state-based 14
Nawfal, Michel 10
nepotism 12
Non Aligned Movement (NAM) 147

oil: control unfriendly actors 33; Gulf crude price and war 51; security 26
oil exporters 43
oil exports: Straits of Hormuz 42
oil installations: attacks on 51
oil market: globalization 49–50, 55–7
oil pipeline: Iran 58
oil price 42; instability (2008) 56; US dollar denomination effect 50
oil production: technology and capital intensity 43
oil revenues: and UAE sovereignty 58

oil revolution (1970–1974) 46
oil spot price spikes: Iranian Revolution 49
oil-exporting countries: nationalization of oil 47
oil-producing countries: and transnational petroleum companies 3
Okruhlik, Gwenn 37; and Conge, Patrick 25–40
Omani terrorists 107
O'Reilly, Marc 6
Organisation of the Islamic Revolution (OIR) 64
Organization of Petroleum Exporting Countries (OPEC) 44; formation 47; price stability measures (1983) 49; quota disagreements (1980s) 105; quotas on production 50
The Origins of Alliances (Walt) 13
Orwellian logic 31–3
Oslo Accords 87

Pahlavi Iran 139
Pahlavi, Shah Muhammad Reza 103–4, 138
Pahlavi state 138
Palestinian Authority (PA) 91, 93
Palestinian independent state 89
Palestinian intifada (2002) 88
pan-Arabism: as ideological tool 120
pan-Islamism: and Saudi Arabia 80
pan-Islamist violence 66
Persian Empire: pre-Islamic 137
Persian Gulf: Arabian Gulf designation Iraq government 120
Peterson, John E. 66
political realism 30–1
political repression: Algeria, Egypt and Saudi Arabia 75
Political Terror Scale (Gibney and Dalton) 74
politicisation 12
Popular Front for the Liberation of Occupied Arab Gulf 107
Port Jebel Ali: American warships 111–12
power cycle theory 20
power of the state: fear 38
power and state relationship 38
Priess, David 13
The Prophet's Guidance on Targeting Emergency Forces (QAP) 71
public-private partnerships: domestic infrastructure 59

QAP campaign 68–72, 79; civilian representatives clemency 72; 'manifesto' 70; operations (2003–2007) 68; preference for Western targets 70

INDEX

Abd Qasim, Prime Minister al-Karim 120, 121

Rahnema, Ali: political biography of Shariati 140
Ramazani, R.K. 147
Ranger, Terence: and Hobsbawm, Eric 153
al-Rasheed, Madawi 77
The Reagan Plan 86
Reagan, President Ronald 85; decontrolled US crude oil prices 49; 'new Cold War' 49
regional deterrence 20
regional security: dimensions 11–18
regional states: 'domestic instability' 29
religious conservatism: Saudi Arabia 76
Revolutionary Guards Corps 9
revolutionary Islamist violence 66; Saudi Arabia 73, 75
Rice, Condoleezza 26
Ricoeur, Paul 141
de la Roche, Senechal 78
Roosevelt, President F.D.: 'original bargain' Saudi Arabia 26
Rosenau, James 4
Royal Netherlands Army: military equipment sales UAE 99
Rushdie, Salman: *fatwa* against 145
Russia: hydrocarbon transit 58

Saad, Joya Blondel 138–9
al-Sabah, Mubarak 44
al-Sadr, Muqtada 91
Sagem Défense Sécurité 99
Sahwa leaders: Saudi Arabia 76
Sahwa movement 67

The Satanic Verses (Rushdie): *fatwa* against 145
House of Saud 32, 61, 75, 116
Saudi Arabia: anti-Western jihadists 68; and the Arab-Israeli peace process 83–95; domestic security incidents 62; Egypt and Syria meeting 84; foreign military presence 67; Hijaz-based civil reformers 63; jobs-for-all policy 74; leftist and Shiite militancy 63–5; as mediator formative stage 84–6; military facilities American corporations 26; mobilisation obstacles to revolutionary activism 75; National Security Advisor 89, 91, 94; OPEC quotas 50; and pan-Islamism 80; patterns of violence 62–72; political diversion 79–81; political grip and US military dependence 39; political order 27; regime legitimacy 75–6; as regional coordinator 83; relationship with USA 28; religious basis 80; religious conservatism 76; rentier economy 76; revolutionary activism 61; revolutionary Islamist violence 73, 75; royal family 32, 61, 75, 116; Sahwa leaders 76; Shiite militants 64; 'special relationship' with USA 25–40; Sunni Islamist violence 65–8, *69*; tension with UAE 106; 'tribal factor' 76; Wahhabism 21, 77
Saudi Arabia Islamist violence 61–82; explanations 72–81; patters *73*
Saudi education systems 78; ethnocentrism 78
Saudi jihadist literature 72
Saudi jihadists 78
Saudi xenophobia 77–9
scholarship: international relations 3–23
Second Khordad Movement in Iran 22
sectarian violence 66
security challenges: actual and potential 11
security eras 43–57
September 11th Commission hearings 109; hijackers flights to USA from UAE 110
September 11th terrorist attack 37, 54
Shariati, Ali 140; ideal man 142; Sufism (Islamic mysticism) 140
Shi'is: imagery of suffering via unjust rulers 145
Shiite militants: Saudi Arabia 64
Shikara, Ahmad 118
Shuhada (martyrs) 142
socialism: and nationalism 32
Soroush, Abdolkarim 150–1
sovereignty: and autonomy 44–5
former Soviet republics: as 'emerging markets' 55
Soviet Union: fall of 55
'special relationship': Saudi Arabia and USA 25–40
state: fear of absolute power 38
state autonomy: constraints 56
state officials: coercion by 14
state power: limits Saudi Arabia 39; morality and use 36
state and power relationship 38
Straits of Hormuz: oil exports 42
'Sudeten Territories' 119
Sunni Islamist violence: ideal-types 66; Saudi Arabia 65–8, *69*
Talabani, President Jalal 111
terrorism incidents: databases 62
terrorist activity: Saudi government responses 79
terrorist attacks: Algeria, Egypt and Saudi Arabia *63*
Tétreault, Mary Ann 41–59
Thucydides: *History of the Peloponnesian War* 30
transnational petroleum companies: and oil-producing countries 3

INDEX

Tripp, Charles 122, 125; and Chubin, Shahram 14
Trucial Oman Levies 98, 106
Republic of Turkey 116

UAE Armed Forces 97, 98, 99; insufficient personnel 101; Iran fear of attack by 103; joint military equipment ventures 100; Lockheed Martins' best customer 100; military equipment 99; military salaries 101
ulama 33
Union Defence Force 99
Union of the People of the Arabian Peninsula (UPAP) 63
United Arab Emirates and Dubai *see* Dubai and United Arab Emirates
United Arab Emirates (UAE) 4; air force advanced equipment 99–100; disputed island territories with Iran 103; foreign policy-making 5; permanent French military base 102; recognition by Saudi Arabia 106; sovereignty and oil revenues 58; successful post-oil states 97–8; tension with Saudi Arabia 106
United Arab Republic: Iraq's refusal to join 121

United Nations General Assembly Resolution (194) 90
United States of America (USA): military ally Saudi Arabia 31; 'special relationship' with Saudi Arabia 25–40
United States Department of State: cables (1950s) 33
US Arms Export Control Act 51
US Marine barracks, Lebanon: bombing of 51
USS *John Kennedy*: Dubai's dry dock service 102
al-Utaybi, Juhayman 66
al-Uyayri, Yusuf 70

vigilantist violence 66
Vitol 57

Wahhabism 61; Saudi Arabia 21, 77
Walt, Stephen: *The Origins of Alliances* 13
war on terror 101–2
Weber, Max 136
Western security umbrella 101–3
Westphalian sovereignty 21
Williams, Raymond 148